History of Universities

VOLUME IV
1984

History of Universities

VOLUME IV
1984

Oxford University Press

History of Universities is published annually as a single volume.

Editor: Charles Schmitt (Warburg Institute, University of London).

Assistant editor: Peter Denley (Westfield College, University of London).

Editorial board:
L. W. B. Brockliss (Hull)
R. J. W. Evans (Brasenose College, Oxford)
J. M. Fletcher (University of Aston in Birmingham)
J. K. McConica (All Souls' College, Oxford and Toronto)
N. G. Siraisi (Hunter College, New York)

Papers for publication in *History of Universities* as well as books for review should be sent to the editor, Dr. C. B. Schmitt, The Warburg Institute, Woburn Square, London WC1H 0AB, England. A leaflet entitled 'Notes for contributors' is available on request from the editor.
Details of subscription rates and terms are available from Oxford Journals Subscription Department, Walton Street, Oxford, OX2 6DP, United Kingdom

History of Universities, Volume IV, first published in 1985 by Oxford University Press, Oxford, England.

British Library Cataloguing in Publication Data:

History of universities. - Vol. 4 (1984)
1. Universities and colleges - History - Periodicals
378'.009   LA173

ISBN 0-19-820085-4
ISSN 0144-5138

This volume was prepared using facilities generously provided by the Computer Unit, Westfield College. It was photoset on the Oxford University Computing Service's Monotype Lasercomp phototypesetter, in 10 on 11-point Times Roman.
Printed in Great Britain at the University Press, Oxford
by David Stanford, Printer to the University

Contents

FINANCING OF UNIVERSITY STUDENTS IN THE MIDDLE AGES: A NEW ORIENTATION

*Paul Trio**

Introduction

Anyone familiar with the historiography of history of universities, and especially with current trends in this field, knows that both the place and the function of the university within society are being more and more emphasised. This so-called 'social history' — understood in its fullest possible sense — was started by American historians such as Hexter and Curtis at the end of the 1950s, but did not reach its full development until the last decade.[1] That may be why research into the social history of universities has not gone much beyond the exposition of a few problems. This paper will focus upon the question of the financing of university studies: in other words, an attempt is made to answer the question as to how and by whom the costs of university training were mainly paid.

The importance of this question lies in the fact that the answer to it may very well provide the key to the whole social history of universities. The subjects which up to very recent times have mostly been researched — such as numerical development and the geographical and social recruitment of the student population — cannot and should not be considered independently from the financial aspect. Unfortunately, this is what all too often has been done. Moreover, the total cost of university studies[2] takes on real significance only when balanced against the income at the disposal of the student in question, as well as the way he is able to obtain it.

As it is, inquiries into the financing problems have remained very modest so that the judgment expressed by F. J. Pegues in 1956, 'The methods by which medieval students financed their education is one phase of student life which has, in particular, been neglected',[3] was bound to be repeated almost unchanged more than twenty years later by the same author as 'one of the more obscure and unexplored questions in the constitutional history of the medieval university'.[4] As a result, the few scattered data available at the present time do not justify any solid conclusions concerning the average share of different sources of income the medieval student had at his disposal in order to pay for his studies. The present article, therefore, shall be limited to defining some important forms of income, and to emphasising those forms which up to this day have scarcely been mentioned in the present literature. It does strike us that, aside from direct financial support from home (i.e. parents and relatives)[5] and earnings from odd jobs,[6] attention has been centred mainly, if not exclusively, on scholarships obtained via colleges and benefices.[7] Without underestimating the importance of both these sources of income, one should be made aware of the number of limitations inherent to such sponsoring.[8]

1. Colleges and thereby incorporated scholarship grants

The first colleges originated in Paris (Collège des Dix-Huit) in 1180, and in Oxford and Cambridge in the second half of the XIIIth century, spreading later to other university towns. Originally, they were charitable institutions endowed by their founder, a wealthy cleric or layman, with the buildings and the regular income needed to guarantee board and lodging for a number of poor students.[9] New scholarship grants were sporadically appended to these colleges.[10] They may be called 'fixed scholarship grants' as opposed to the 'flying grants'. The founder entrusted the college with an income and made it the administrator of the foundation, in charge of cashing the money and ensuring payment to its resident bursars. Only the nomination of the candidates remained in the hands of a donor appointed by the founder.[11]

    With regard to the importance of these colleges and the scholarship foundations connected with them later, two important qualifications should be stressed, aside from the geographical[12] and chronological[13] ones, often specified in the founding document. First, such scholarships seldom covered more than the cost of lodging.[14] Their value also suffered from other financial difficulties (not discussed in this article), e.g. inflation which, especially from the XVth century on,[15] led to a gradual devaluation of the scholarships. As a result, such scholarships were then usually granted as a supplementary income to non-indigent students.[16] The second qualification was even more significant: the number of students benefiting from such scholarship grants always represented only a small minority of the total student population.[17] According to a rough estimate given by Pegues,[18] the University of Paris, in the XIIIth and even in the XIVth century, had about 400 students in colleges out of a total student population of *ca.* 6000; by 1550, according to L. W. B. Brockliss,[19] the proportion was about 600 out of a total of some 10.000 students. For Oxford in the middle of the

XIVth century, the figures given by E. F. Jacob are 300 out of 1200 students,[20] and at Cambridge at the end of the XIVth century, 137 scholarship grants were founded, of which seldom more than 80 were handed out.[21] Finally, in 1530 at Louvain, one seventh of the student body — 200 out of ca. 1450 — benefitted from a college bursary.[22]

2. Benefices

As early as 1219, the papal bull *Super speculam* made known the desire of the papacy to grant privileges to whomever sought knowledge by studying at a *studium generale*: Pope Honorius III relieved clerics who wanted to study theology from the residence obligation for five years without loss of income.[23] This preferential treatment found expression especially in the granting of benefices: in fact, each *scholaris* who had the status of *clericus* (tonsure and celibacy) enjoyed the *beneficium competentiae* or was entitled to a benefice.[24] Consequently, student-clerics applied to the pope for a benefice which was to serve as a kind of scholarship. Such a petition could be made individually or collectively (hence the roll-form), preferably through an eminent ecclesiastical or secular person, or via an institution of distinction, in order to speed up the papal response to the request. Not surprisingly, the university, being favoured by the popes, made it its duty to regularly recommend its *suppositi* via the so-called *rotuli beneficiorum* or *nominandorum*.[25] This was done for the first time by the University of Paris in 1317.

Of particular interest, of course, is the question whether and to what extent such petitions were effective. There is the fact that even when the pope granted his *fiat* — which happened in most cases — this did not necessarily lead to the immediate transfer of a benefice.[26] Much depended, indeed, on the collator who had to consent to the (transfer of the) benefice. For this and other reasons, many historians have their doubts about deducing from a papal grant the actual possession of a benefice. Nevertheless, to speak in this connection with A. Budinzky of a 'Recht von übrigens ziemlich illusorischem Werthe'[27] is an unwarranted conclusion. Although research on this matter remains to be done,[28] the regular and frequent dispatching of these *rotuli* indicates that not all applications were fruitless.[29] Finally it should be mentioned here that the expectations of acquiring a benefice thanks to papal favour were greatly reduced when the Great Schism had its effect, and, in a later period, when under the influence of the Conciliar Theory, sovereigns and local ecclesiastical collators contested papal reservations. It comes as no surprise, therefore that the practice of sending *rotuli* to the pope by the universities declined rapidly in the course of the XVth century.[30] That the universities and their members had to appeal more and more to a local bishop or other patrons — which had been possible and had been done previously — did not seem to please them. The numerous complaints recorded for those years about this situation suggest that they would have preferred a papal favour and expected more benefit from it.[31]

But, whatever form of assistance may have been used in reserving benefices for university students — whether from the pope or other patron, or by conciliar decrees or concordats[32] — only systematic research will prove how many students were actually granted a benefice for scholarship. The number of inquiries conducted so far in this matter is much too small to warrant any general conclusion. Here follow a few figures obtained from limited investigations. F. J. Pegues calculated, on the basis of the number of exemptions for ecclesiastical benefices in episcopal registers, that around the year 1500 in Oxford, about 900 out of about 1200 students were supported in their studies in this way.[33] Between the years 1372 and 1418, of the 199 Scandinavian students in the Faculty of Law in Prague, at least 51 were provided with an ecclesiastical benefice.[34] During the years 1497-98, in three rural deaneries in the Louvain area (Louvain, Geldenaken and Zoutleeuw), 102 benefices were taken by *suppositi* residing in Louvain.[35] Concerning an important chapter, St. Donatian in Bruges (Diocese of Tournai), R. De Keyser noticed that, over the period 1350-1450, only 40 out of the 182 university-taught canons finished their studies with the help of a canonry, and this exclusively for studies in higher faculties.[36] If here, too, geographical and chronological differentiation is to be taken into account, the question of the extent to which study expenses could be covered by a benefice still remains unanswered.[37]

Despite all the reservations expressed above, the opinion still prevails that most university students financed their studies thanks to an ecclesiastical benefice.[38] In the following pages, the present article does not intend to challenge such statements but merely to reopen the discussion by pointing out other forms of financing, less known or not known at all. The examples relate to the Low Countries.

3. Flying Grants

Free or 'flying' grants (*bursae volantes*), as they were formerly called, were scholarship grants not tied to any particular college or boarding house. By these a founder — in a testamentary disposition with perpetual character — provided one or more students a certain income (most paid yearly) and entrusted the administration of his foundation and the annual nominations of the bursars to his relatives, and/or to an institution such as an abbey, but never a college. Apart from having to fulfil a number of conditions, of which poverty, studiousness and the choice of subjects were most often stipulated, the beneficiaries of a flying grant were not obliged to reside in any particular college or boarding house; sometimes, not even a particular university was designated.[39] E. De Maesschalck thought this form of financing was extremely rare at Louvain University.[40] His assertion, while remaining open to dis- cussion,[41] needs a more systematic investigation to arrive at a decisive answer. The following examples pertaining mainly to the XIIIth century should indicate the relative importance of flying grants in financing studies.

An early and significant instance of a flying scholarship foundation is that of Margaret of Constantinople, Countess of Flanders and Hainaut (1244-1278). In her last extensive will made in November 1273, she donated the sum of £300 to be put out at interest, and its annual yield to be distributed among students from Flanders and Hainaut attending the University of Paris.[42] The distribution was to be made by one of three persons, viz. the chancellor of Paris, the prior of the Dominicans, or the guardian of the Franciscans, or by two of those three. What moved Margaret to this sudden affection for young people from her domain who studied at the Paris *studium*, remains an intriguing question. Possibly she felt a special affection for the city of Paris and its cultural charm, having spent a few years at the French court.[43] Another explanation is suggested by the fact that the scholarship was founded by testamentary disposition. Such acts — in medieval times at any rate — often represented a last chance for people to correct errors committed during their lifetime and to atone for their sins. Now one of Margaret's 'sins of omission' seems to have been that she neglected to grant to the *scolares* the exemption they usually enjoyed from paying toll and other duties on their travels to and from the *studium*.[44] In a letter dated 18 March 1251, Pope Innocent IV reprimanded the Countess for this omission.[45] It may very well be, then, that Margaret when making her will used this scholarship foundation as a way to make up for her negligence affecting the *scolares* of her domain studying in Paris.

In addition to this royal initiative, mention should be made of other flying grants donated by less illustrious persons from Flanders who had ample financial means. The first known flying grant dates back to 1224/25 n.s, when Matthew de Sancto Piato, cantor of the Notre Dame Cathedral of Tournai,[46] donated property and income to poor clerics from Tournai (diocese?) studying in Paris. The *scholasticus* of the chapter was entrusted with the administration and distribution of these incomes; he also, assisted by men of integrity (canons of the chapter?), nominated the candidates for this scholarship who had to prove good conduct in order to qualify. In addition, the founder stipulated that in the selection of candidates priority ought to be given to his nephews, provided, of course, they met the above conditions.[47] In April 1228 or 1-14 April, 1229 n.s., Matthew made some alterations in his will: leaving the grant itself unchanged, he now stipulates that the *scholasticus* should be assisted by the cantor of the chapter in administering the foundation; family preference is no longer mentioned.[48] Some of Matthew's arrangements are rather vague. Thus, not a single word is said about the amount to be paid out, or about the number of beneficiaries of the grant.

Such is not the case with the foundation made by Peter of Harelbeke, who held the office of archdeacon of the Tournai Diocese from 1256 till 1277, when he died.[49] In the obituary of the cathedral chapter of Notre Dame of Tournai, he is given the title of *magister*.[50] From the same obituary comes all the information we possess about his scholarship foundation, which must be dated between 1254 and the date of his death. From an annual interest of £10 Fl(emish), donated by Peter, the dean and chapter would pay — at times determined by themselves — a weekly amount of 3 s.par. to a cleric meeting the following conditions : he had to be a native of the archdeaconry of Tournai[51]; he had to be studying theology in Paris; he had to be studious, well-mannered, and actually staying at school. The period for which the scholarship could be granted to one person would normally be three years, but might be shortened or lengthened at the discretion of the dean and chapter. In selecting a candidate, dean and chapter had to give preference alternately to a Flemish-speaking and a French-speaking student. Besides his scholarship, Peter of Harelbeke donated some textbooks to the chapter to be available for use by the beneficiary of the scholarship[52]; these included the *Sententiae*, the Book of the Pericopes, the four Gospels with glosses in two volumes, the Acts of the Apostles, the Canonic Letters, and the Apocalypse of St. John in one volume. The selection of the books donated, and the title of Magister, which he carried, suggest that Peter himself had attended the Faculty of Theology in Paris.[53]

The scholarship established by Arnulf of Maldegem was much larger. He was a canon of the chapter of Notre Dame of Tournai, who died on 2 February 1276. As a nobleman, he possessed a considerable fortune which enabled him to found, among many other donations, a hospital in Maldegem.[54] The first mention of the creation of several flying grants goes back to June 1261.[55] In exchange for various sorts of income, the abbot and monastery of St. Peter's Abbey in Ghent take on the obligation of paying — annually and for all time — the sum of £50 Fl., new coins, to ten Flemish-speaking students: this amounted to an annual payment of 100 s.fl. to each student, to be paid before the name day of St. Remy, October 1st. In appointing the bursars each year around the Feast of the Exaltation of the Cross (October 14th), the abbey had to be guided by the following requirements: they had to be natives of the castellany of Bruges or Ghent,[56] had to prove to be of good reputation, and had to be most suited for studies. Moreover, the abbey should refrain from favouring its own monks and ministers, or their relatives or acquaintances: only the best, the most gifted should be chosen in good faith, without paying attention to the personal prestige of the candidates. Finally, it is stipulated that a bursar shall forfeit his right to full payment if he does not attend school for at least seven months.[57]

In December 1263,[58] the donor added another £20 Fl. to the original fifty and, while leaving the amount and date of payments unchanged, altered some of the dispositions of the original foundation, as far as these £20 were concerned. Thus, the right of choosing the candidates is now reserved to the abbot; candidates must come from the castellany or the deanery of Bruges[59]; assurance must be given that the bursars actually attend school and reside in the city of the *studium* for the full seven months, and if they do not, they should reimburse the abbey pro rata of the time of their absence; finally, it is strongly emphasised that the candidates must be poor students, that is, unable to support themselves by means of a benefice or their patrimony. About 1264, the abbot states that, in accordance with previous arrangements, after the death of Arnulf of Maldegem he and the abbey will distribute, in exchange of sufficient income, annually and for all time, the sum of £70 Fl. among poor *scolares* studying in Paris or wherever such a *studium* exists.[60]

In March 1268 n.s., the St. Peter's Abbey of Ghent received from Arnulf of Maldegem another grant of £100 Fl. of annual income, to be paid to the chapter of Tournai in two portions of £50 each, respectively on January 1st, and on the Feast of St. John the Baptist, June 24th.[61] On 8 December 1269, the abbot asked the bishop of Tournai to ratify the agreement between the abbey and Arnulf, providing £170 to poor students.[62] It was not until 24 January 1276 n.s.[63] that it became known, through the reading of Arnulf's will, how the £100 should be distributed by the chapter of Notre Dame of Tournai.[64] The chapter, or two people (canons?) appointed by the chapter, are to distribute the above sum around Christmas time to poor students in Paris or some other *studium generale*. In choosing the beneficiaries of the grant, the chapter is to take into account the following conditions: candidates must come from the Tournai Diocese and speak Flemish[65]; they must be the ones most in need of support, and most suited to study, particularly of theology; neither personal prestige nor social status of the candidates should affect the choice. Besides giving financial help, the chapter is expected to further the interests of these poor students in other matters as well. Such were the arrangements made by Arnulf of Maldegem. Extracts of bills coming from the cathedral chapter of Notre Dame of Tournai show that these payments were still awarded in the early years of the XVth century.[66]

The last known flying scholarship of the XIIIth century was established by Henry van der Muiden. F. Huet, who in 1838 published a biography of Henry of Ghent, the well-known XIIIth century philosopher and theologian from the Tournai Diocese, discovered a will, which has since vanished. In this a certain Henricus de Muda, archdeacon of Tournai, donated a yearly income to the city of Ghent from which to support two students in Paris. At least one of the two had to be a relative of the benefactor and a student in theology. The same Henry also donated a number of manuscripts of theology and other 'sciences' to St. Bavo's Abbey and to the convent of the Dominicans, both located in Ghent.[67] Since these data correspond to what was at the time generally accepted about the life of Henry of Ghent, F. Huet attributed this will to him. This attribution, however, can no longer be maintained after N. De Pauw's more scholarly investigation into the life of the great philosopher. While not impugning the genuineness of the will, De Pauw was of the opinion that the author of the will probably lived in the neighbourhood of St. Bavo's Abbey, where he got in touch with a Henricus de Muda, priest and monk, whose name is indeed mentioned in the obituary of the abbey.[68] Further research on our part has brought to light some possibly useful supplementary information. First, a remark about the foundation itself. The town accounts of Ghent of the XIVth and XVth centuries regularly record expenses for two students at the University of Paris[69]: curiously enough, one of these bursars was a student in theology. When P. Rogghé noticed that several of these bursars were later employed in municipal services, he concluded that the city of Ghent used these scholarships in order to train a solidly skilled staff.[70] But even if nothing was known about a former scholarship grant on the part of the city, it would remain doubtful that the city would subsidise students of theology rather than of arts or law. A second remark concerns the founder himself. N. De Pauw's theory that this Henry was a monk of St. Bavo's Abbey of Ghent must be discarded for the simple reason that the Henry of the will was an archdeacon of the Tournai Diocese and therefore could not possibly be mentioned in the obituary of the abbey as a monk. A more likely candidate might be a Henry of Ghent, canon of the chapter of Notre Dame of Courtrai, who died in 1295[71]; he had been a professor of theology in Paris for some time,[72] which would readily explain his donation of books mentioned in the will.

A few conclusions and remarks about these flying grants seem justified. Looking at the origin of the donors, one is at once struck by the central role played by the city of Tournai. Matthew de Sancto Piato and Arnulf of Maldegem were canons of the cathedral chapter, whereas Peter of Harelbeke and Henry van der Muiden must have resided mostly in Tournai on account of the function of archdeacon of the diocese. The important part played by the chapter in these matters most likely resulted from its task as administrator assigned to it by several founders.

The flying grants, however, are not the only proof of frequent aid to students from the Tournai region. In the first place, there is the fact that several fixed grants were also created in the same region. Two of them were destined for students of theology at the College of the Sorbonne in Paris. In October 1266, Nicholas, archdeacon of the Tournai Diocese for Flanders, bequeathed the sum of £50 par. to the Sorbonne in order to support five Flemish-speaking *magistri*.[73] A few decades later, Michael de Warenghien, Bishop of Tournai himself (1284-1291), established a fixed grant for two French-speaking *magistri* from the city or diocese of Tournai: each bursar was to receive £10 par. annually.[74] It is significant that the nomination right for both grants belonged to the Bishop of Tournai. The donations of manuscripts to the Sorbonne and to the cathedral chapter of Notre Dame of Tournai are equally noteworthy.[75] Later, in the XIVth and XVth centuries in the region of Tournai, there is a constant demonstration of concern for university students, particularly those in Paris.[76] All this suggests that Gilles li Muisis, abbot of St. Martin's in Tournai, was not exaggerating when he stated that in his time 73 people from the city of Tournai alone were studying in Paris around 1350.[77] From this preliminary research, the favourable atmosphere with regard to financial support of students (indirectly as well as by providing 'expensive' textbooks) emerges as typical of Tournai. Further systematic research may prove that the same trend prevailed in other places as well. In any case, it may be safely concluded that these flying grants were of considerable importance for the financing of studies. At the end of the XIIIth century, the 35 people who enjoyed a flying scholarship unmistakably outnumbered the seven students entitled to a fixed grant.[78] This favourable attitude accounts for the large number of foundations. Even those who themselves never studied and, consequently, were unaware of the needs of university life and felt no nostalgia for student life,[79] living as they did in a milieu favourable to university life, did feel more inclined to endow some form of financial support to university students in order to fulfil their charitable obligations.

The Faculty of Theology of Paris appears to have been chosen by preference, although in many cases the choice of place (such as Bologna and Montpellier) as well as of subject (arts, medicine, or law) was left to the bursar's personal decision. Conditions regarding language and place of origin of the candidates often imposed by the founders are not treated here because they are of minor importance.[80]

The notion of *pauper*, however, requires some explanation, since it is one of the standard requirements a bursar had to meet, besides being well-mannered, eager to study, and regular school attendance.[81] In the will of Arnulf of Maldegem a *pauper* is one who 'cannot sufficiently support himself either from a benefice or from income from his patrimony'. He should not be thought of, then, as a *nihil habens*.[82]

How much were the bursars paid?[83] The grant of Peter of Harelbeke amounted to 3 s. par. weekly per bursar, that of Arnulf of Maldegem only about 2 s. par. weekly, or respectively £7.15 s. par. and £5 par. annually. Bishop Warenghien gave each student of theology £10 par. annually, which meant about 4 s. par. weekly. These sums come very close to those from grants donated by the English kings in the XIIIth century, viz. from £5 to £10 annually, or 2 to 4 s. par. weekly.[84] There too, presumably, these amounts were intended to pay for room and board only, and not for the often high enrollment fees — as was the case in grants obtained via colleges.

4. Patronage

A last form of financial aid to pay for study expenses is patronage, in the form of a temporary bequest of money or goods, e.g. books, to university students. This may be a direct and unique allocation of the donation to the students, and therefore mostly without registration by an Act, or a written disposition concerning a regular payment but limited to a certain period of time.

a. Individual Patrons

The French and English kings are well-known for their patronage of students. Presumably already in the XIIth, and certainly in the XIIIth centuries, they provided some students with financial assistance whatever their reasons for sponsoring them may have been. Up to the end of the XIIIth century under the reign of Philip the Fair (1285-1314), there was an entry provided *pro bursis scolarium* in the expense column of the treasury accounts.[85] Not surprisingly, on account of their temporary character, many cases of patronage by donors of lesser rank have never been registered, or, even if they were, have left no trace in any surviving archives.[86]

b. Institutions

Setting aside the better known forms of financial assistance to university students by towns[87] or religious institutions,[88] it might be useful to stress a number of lesser-known forms, and particularly the so-called charitable institutions. A distinction has to be made in this connection between those that considered support of university students as secondary within the framework of their large-scale charity, and those that made such support their main concern. A whole range of institutions such as poor-tables, tables of the Holy Ghost, and the like belong to the former kind. For example, the 'Common Purse' of Ypres undertook to bear all expenses of a burgher of Ypres studying in Louvain.[89]

The second category is made up of those institutions almost exclusively established for the purpose of rendering financial support to university students. Thus cities such as Ypres and Douai know the existence of student-confraternities in the XIVth century, providing at any rate in the beginning, financial help to students.[90] In Tournai a foundation was established for 'poor' university students coming from the region of Tournai. This foundation, already in effect before 1484, was created, and later occasionally enriched, with property and revenue by wealthy clergymen and lay people.[91] Seven registers of accounts of this foundation, extended over the period 1484-1522, have survived.[92] They record the incomes from rents and interests and the expenses for scholarship grants; as they mention the amount paid to each individual, the name of the bursar, and mostly that of the university he attended, they are very important and useful to the researcher.[93] The foundation in question was administered by the *scholasticus* and the cantor of the chapter of Notre Dame of Tournai.[94]

What conclusions may be drawn from these accounts? In the period 1484-1522, 84 boys were supplied with a grant, often for several years; 62 of them resided in Paris, four in Louvain, one in Montpellier, and for the others no university town was given.[95] As far as these 67 students were concerned — whether the remaining ones were actually university students cannot be ascertained[96] — the distribution of grants is as follows:

		11	12	16	18	24	in £Fl.
	1		9	1	11	4	
number of	2	1	3		2	5	
years a	3		6		5	2	
grant was	4		6		7		
given	5		1		1	1	
	6		2				
		1	27	1	26	12	number of bursars

It is not clear which standards the administrators of the foundation applied in determining the amount and duration of each grant: most likely, for the amount need was the dominant factor. Since this financial aid ran mostly for only a limited number of years, it may be assumed that most of the bursars were students of the Faculty of Arts. What was said above about flying grants applies here also, viz. that they represented an important supplementary income to students but hardly ever covered the total cost of their studies.[97] In our view, these institutions played a very important part by raising all kinds of funds through 'small' testamentary dispositions. Each fund by itself would not have sufficed to maintain an independent scholarship grant, but, joined together, they enabled less wealthy prelates or lay people to effectively favour university students in their will.

Summary

Only college foundations and scholarships incorporated by these have been investigated in recent times. The conclusion was that only a small percentage of the toal student population was eligible for such financial support. This explains why most historians dealing with this problem sought a solution in the granting of ecclesiastical benefices, together with direct financing by the parents — which is obviously difficult to check. A benefice was probably one of the prevailing forms of scholarship, but its role should not be overestimated! All investigation into the actual share of benefices in covering the total expenses for university studies remains to be done.

An examination of other forms of financial support to university students such as flying scholarship and patronage led us to modify somewhat the traditional outlook. Although these ways of financing were most limited to bring supplementary relief in the all too heavy cost of university training, on the whole it would seem to us that they have played an important part next to colleges and benefices. Only a more systematic investigation — even for Flanders — will provide a more decisive answer on the importance, in quantity as well as in quality, of these 'non-traditional forms' of study financing.[98]

Langemarkstraat, 24
B-8688 Zonnebeke, Belgium

REFERENCES

* Research Assistant of the National Fund for Scientific Research (Belgium), K. U. Leuven.

1. See on this especially: J. Scheurkogel, 'Nieuwe universiteitsgeschiedenis en late middeleeuwen', *Tijdschrift voor geschiedenis*, 84 (1981): 194-204, with further bibliography on p. 194 n. 10; also N. Hammerstein, 'Neue Wege der Universitätsgeschichtsschreibung', *Zeitschrift für historische Forschung*, 5 (1978): 449-463, and idem, 'Nochmals Universitätsgeschichtsschreibung', *ibidem*, 7 (1980): 321-336. For a survey of the various social themes within the history of universities, and the relevant bibliography, see H. De Ridder-Symoens, 'Universiteitsgeschiedenis als bron voor sociale geschiedenis', *Tijdschrift voor sociale geschiedenis*, 10 (1978): 87-115; also, just about every introduction to monographs and articles dealing with the social history of universities: for example R. Chartier and J. Revel, 'Université et société dans l'Europe moderne: position des problèmes', *Revue d'histoire moderne et contemporaine*, 25 (1978): 353-357, and J. Paquet, 'Recherches sur l'universitaire "pauvre" au moyen âge', *Belgisch tijdschrift voor filologie en geschiedenis*, 56 (1978):

14   *History of Universities*

301-303. Although somewhat reluctantly at first, German historiography has now joined in this 'new' trend; see R. C. Schwinges, 'Pauperes an deutschen Universitäten des 15. Jahrhunderts', *Zeitschrift für historische Forschung*, 8 (1981): 285-286. For recent developments in Italian historiography of universities, see among others P. Denley, 'Recent Studies on Italian Universities of the Middle Ages and Renaissance', *History of Universities*, 1 (1981): 193-205.

2.   Research into such calculation of costs is still in its initial stage: the main studies dealing with its various aspects have been analysed by H. De Ridder-Symoens, *art. cit. n. 1*, pp. 100-101. See also J. Paquet, 'L'universitaire "pauvre" au moyen-âge: problèmes, documentation, questions de méthode', in *The Universities in the Late Middle Ages*, eds. J. IJsewijn and J. Paquet, *Mediaevalia Lovaniensia*, series I, studia VI (Louvain, 1978), p. 414 n. 30 and J. Paquet, 'Coût des études, pauvreté et labeur: fonctions et métiers d'étudiants au moyen âge', *History of Universities*, 2 (1982): 16-17; also the calculation of expenses at the University of Paris in the XVth-XVIth centuries in L. W. B. Brockliss, 'Patterns of Attendance at the University of Paris, 1440-1800' *The Historical Journal*, 21 (1978): 528-530. Such calculation is, indeed, fairly complicated, and not just because of the problems concerning the sources (regarding these, see J. Verger, 'Le coût des grades: droits et frais d'examen dans les universités du midi de la France au moyen âge', in *The Economic and Material Frame of the Mediaeval University*, ed. A. L. Gabriel, *Texts and Studies in the History of Mediaeval Education*, 15 (Notre Dame, 1977), p.19). Also when the exact expenses of one particular student during a number of years have been calculated (for instance J. Wils, ed., 'Les dépenses d'un étudiant à l'université de Louvain (1448-1453)', *Analectes pour servir à l'histoire ecclésiastique de Belgique*, 32, ser. III, 2 (1906): 489-507; for the most thorough analysis of this edition, see E. De Maesschalck, 'De criteria van de armoede aan de middeleeuwse universiteit te Leuven', *Belgisch tijdschrift voor filologie en geschiedenis*, 58 (1980): 347-348). Still, this is only one particular case which cannot be generalised as such. The range of varying factors (geographical, chronological and sociological) which determined the cost have been summarised best in S. Stelling-Michaud, 'L'histoire des universités au moyen âge et à la renaissance au cours des vingt-cinq dernières années', in *Comité international des sciences historiques, XIe congrès international des sciences historiques, 1960. Rapports* I (Uppsala, 1960), p. 119: 'Les frais d'entretien variaient fortement selon la condition sociale des étudiants et le niveau de vie de la ville universitaire, à une époque donnée, compte tenu du pouvoir d'achat de l'argent et des revenus'. To illustrate this with two extremes: how much more will be spent by a son of nobility studying at the Faculty of Law in Orléans (average calculation of costs by H. De Ridder-Symoens, 'La vie et l'organisation matérielle de l'ancienne université d'Orléans', in *The Economic and Material Frame . . .*, pp.44-45) compared with a matriculated *pauper* at the Faculty of Arts in Paris! Concerning the phenomenon of the *pauper* in the medieval universities, quite a lot has been published the last few years. Most publications show that such *pauper* was often exempted from the so-called school expenses (matriculation fees, college fees, *collectae* in general and the examination and promotion fees) or these costs were reduced, mainly as long as this *pauper* was a student of the Faculty of Arts. This exemption often consisted of a loan not bearing interest: M. Ditsche, 'Zur Studienförderung im Mittelalter', *Rheinische Vierteljahrblätter*, 41 (1977): 51-62; J. Verger, *art.cit.*, pp. 19-36 (concerning the universities of Toulouse, Montpellier and Avignon) and J. Paquet, *art. cit.*, (n. 1), pp. 314 and 341-344. In this connection I refer to the existence at university centres of funds providing loans not bearing interest: S. Stelling-Michaud, *art.cit.*, p.119; E. Mornet, 'Pauperes scolares. Essai sur la condition matérielle des étudiants scandinaves dans les universités aux XIVe et XVe siècles', *Le moyen âge*, 84 (1978): 87, and G. C. Boyce, *The English-German Nation in the University of Paris during the Middle Ages* (Bruges, 1927), pp. 166-167 and 172. Besides money, books also were lent in this way: J. Veillard, 'Le registre de prêt de la bibliothèque du collège de Sorbonne au XVe siècle',

in *The Universities in the Late Middle Ages* . . . , pp. 276-292. But, apart from the general calculation of costs, circumstances such as illness, war, poor harvest, etc. involving extra expenses, should be taken into account: C. H. Haskins, 'The Life of Mediaeval Students as Illustrated by Their Letters', in *Studies in Mediaeval Culture* (New York, [1929]), pp. 11 ff. See also J. Paquet, *art. cit.* (n. 1), pp. 320-322.

3.   'Royal Support of Students in the Thirteenth Century', *Speculum*, 31 (1956): 454.

4.   'Philanthropy and the Universities in France and England in the Later Middle Ages', in *The Economic and Material Frame* . . . (n. 2), p. 69. Parallel to this are the findings of A. -L. Gabriel (*Preface*, in op. cit., p. 12) stating that the economic history of medieval universities — with which the financing aspect is highly linked — still has to be written. See also A. B. Cobban, *The Medieval Universities: Their Development and Organization* (London, 1975), p.237.

5.   In the letters from *formulae*-books (for the *ars dictaminis*) the parents are mostly asked for money: C. H. Haskins, *art. cit.* (n. 2), pp. 8 ff.; H. G. Richardson, 'Business Training in Medieval Oxford', *American Historical Review*, 46 (1941): 265-266; and T. H. Aston, G. D. Duncan and T. A. R. Evans, 'The Medieval Alumni of the University of Cambridge', *Past and Present*, 86 (1980): 49-50. Of course in itself this is no proof of the relative preponderance of parents paying for university studies. It is fairly logical that, in contrast to foundations of scholarship grants by which the amount of annual payment was fixed in advance, the payment by parents was a fluctuating amount certainly influenced by the students' requests. Although there is a scarcity of sources, I agree with T. H. Aston, et al., *art. cit.*, p.50: ' . . . we are disposed to believe that family support was probably the most important single element in the maintenance of scholars (at medieval Cambridge, and Oxford as well)'.

6.   An enormous range of 'professional activities' has been found among university students: from beggar, copyist and clerk, to *pedagogus* and teacher: J. Paquet, 'Coût des études, pauvreté et labeur . . . ', (n. 2), pp. 21-52; some wide-spread data, among others, in E. Mornet, *art. cit.* (n. 2), pp. 53-102 (passim) and H. De Ridder-Symoens, 'La vie et l'organisation . . . ', (n. 2), p. 45. More generally J. Verger, *Les universités au moyen âge, Collection SUP, L'historien*, 14 (Paris, 1973), p.71, and J. -G. Goglin, *Les misérables dans l'Occident médiéval, Points, Histoire*, 25 (Paris, 1976), p.128.

7.   One of the exceptions is the study of T. H. Aston, et. al., *art. cit.* (n. 5), pp. 40-51, concerning the University of Cambridge.

8.   In this cursory survey the German situation is rarely mentioned. For an explanation see R. C. Schwinges, *art. cit.* (n. 1), p. 287: 'Eine nennenswerte Zahl von Förderungsmassnahmen, von denen auch mittellose Universitätsbesucher profitieren konnten, wurde jedoch erst seit der 2. Hälfte des 16. Jahrhunderts evident'. See there also for the existing literature concerning this subject (to which should be added H. Boockman, 'Die Rechtsstudenten des deutschen Ordens. Studium, Studienförderung und gelehrter Beruf im späten Mittelalter', in *Festschrift für Hermann Heimpel*, II (Göttingen, 1972), pp. 315-316 and 367-368).

9.   A good general survey is given by J. Verger, *op. cit.* (n. 6), pp. 71-72.

10.   Or the original scholarship foundation was enriched with new donations: examples of this in F. J. Pegues, *art. cit.* (n. 4), pp. 71-73.

11.   Especially elaborated for Louvain: E. De Maesschalck, *Kollegstichtingen aan de universiteit te Leuven (1425-1530). Pogingen tot oplossing van armoede- en tuchtproblemen*, unpublished doctorate thesis K. U. L., 3 vols. (Louvain, 1977). Special thanks to the author for having granted me access to his thesis. The same author gave a summary in 'Beurzen en colleges te Leuven in de 15de en 16de eeuw', *Spiegel historiael*, 13 (1978): 556-563. A few examples of fixed scholarships for Paris in F. J. Pegues, *art. cit.* (n. 4), pp. 76-77.

12.   In the XIIIth century universities of southern Europe, such as Bologna, had few colleges; in fact they were especially centres for law students from better classes: see J. Verger, *op. cit.* (n. 6), p. 71; also A. B. Cobban, *op. cit.* (n. 4), pp. 151-152. For Orléans, see H. De Ridder-Symoens, 'Les origines géographique et sociale des étudiants de la nation germanique de l'ancienne université d'Orléans (1444-1546): aperçu général', in *The Universities in the Late Middle Ages* . . . (n. 2), pp. 464-465.

13.   F. J. Pegues places the culminating point of the founding of colleges in the first half of the XIVth, and the XVth centuries: *art. cit.* (n. 4), pp. 70-74. See also A. B. Cobban, *op. cit.* (n. 4), p. 129.

14.   In general: A. B. Cobban, *op. cit.* (n. 4), pp. 204-207, and J. Paquet, *art. cit.* (n. 1), p. 312. Recent thorough inquiries have provided clear evidence. For Louvain: E. De Maesschalck, *art. cit.* (n. 2), pp. 346-351, and idem, 'Scholarship Grants and Colleges, Established at the University of Louvain up to 1530', in *The Universities in the Late Middle Ages* . . . (n. 2). For Paris: L. W. B. Brockliss, *art. cit.* (n. 2), p. 534.

15.   E. De Maesschalck, 'Scholarship . . . ', (n. 14), pp. 489-490; idem, 'Beurzen en colleges . . . ', (n. 11), pp. 558-559 and L. W. B. Brockliss, *art. cit.* (n. 2), p. 535.

16.   Regarding the so-called 'aristocratisation progressive de la population des collèges' (already from the end of the XIVth century), see J. Le Goff, *Les intellectuels au moyen âge, Le temps qui court*, 3 (Paris, 1960), 2nd ed., pp. 139 ff.; J. Paquet, *art. cit.* (n. 1), p. 344; idem, *art. cit.* (n. 2), p. 418; J. -G. Goglin, *op. cit.* (n. 6), p. 131; and others L. W. B. Brockliss, *art. cit.* (n. 2), pp. 534-537.

17.   In general: F. J. Pegues, *art. cit.* (n. 4), pp. 69 and 76. See also A. B. Cobban, *op. cit.* (n. 4), pp. 130-138, and J. Verger, *op. cit.* (n. 6), p. 173.

18.   F. J. Pegues, *art. cit.* (n. 4), p. 75 (The figure of the total student population is based on H. Rashdall, *op. cit.* (n. 24), III, pp. 328-332).

19.   L. W. B. Brockliss, *art. cit.* (n. 2), p. 534.

20.   E. F. Jacob, 'English University Clerks in the Later Middle Ages: the Problem of Maintenance', *Bulletin of the John Rylands Library Manchester*, 29 (1945): 313 (new edition in *Essays in the Conciliar Epoch* (Manchester, 1963), 3rd ed.). Wrongly quoted in F. J. Pegues, *art. cit.* (n. 4), p. 75. For the total size and the figure of secular colleges see also the estimate of T. H. Aston, 'Oxford's Medieval Alumni', *Past and Present*, 74 (1977): 6-7, where the authors are convinced that Oxford colleges mustered at most 200 and perhaps only 150 out of about 1600 scholars (including 250 friars) during the first half of the XVth century.

21.   F. J. Pegues, *art. cit.* (n. 4), p. 75 (based on Cobban, *The King's Hall*, pp. 44-45). Cambridge may have contained between 400 and 700 scholars (including 200 friars) in the 1370's and 1380's: T. H. Aston, et al., *art. cit.* (n. 5), pp. 12-13. For calculations concerning the mid-fifteenth century: *ibidem*, pp. 14 ff.

22.   E. De Maesschalck, *Scholarship* . . . (n. 14), p. 485. These figures are gathered from a 1526 census, and somewhat adapted by the author.

23.   C. Lefebvre, 'Grade académique', in *Dictionnaire de droit canonique*, V (1953), col. 977. Later these privileges were extended in time and applicable to other branches as well: F. J. Pegues, *art. cit.* (n. 4), p. 76. On the regular reconfirmation of these privileges for some important universities see P. Kibre, *Scholarly Privileges in the Middle Ages: the Rights, Privileges and Immunities of Scholars and Universities at Bologna, Padua, Paris and Oxford*, Mediaeval Academy of America, publ. no. 72 (London, 1961), XVI-446 pp.

24.   On the status of *clericus* and the privileges connected with it see H. E. Feine, *Kirchliche Rechtsgeschichte. Die katholische Kirche* (Cologne - Vienna, 1972), 5th revised ed., pp. 391-395; W. Nolet and P. C. Boeren, *Kerkelijke instellingen in de middeleeuwen* (Amsterdam, 1951), pp. 86-106; P. Kibre, *op. cit.* (n. 23), pp. 7-8; and H.

Rashdall, *The Universities in Europe in the Middle Ages*, revised ed. by F. M. Powicke and A. B. Emden (Oxford, 1936), III, pp. 393-396. On the usurpation of clerical privileges by university students, see P. Kibre, *op. cit.* (n. 23), pp. 3-17. The number of clerics among the university population is difficult to estimate. More numerous in the north than in the south, and declining towards the end of the Middle Ages, the clerics must have formed for a long time a great majority, especially since their return to civil life posed no problem as long as lower ordinations were not received: S. Stelling-Michaud, *art. cit.* (n. 2), p. 114; H. De Ridder-Symoens, *art. cit.* (n. 1), pp. 106-107, and J. Verger, *op. cit.* (n. 6), pp. 80-81 and 111.

25.   D. E. R. Watt, 'University Clerks and Rolls of Petitions for Benefices', *Speculum*, 34 (1959): 213-229; J. Verger, 'Le recrutement géographique des universités françaises au début du XVe siècle, d'après les suppliques de 1403', *Mélanges d'archéologie et d'histoire de l'École française de Rome*, 82 (1970): 855-870; P. Kibre, *op. cit.* (n. 23), pp. 227 ff., and E. F. Jacob, 'Petitions for Benefices from English Universities during the Great Schism', in *Essays in the Conciliar Epoch* (Manchester, 1963), 3rd revised ed., pp. 223-239. See also U. Berlière, *Suppliques de Clément VI (1342- 1352)*, *Analecta Vaticano-Belgica*, ser. 1: *Publication de l'Institut historique belge de Rome. Documents relatifs aux anciens diocèses de Cambrai, Tournai, Thérouanne et Liège*, I (Bruges, 1906), pp. IX-XXXIII.

26.   D. E. R. Watt, *art. cit.* (n. 25), p. 223, and E. F. Jacob, *art. cit.* (n. 25), p. 224: 'Petitions for provisions . . . should . . . be regarded as the approach to promotion rather than as promotion itself'.

27.   A. Budinszky, *Die Universität Paris und die Fremden an derselben im Mittelalter. Ein Beitrag zur Geschichte dieser hohen Schule* (Berlin, 1876; unchanged reprint, Aalen, 1970), p. 53. Many authors have shared his view, although in a more nuanced form: for example: J. -G. Goglin, *op. cit.* (n. 6), p. 130; C. Tihon, 'Les expectatives in *forma pauperum*, particulièrement au XIVe siècle', *Bulletin de l'Institut historique belge de Rome*, 5 (1925): 91-94, and J. Verger, *op. cit.* (n. 6), p. 129 (the lavishness with which the pope granted benefices was the cause of too many candidates being entitled to one and the same benefice). See also the conclusion of T. H. Aston et al., *art. cit.* (n. 5), p. 42: 'How large a proportion of those in higher study was thus financed out of ecclesiastical revenues it is probably impossible to know, . . . '.

28.   Some interesting indications about this are to be found in J. Verger, *art. cit.* (n. 25), pp. 864-865.

29.   Compare with the inquiry into the actual result of a number of cases in E. F. Jacob, *art. cit.* (n. 25). Some were successful (often after several attempts); others were not. Hence his conclusion (p. 239): 'The proportion is hard to determine'. That a highly graduated student had better chances of succeeding than a student of the Faculty of Arts (if he was admitted to the roll: see J. Verger, *art. cit.* (n. 25), p. 866) is quite obvious: J. Verger, *art. cit.* (n. 25), p. 871; idem, *op. cit.* (n. 6), pp. 128 ff.; D. E. R. Watt, *art. cit.* (n. 25), p. 219, and E. Mornet, *art. cit.* (n. 2), p. 88 n. 104. Determinant too were wealth and the relations linked with it, as these highly increased the chances of getting a benefice: C. Renardy, *Le monde des maîtres universitaires du diocèse de Liège, 1140-1350. Recherches sur sa composition et ses activités*, in *Bibliothèque de la Faculté de Philosophie et Lettres de l'Université de Liège*, 228 (Paris, 1979), p. 173.

30.   D. E. R. Watt, *art. cit.* (n. 25), p. 224, and J. Verger, *op. cit.* (n. 6), p. 129. On the heavy opposition to the papal right of reservation in France, see P. Kibre, *op. cit.* (n. 23), pp. 232-240; in England: E. F. Jacob, *art. cit.* (n. 20), pp. 318 ff. This did not prevent the University of Louvain, in 1483 and 1513, from obtaining from the pope far-reaching privileges in order to reserve benefices in the Netherlands for its *suppositi*: M. Bruwier, 'Les conflits juridictionnels et bénéficiaux entre l'université de Louvain et l'évêque de Liège de 1425 à 1568', *Revue d'histoire ecclésiastique*, 44 (1949), pp. 575 ff.

18 *History of Universities*

31. E. F. Jacob, *art. cit.* (n. 20), p. 314, and P. Kibre, *op. cit.* (n. 23), pp. 234 ff.

32. Like the Council of Constance (1417), the Council of Basel (1436), or the Pragmatic Sanction of Bourges (1438). See the main bibliography in R. De Keyser, 'Chanoines séculiers et universités: le cas de Saint-Donatien de Bruges (1350-1450)', in *The Universities in the Late Middle Ages* . . . (n. 2), p. 586 n. 6. See also J. Verger, *op. cit.* (n. 6), p. 129.

33. *Art. cit.* (n. 4), p. 76. The figure of the size of Oxford must be estimated higher, see n. 19 and T. H. Aston et al., *art. cit.* (n. 5), p. 13. The question still remains whether an exemption was granted only because of studies. Was the possession of two or more benefices by one and the same person taken into account?

34. E. Mornet, *art. cit.* (n. 2), pp. 65-66.

35. C. Buve, 'Lijst van eenige pastoors en beneficianten die de lessen der Hoogeschool volgden in de 16de eeuw', *Bijdragen tot de geschiedenis, bijzonderlijk van het aloude hertogdom Brabant*, 1 (1902): 282-289.

36. *Art. cit.* (n. 32), pp. 590-591. J. Pycke, 'Les chanoines de Tournai aux études, 1330-1340', in *The Universities in the Late Middle Ages* . . . (n. 2), pp. 602-603, does mention the custom of continuing to study through the income of a canonry, but gives no exact figures.

37. Consideration in E. Mornet, *art. cit.* (n. 2), p. 88, and in H. Boockman, *art. cit.* (n. 8), p. 368. More optimism in T. H. Aston et al., *art. cit.* (n. 5), p. 41.

38. F. J. Pegues, *art. cit.* (n. 4), p. 76. See also E. F. Jacob, *art. cit.* (n. 20), p. 313.

39. Elaborated on the basis of following examples and H. De Vocht, *Inventaire des archives de l'université de Louvain (1426-1797) aux Archives générales du royaume à Bruxelles* (Louvain, 1927), pp. XX and 21. Compare also with E. De Maesschalck, 'Beurzen en colleges . . . ' (n. 11), p. 557, and idem, 'Scholarship . . . ' (n. 14), p. 484. However, I do not agree with the statement expressed there implying that flying grants should be understood as 'a certain income, with which he could do whatever he wanted'. What follows should give evidence of this.

40. 'Scholarship . . . ' (n. 14), p. 484.

41. To base conclusions only on what is kept in the archives about the university of Louvain (especially H. De Vocht, *op. cit.* (n. 39), no. D: 'Les fondations volantes', nos. 4503-3661), as the author does, seems rather precarious. Indeed, documents in connection with a flying grant for a long time were kept in sole custody of the donor, often a private person. There was a real danger of these documents disappearing after some time. Who keeps papers of a scholarly foundation that has been usurped in the course of time, or which has simply lost its significance due to the devaluation of incomes (especially with very old foundations)? How many flying grants were still being paid off when, on 4 July 1761, the Austrian government had all existing flying scholarship grants in the Southern Netherlands — including those founded for students at a foreign university — transferred and fixed to the university of Louvain (*Ibidem*, p. XX)? The flying grants transferred then (together with the documents) seldom go back beyond the XVIth century. Compare with M. Goyens, 'De familiebeurzenstichtingen', *Vlaamse stam*, 5 (1969): 237-238 (French version 'Les fondations des bourses d'études', *Le parchemin*, 17, no. 146: 80-85), and idem, 'De beurzenstichtingen ingelijfd bij de colleges van de universiteit van Leuven', *Vlaamse stam*, 10 (1976): 505-515 (French version 'les fondations des bourses d'études des collèges de l'université de Louvain: Fondations de collateur — parent vacantes', *L'intermédiaire des généalogistes*, 161 (1972): 261-274). Our assumption concerning the real importance of flying grants for Louvain has very recently been confirmed by P. Vandermeersch, *op. cit.* in n. 87 below, I, p. 116.

42. ' . . . as escoliers de la terre de Flandres et de Haynau à Paris, trois cens livres
pour achater rente à départir chascun an par le consel dou chancelier de Paris, dou
prieus des préecheurs et dou gardyen des frères meneurs u des deux de ces trois, . . . ': E.
Hautcoeur, ed., *Cartulaire de l'abbaye de Flines* (Lille-Paris-Brussels, 1873), No.
CLXXXII, pp. 201-202. For the placing of this will in the context of Margaret's life and
of the Flemish political background, see T. Luyckx, *De grafelijke financiële
bestuursinstellingen en het grafelijk patrimonium in Vlaanderen tijdens de regering van
Margareta van Constantinopel (1244-1278)*, in *Verhandelingen van de Koninklijke
Vlaamse academie voor wetenschappen, letteren en schone kunsten van België. Klasse der
letteren*, 39 (Brussels, 1961), pp. 282-287.

43. From September 1208 to February 1212: see T. Luykx, *op. cit.* (n. 42), p. 300;
compare also with A. Wauters, 'Marguerite de Constantinople', in *Biographie
nationale*, XIII (Brussels, 1895), cols. 612-629.

44. Concerning this privilege see P. Kibre, *op. cit.* (n. 23), pp. 85 ff.

45. H. Denifle and A. Chatelain, eds., *Chartularium universitatis Parisiensis*, I (Paris,
1889), no. 196, p. 222. See also P. Kibre, *op. cit.* (n. 23), p. 100.

46. For biographical data concerning this canon, as well as some other founders
mentioned below, consult in the first place J. Pycke, *Le chapitre cathédral Notre-Dame
de Tournai de la fin du XIe à la fin du XIIIe siècle: son organisation, sa vie, ses membres*,
unpublished doctoral thesis U. C. L., 2 vols. (Louvain, 1976), IX-502 and 301 pp. Until
the publication of this report, we have to rely on fragmentarily gathered notes. For the
bibliography on the chapter of Tournai, see J. Pycke, 'Bibliographie relative à l'histoire
de Tournai', *Annales de la Société royale, d'histoire et d'archéologie de Tournai*, 24
(1974): 129-436. Matthew, who had been cantor since 1205, was not to die until 30
October 1233: thus C. Vleeschouwers, 'Het oudst bewaarde martyrologium-
necrologium van het kathedraal kapittel van O. -L. -Vrouw-Doornik', *Archief en
bibliotheekwezen in België*, 49 (1978): 599-560, where he argues against the earlier date
30 October 1228, proposed by J. J. Vos in his *Les dignités et les fonctions de l'ancien
chapitre de Notre-Dame de Tournai*, II, (Bruges, 1898), pp. 17-18 — an uncritical study
often based on unreliable sources, according to C. Vleeschouwers, *art. cit.*, p. 593.

47. Archives of the chapter of Tournai (hereafter ACT.), *Cartularium* D4, f. 25ʳ-
25ᵛ (A. Pasture, 'Les archives du chapitre cathédral de Tournai. Inventaire sommaire',
Archives, bibliothèques et musées de Belgique, 25 (1954): 32, 'Grandes archives ou
archives anciennes, section I: les grandes cartulaires'). Some general remarks
concerning this *cartularium* in C. Vleeschouwers, 'Les cartulaires des évêques de
Tournai. Étude diplomatique et notes sur l'histoire et la composition de ces cartulaires
ainsi que leurs scribes', *Bulletin de la Commission royale d'histoire*, 143 (1977): 63-72.
As a matter of fact, it is an indirect donation. First, property and income go to two
clerics and only after their death — or rather if they don't meet specific conditions — to
the students mentioned. Further down it reads: ' . . . pauperum erit clericorum
Tornacensium Parisius studentium laudabilis vite libenter [adiacencium]. Ita quod
proventus predictorum reddituum distribuet scolasticus predictis clericis de consilio
proborum virorum, predictos scolares cognoscencium, precipue aliquibus de
nepotibus predicte cantoris si aliquis ex eis inter ipsos scolares ydoneus . . . ' (f. 25ᵛ).

48. ACT., D4, f. 24ᵛ-25ʳ .

49. E. Warlop, '"Pariteit" in het bisdom Doornik in de XIIIe eeuw', in *Horae
Tornacenses* (Tournai, 1971), pp. 60-64. See also J. -J. Vos, *op. cit.* (n. 46) I, pp. 249, 251
and II, p. 74.

50. E. Warlop, ed., *art. cit.* (n. 49), pp. 66-67: ' . . . ita quod decanus et capitulum
dicte ecclesie dent in perpetuum singulis septimanis de dicto redditu tres solidos

parisiensium uno clerico oriundo de archidyaconatu Tornacensi, quamdiu erit in scolis docili et bene [morigerato], ad tres annos vel plus aut minus prout viderit expedire, vicissim nunc de lingua gallica nunc de flaminga studenti Parisius in theologia, qui tantum dictam subventionem pro rata temporis quo erit in scolis percipiet. Ordinavit nichilominus memoratus archidyaconus quod refectorarius bursam portans dictum redditum recipiat et ministret eidem scolari diversis temporibus prout dictis decano et capitulo videbitur expedire, et habeat quinque solidos parisiensium pro labore'.

51.   Concerning the division of the diocese of Tournai into archdeaconries and deaneries, see É. De Moreau, *Histoire de l'église en Belgique, tome complémentaire. Circonscriptions ecclésiastiques. Chapitres, abbayes, couvents en Belgique avant 1559*, by J. Deharveng and A. De Ghellinck (Brussels, 1948).

52.   About the donation of these manuscripts: A. Derolez, 'Notice sur les livres et la bibliothèque de la cathédrale de Tournai au moyen âge', in *Horae Tornacenses* (Tournai, 1971), pp. 72-73, and J. Pycke, 'Matériaux pour l'histoire de la bibliothèque capitulaire de Tournai au moyen âge', *Scriptorium*, 33 (1979): 79. The expression 'textbooks' is most appropriate here, since the *Sententiae* of Lombard, together with the Bible, were the only textbooks a student of theology was normally acquainted with: H. Rashdall, *op. cit.* (n. 24), I, p. 474.

53.   Not mentioned in H. Denifle and A. Chatelain, *op. cit.* (n. 45).

54.   Biographical data in E. Warlop, *De Vlaamse adel vóór 1300* (Handzame, 1968), II, vol. 2, no. 141/23, and C.-J. Voisin, 'Testament d'Arnould de Maldenghem, chanoine de Tournay', *Annales de la Société d'émulation pour l'étude de l'histoire et des antiquités de la Flandre*, 2nd. series, 7 (1849): 345 ff. Nothing special in J. -J. Vos, *op. cit.* (n. 46), II, p. 18. About his foundation in Maldegem in particular, see J. De Smet, 'Het hospitaal van Maldegem in de XIIIde eeuw', in *Album Antoon Viaene* (Bruges, 1970), pp. 205-209.

55.   A. Van Lokeren, ed., *Chartes et documents de l'abbaye de Saint-Pierre au Mont Blandin à Gand* (Gent, 1868), I, no. 859, p. 379: '. . . et has L libras Flandrenses novor. distribuemus annis singulis in perpetuum X scolaribus Flamingis, ex officio Brugensi vel Gandensi oriundis, qui erunt melioris nominis et magis dociles videbuntur, et illos singulis annis circa Exaltationem sancti Crucis eligemus et unicuique ipsorum sicut dictum est C sol. Fland[r]enses ante festum sancti Remigii in subsidium studii sui conferemus, conditione tali quod septem mensibus ad minus oportebit stare in scolis unumquemque scolarium predictorum; debemus autem non nostros vel monachorum nostrorum seu servientium nostrorum presentes vel familiares vel notos preferre, sed meliores et magis dociles eligere bona fide et sine personarum acceptione'.

56.   *Officium* in the sense of a territorial juridical circumscription (see Du Cange, *Glossarium ad scriptores mediae et infimae Latinitatis*, IV (Paris, 1845), col. 705) presumably refers to 'castellany', units into which the county of Flanders had been subdivided since the XIth century: A. C. F. Koch, 'De rechterlijke organisatie van het graafschap Vlaanderen tot in de 13de eeuw', *Handelingen van de maatschappij voor geschiedenis en oudheidkunde te Gent*, new series, 5 (1951): 1-214.

57.   The act of 1264, which follows, shows clearly that *studia generalia* are meant. These fifty pounds were still awarded to *decem pauperibus scholaribus Flamingis Flamingantibus Parisius in facultate arcium studentibus et personaliter residentibus* in 1466. See a Public Act of 18 April 1466 in the Archives of the Government of Ghent: *Inventaire des archives de l'abbaye de Saint-Pierre*, 1898, 34^{II}, nr. 124 (2).

58.   A. Van Lokeren, *op. cit.* (n. 55), I, no. 859, p. 380: 'Post ipsius vero decessum XX libre de dictis XXX in subsidium pauperum scholar[i]um Parisius vel alibi ubi vigebit studium commorantium perpetuo singulis annis in festo sancti Remigii per manum nostram, abbatis scilicet vel alterius, qui pro tempore fuerit, distribuentur. Ita quod nos abbas et nostri successores scolaribus de officio vel decanatu Brugensi oriundis sub

acceptatione predictorum tenebimur fideliter departiri et cuilibet scolari conferre C sol. Flandrenses ad studii sui continuationem, recepta prorsus cautione a quolibet scolari vel ejus propinquis quod septem mensibus ad minus infra annum stabit vel erit in scolis et in civitate ubi studium vigebit, et si breviori tempore ibidem steterit, pro rata temporis quo absens fuerit, restituet nobis vel nostris post nos successoribus pecuniam supradictam; tenebimur etiam bona fide et in periculo anime nostre diligenter inquirere a bonis et fide dignis ut meliores et magis dociles eligamus ad dictam pecuniam assignandam et quod ad eam nullum admittemus beneficiatum aut de suo patrimonio tantum habentem quod possit inde sustentari'.

59. É. De Moreau, *op. cit.* (n. 51).

60. A. Van Lokeren, *op. cit.* (n. 55), I, no. 748, pp. 334-335. Concerning the £50 separately, another act of May 1265 in *Ibidem*, no. 772, pp. 350-351.

61. *Ibidem*, no. 788, pp. 354-355. Also *Ibidem*, no. 859, pp. 378-379.

62. *Ibidem*, no. 859, p. 380.

63. And not 23 January 1276 n.s., as in C. Vleeschouwers, *art. cit.* (n. 46), p. 602; nor 24 January 1275, as in C. -J. Voisin, *art. cit.* (n. 55), p. 386 n. 29.

64. Editions: C. -J. Voisin, *art. cit.* (n. 54), pp. 354-386 (according to ACT., D4, f. 21ᵛ-22ᵛ); Lalaing, *Maldegem la loyale. Mémoires et archives* (Brussels, 1849), pp. 379-389, and A. Van Lokeren, *op. cit.* (n. 55), I, no. 859, p. 376: 'In primis itaque lego pauperibus scolaribus seu ad opus pauperum scolar[i]um Parisius, vel alibi ubi studium sollempne vigebit seu vigere continget, CL libras annui et perpetui redditus, quas CL libras viri religiosi abbas et conventus Sancti Petri Gandensis annuatim et in perpetuum solvere tenebuntur, . . . De quibus CL libris Flandrensis monete, C libre annis singulis circa festum Natalis Domini per capitulum Tornacense, seu duos de dicto capitulo ad hoc per dictum capitulum deputandos predictis pauperibus scolaribus, precipue magis indigentibus et docilibus, dummodo ipsi scolares fuerint Tornacensis dyocesis atque nationis Flaminge, distribuentur . . . , . . . et volumus quod in distributione, ut dictum est, facienda, non habeatur affectus ad personas, sed subveniatur magis indigentibus scolaribus et docilibus et maxine studentibus et ad proficiendum habilibus in theologica facultate . . . et ut ipsum capitulum animo libentiori dictis pauperibus subveniat et eorum causam agendo cum maiori sollicitudine hiis intendat, . . . '.

65. For the meaning of *natio*, see n. 80; also P. Kibre, *The Nations in the Mediaeval Universities*, in Mediaeval Academy of America, publ. nr. 49 (Cambridge, Massachusetts, 1948), pp. 3 ff.

66. C. -J. Voisin, *art. cit.* (n. 54), pp. 371-372 (latest quotation from 1406). The Archives of the Government of Ghent possess some receipted letters, dating from 1484, 1489, 1503 and 1511-1567, in which the chapter of Tournai declares that, according to the disposition of Arnulf of Maldegem, it has received the annual payment of £100 from St. Peter's abbey to be distributed to poor university students, *pauperibus scolaribus Flamingis Flamingantibus Tornacensis dyocesis in theologia Parisius vel alibi ubi vigeat studium universale studentibus* (7 October 1489): *Inventaire des archives de l'abbaye de Saint-Pierre*, 1898, 34ᴵᴵ, nr. 124 (1).

67. *Recherches historiques et critiques sur la vie, les ouvrages et la doctrine de Henri de Gand, surnommé le docteur solennel* (Ghent, 1838), pp. 63-64.

68. 'Dernières découvertes concernant le docteur solennel, Henri de Gand, fils de Jean le Tailleur (Formator ou de Sceppere)', *Bulletin de la Commission royale d'histoire*, 4th series, 16 (1889): 60-62. A recent biography of the philosopher Henry of Ghent, also called *Henricus ad Plagam*, is R. Macken, 'Hendrik van Ghent (Hendricus de Gandavo, wijsgeer en theoloog)', in *Nationaal biografisch woordenboek*, VIII (1979), cols. 377-395.

69.   Mainly P. Rogghé, 'De Gentse klerken in de XIVe en XVe eeuw. Trouw en verraad', *Appeltjes van het Meetjesland*. *Jaarboek van het Heemkundig genootschap van het Meetjesland*, 2 (1960): 27 (for the XIVth century) and p. 111 (for the XVth century). See also the extracts from the town bills quoted by M. Heins, *Les écoles au moyen âge à Gand. Esquisse historique* (Ghent, [1885]), p. 13, and F. De Potter, *Gent, van den oudsten tijd tot heden. Geschiedkundige beschrijving der stad* (Ghent, 1882-1933), III, p. 127; IV, pp. 163-167 and V, p. 169. Mention of these expenses in the town bills reads as follows: 'Item meester Niclause von Dronghine tulpen to sire scole te Pariis, 40 lb'. See N. De Pauw and J. Vuylsteke, eds., *De rekeningen der stad Gent. Tijdvak van Jacob van Artevelde, 1336-1349*, I: *1336-1339* (Ghent, 1874), p. 454 (a° 1339). Among the expenses in the first half of the XIVth century, annual amounts of £40, £50 or £60 per person are found.

70.   P. Rogghé, *art. cit.* (n. 69), p. 27.

71.   About him see N. De Pauw, *art. cit.* (n. 68), p. 47.

72.   L. Delisle, *Le cabinet des manuscrits de la Bibliothèque nationale*, II (Paris, 1874), p. 154. One of the manuscripts he donated to the Sorbonne carries this inscription: 'Ex legato magistri Henrici de ecclesia, quondam in ecclesia beate Marie Cortracensis decani, professoris in Sacra theologia, quondam socii de magna Sorbona, anima ejus in pace requiescat, nam flos fuit Flamingorum'. See also J. -J. Vos, *op. cit.* (n. 46), I, p. 253, where a *Henricus de Muda*, archdeacon of Tournai, is mentioned: is this one and the same person?

73.   Edition in H. Denifle and A. Chatelain, *op. cit.* (n. 45), I, no. 413, p. 460, and in L. Delisle, *op. cit.* (n. 72), II (1874), p. 164. See also an analysis in P. Kibre, *op. cit.* (n. 23), p. 386. This Nicholas may have donated a number of manuscripts to the Sorbonne also, some of which marked *ad usus Flamingorum*: L. Delisle, *op. cit.* (n. 72), III (1881), p. 9, no. 1-7-10-11 and p. 23 no. XXII; II (1874), p. 164. About this see also A. Derolez, *art. cit.* (n. 52), p. 78. Some biographical data in J. -J. Vos, *op. cit.* (n. 46), I, pp. 249-250 and II, pp. 19 and 183. This Nicholas might be identified with Nicholas of Tournai, professor of theology in Paris, at the beginning of the XIIIth century (thus P. Glorieux, *Répertoire des maîtres de théologie de Paris au XIIIe siècle. Études de philosophie médiévale*, 17 and 18, I (Paris, 1933), no. 131, pp. 296-297), the same who probably donated some manuscripts to the chapter of Notre Dame of Tournai as well (supposition made by A. Derolez, *art. cit.* (n. 52), p. 71).

74.   According to a document of 4 September 1295 whereby Jean de Vassoigne, his successor (1292-1300), promised to honour the foundation. Translation in A. D'Herbomez, 'Le collège de Tournai à Paris', *Revue tournaisienne*, 4 (1908): 180; partially quoted in *Gallia christiana; . . .*, III (Paris, 1725), col. 222. See also L. Delisle, *op. cit.* (n. 72), II (1874), p. 163, who made the assumption that de Warenghien had donated a manuscript to the Sorbonne *ad usus magistrorum Flamingorum*. On both bishops see E. I. Strubbe and L. Voet, *De chronologie van de middeleewen en de moderne tijden in de Nederlanden* (Antwerp-Amsterdam, 1960), p. 248. I was not able to consult the study of C. De Warenghien, *Un prélat au XIIIe siècle: Michel de Warenghien, évêque de Tournai de 1284 à 1291* (Paris, 1919), 103 pp.; some information in J. -J. Vos, *op. cit.* (n. 48), I, pp. 256, 260 and II, pp. 22, 111.

75.   To the examples already quoted should be added the case of one Hanibaldus who donated manuscripts to the Sorbonne for use by the Flemish-speaking students from the diocese of Tournai: L. Delisle, *op. cit.* (n. 72), II (1874), p. 154. On donations to the chapter of Tournai, see J. Pycke, *art. cit.* (n. 52), pp. 76-83. Although only one donation explicitly stated that the manuscripts were to serve *scolaribus Tornacensius docilibus in Sacra Pagina ubi vigebit studium studentibus* (p. 80), the author feels inclined to conclude that, as far as the library of the chapter is concerned, 'Sa nature nous échappe, mais on peut supposer qu'elle était constituée principalement d'ouvrages généraux à l'usage des boursiers' (p. 76).

76.   As manifested by scholarship foundations: F. F. J. Lecouvet, 'Instruction

publique au moyen âge, I: L'abbaye de Saint-Pierre à Gand et l'université de Paris', *Messager des sciences historiques, des arts et de la bibliographie de Belgique* (1855): 172-173, and F. Hennebert, 'Jacques Despars et la fondation de bourses d'études (1448)', *Bulletin de la Société historique et littéraire de Tournai*, I (1849): 156-164. By donations of books to the chapter: J. Pycke, *art. cit.* (n. 52), and A. Derolez, *art. cit.* (n. 52). Even by foundations of two colleges for students of Tournai: in Padua (1342) (F. F. J. Lecouvet, *art. cit.*, p. 173), and in Paris (A. D'Herbomez, *art. cit.* (n. 74), pp. 179-186).

77.   C. V. Langlois, *La vie en France du moyen âge de la fin du XIIe au milieu du XIVe siècle d'après des moralistes du temps* (Paris, 1926), pp. 345-346.

78.   35 must be considered a minimum; the number of bursars benefiting from the foundation by Matthew de Sancto Piato is not known; and I have based the calculation of the number of bursars out of the £100-foundation on the same dividing-key as was used for the £70-foundation, i. e. 100 s. per student.

79.   Motives for scholarship grants and college foundations in A. B. Cobban, *op. cit.* (n. 4), pp. 124-126, and A. L. Gabriel, 'Motivation of the Founders of Mediaeval Colleges', in *Beiträge zum Berufsbewusstsein des mittelalterlichen Menschen*, ed. P. Wilpert, *Miscellanea mediaevalia*, 3 (1964), pp. 61-72 (re-edition in *Garlandia: Studies in History of the Mediaeval University* (Notre-Dame - Frankfurt am Main, 1969), pp. 211-223). Thus, for instance, the influence exerted in the XIIIth century by works like *De Disciplina scolarium* (written about 1230-1240). See also the remarks in H. De Ridder-Symoens, 'Brabanders aan de rechts-universiteit van Orléans (1444-1546). Een socio-professionele studie', *Bijdragen tot de geschiedenis*, 61 (1978): 294.

80.   Concerning the language problem some information is given by E. Warlop, *art. cit.* (n. 49). The new data, presented here, make it possible to deal with the considerations of Warlop in a somewhat broader perspective.

81.   Except in the case of the foundation of Peter of Harelbeke. Such a condition is not known either for the foundation by Henry van der Muiden; but this may be due to a defective text tradition.

82.   Identical findings in J. Paquet, *art. cit.* (n. 1), pp. 306-320 and 348; N. Ditsche, *art. cit.* (n. 1), pp. 51-55; E. De Maesschalck, *art. cit.* (n. 2), pp. 345 and 353, and H. De Ridder-Symoens, *art. cit.* (n. 1), p. 97 (with bibliography).

83.   In the calculation it is assumed that £1 Fl. equals £1 par. : see H. Van Werveke, *De Gentse stadsfinanciën in de middeleeuwen. Mémoires de l'Académie royale de Belgique. Classe des lettres et des sciences morales et politiques*, Collection - 8⁰ , 2nd. series, 34 (Brussels, 1934), pp. 107-110.

84.   F. J. Pegues, *art. cit.* (n. 3), p. 462. But there is an enormous difference between 2 s. and 4 s. !

85.   F. J. Pegues, *art. cit.* (n. 3), pp. 454-462. Patronage of the English kings in the XIVth and XVth centuries in T. H. Aston et al., *art. cit.* (n. 5), pp. 43-44. Another instance is that of Maximilian of Austria who had a protégé studying in Louvain and Paris (beginning of XVIth century): J. Wils (ed.), 'Dépenses d'un étudiant allemand aux universités de Louvain et de Paris', *Revue du Nord*, 9 (1923): 287-288.

86.   A few more indications from the *ars dictaminis*: C. H. Haskins, *op. cit.* (n. 2), pp. 8 ff., and H. G. Richardson, *art. cit.* (n. 5), p. 267. See also some examples for Cambridge in T. H. Aston et al., *art. cit.* (n. 5), pp. 43 ff.

87.   A clear example is the student in Padua whose expenses were studied by J. Le Goff. This young man was financially supported by the town of Syracuse (Sicily): 'Dépenses universitaires à Padoue au XVe siècle', *Mélanges d'archéologie et d'histoire. Moyen âge. Temps modernes*, 68 (1956): 386-387. Scholarships granted in the XVth century by the city of Bruges are mentioned in L. Gilliodts-Van Severen, *Inventaire des archives de la ville de Bruges*, V (Bruges, 1876), pp. 512-513. However, these grants were mostly no more than a premium on occasion of the promotion by a citizen: P. Vandermeersch, *Een onderzoek naar de relatie stad-universiteit in de periode van het*

late-humanisme. Bruggelingen te Leuven en aan buitenlandse studia, unpublished licentiate thesis R. U. G. (Ghent, 1983), I, pp. 101-103 (with thanks to the author for access to his thesis). Maybe real support by the city was only intended as a means of recruiting university-taught municipal staff especially in the XIIIth and XIVth centuries, when a university training was less common.

88.   Especially for their own members. In the chapter of St. Donatian of Bruges certain students of theology were paid yearly grants: R. De Keyser, *art. cit.* (n. 31), p. 587. Also in the abbey of Tongerlo (Prémontré, diocese of Cambrai) there are indications that canons were being assisted in their studies out of the *mensa conventualis* (beginning of the XVth century): thus H. De Ridder-Symoens and L. Milis, 'Tongerlo en zijn studenten op het keerpunt van de middeleeuwen en de moderne tijden', *Ons geestelijk erf,* 45 (1971): 319. See also the patronage of the dean and chapter of Wells to the son of a knight: T. H. Aston et al., *art. cit.* (n. 5), p. 43.

89.   The Common Purse was a unification — at least, that was what it intended to be — of all charitable institutions which at that time were providing support to poor people (poor-tables, hospitals, foundations with distributions, etc.). It was founded 3 December 1525, to fight poverty in a more rational way: J. Nolf, *La réforme de la bienfaisance publique à Ypres au 16e siècle,* in *Université de Gand. Recueil de travaux publiés par la Faculté de Philosophie et Lettres,* 45 (Ghent, 1915), pp. XXVI-XXIX. An undated letter from the middle of the XVIth century provides information about a similar scholarship grant: see *ibidem,* no. XXXIX, pp. 207-208.

90.   P. Trio, *De O. L. V. -broederschap van de scholieren van Parijs te Ieper gedurende de late middeleeuwen (ca. 1330-1600),* unpublished licentiate thesis K. U. L., Louvain, 1981), I, pp. 226-227, and 296-297. An extensive article on these student-confraternities is in preparation, but see idem, 'De statuten van de laat-middeleeuwse clericale O. L. V.-broederschap van de studenten van Parijs te Ieper', *Handelingen van de Koninklijke commissie voor geschiedenis,* 148 (1982): 91-142.

91.   E. De Bethune-Sully, 'Les escholiers tournaisiens à Paris', *Bulletin de la Société d'études de la province de Cambrai (Histoire et Archéologie. Flandre, Tournaisis, Cambrésis, Hainaut, Artois)* (1972-73): 3-4.

92.   ACT., nos. 594-597 (A. Pasture, *art. cit.* (n. 47), p. 53. Section XVI: 'fonds spéciaux et petits offices, X. Ecoliers de Paris'). Actually, the bills extend to 1535 and the series resumes in 1562, continuing until the end of the XVIIIth century. However, the notes from 1522 till 1535 are very fragmentary.

93.   These bills are more or less reproduced in E. De Bethune-Sully, *art. cit.* (n. 91), pp. 1-63. Obviously, these documents are awaiting a critical edition with an elaborate study based on other sources. In the meantime, the publication of E. De Bethune-Sully remains sufficiently useful to present this interesting form of financing studies to a wider range of people.

94.   A. Pasture, *art. cit.* (n. 47), p. 207. A link between this foundation and the flying grants of the XIIIth century is not unlikely.

95.   That Tournai preferred the *studium generale* of Paris to that of Louvain, even in the XVth century, was already suggested in G. Cardon, *La fondation de l'université de Douai* (Paris, 1892), pp. 24-25 and 95. Orléans, and other 'rich' universities with important higher Faculties, must have been beyond the means of these 'poor' bursars.

96.   Some of these bursars were explicitly identified as non-university students.

97.   L. W. B. Brockliss has calculated that, in Paris in the XVth and XVIth centuries, the total expenses for a student from the provinces averaged £75 annually: *art. cit.* (n. 2), pp. 528-530. Compare with H. Boockman, *art. cit.* (n. 8), p. 367.

98.   I wish to express my sincere thanks to Professor Dr. R. De Keyser (K. U. Louvain), and especially to Dr. H. De Ridder-Symoens (R. U. Ghent) who has been most generous in giving aid, counsel, and encouragement. I am deeply indebted to P. Beersaerts for typing the manuscript, to V. De Clercq for the correction of the English text, and to Dr. J. Goossens (K. U. Louvain) for the revising.

PHILOSOPHY AT OXFORD AND CAMBRIDGE
IN THE FIFTEENTH CENTURY

Damian Riehl Leader

The important place given to the three philosophies in the curricula of
the universities in the Middle Ages is beyond dispute. Natural
philosophy, moral philosophy, and metaphysics were studied not
only for their own sake, but as a propaedeutic to scholastic theology.
In spite of this fundamental role, however, little has been written of
the study of philosophy in the English universities in the fifteenth
century other than that it was Aristotelian, realist, and only a sterile
continuation of the more fruitful age that preceded it.[1]

This view, although broadly true, has never been subjected to close
scrutiny. The present study will examine not only the place of the
three philosophies in the curricula of the faculties of arts at Oxford
and Cambridge, but will also focus on each of the philosophies
individually. The sources for this study are the university statutes and
graces (dispensations granted by the universities to individual
students taking degrees), and all of the surviving fifteenth-century
university, college, and private library catalogues. A particularly
fruitful source has been the surviving philosophical manuscripts
which were written or used by English masters or scholars during that
century.[2]

The resulting picture contrasts sharply with that of the continental
universities, where diverse philosophical schools co-existed in the
later Middle Ages. Chairs in philosophy existed simultaneously in the
viae Thomae, Scoti, and Ockham at many German, Italian, and
Spanish universities.[3] This was not the case at either Oxford or
Cambridge. The nominalist philosopher William of Ockham was
little read after the late fourteenth century, and although the logical
works of William Heytesbury, John Dumbleton, and others who held
nominalist positions were known, their philosophy was not read
ordinarily at either university, and their surviving manuscripts were
rarely used except for the parts on logic. Both universities were
dominated by followers of Scotus, Oxford particularly. But dozens of
other realist Aristotelian commentators besides Duns Scotus and his
followers were also known and read, and there are many exceptions
to such a generalisation.

The student of philosophy in fifteenth-century England knew
Scotism primarily through the writings of the Subtle Doctor's
fourteenth-century Catalonian followers Joannes Canonicus (or

Marbres), and Antonius Andreas. The former was a canon of Tortosa and master of arts at Toulouse whose best known writing is *Questiones super VIII libros physicorum*, written in 1321-23.[4] The latter, known as *Doctor dulcifluus* or *Scotellus*, was a Franciscan who studied under Scotus in Paris and taught there 1304-07. Andreas wrote several philosophical works, the most widely diffused of which was the *Questiones super XII libros metaphysicae*.[5] Both Johannes Canonicus and Antonius Andreas agreed with Scotus on all essential points of doctrine, including the univocity of being, the plurality of forms, denial of the real distinction between essence and existence, *haecceitas* as the principle of individuation, the quantification of matter prior to form and quantity, and actual formal distinctions.[6]

   Another general characteristic of philosophy at both Oxford and Cambridge was that students approached the subjects through textbooks organised into *questiones* that were adapted from and useful for disputations in the schools. The basic texts of Aristotle were rarely studied alone, and the manuscripts of even such popular commentators as Aquinas and Averroes were used less frequently that the *questiones* of their now obscure successors. The use of this format was found in the study of the seven liberal arts as well.[7]

   A third characteristic to bear in mind was the interpenetration of logic and philosophy, which was particularly evident in the polemical tracts of the nominalist controversy. Although the discussion of universals was, strictly speaking, the province of metaphysics, the basis of the contest was familiar even to first-year students who were exposed to Porphyry's *Isagoge*, from which the discussion arose. A very active group of Oxford masters, centred at Merton and Queen's colleges between 1380 and 1420, produced many commentaries on Porphyry that were forums for discussing universals and enjoyed wide circulation in fifteenth-century Oxford. William Penbegyll,[8] John Sharpe,[9] Robert Alyngton,[10] William Milverley,[11] John Chilmark,[12] and other Oxonians all wrote similar realist commentaries that usually rehearsed the opinions of Burley, Wyclif, Scotus, and others, and countered the arguments of Ockham.[13] Many more general logical works were also written as aids to philosophical disputations. William Heytesbury's *Regulae solvendi sophismata* was one of the most popular of this genre. Primarily a logical treatise, many philosophical questions arise in the later chapters, the last of which is 'devoted entirely to questions of physical motion.'[14]

   The university statutes say nothing about Scotism, *questiones*, or realist logic, but insist only on the central position of Aristotle. At Cambridge the late fourteenth-century statute for taking the M.A. required three years of reading or hearing the[15]

... libros aristotelis phisicorum, celi et mundi, de generacione, metheorum, de anima, de sensu et sensato, de sompno et vigilia, de memoria et reminiscentia, de morte et vita, de plantis, de motu animalium, metaphisicam, et omnes libros ethicorum . . .

For the Cambridge undergraduate in the mid-fifteenth century, his first two years were devoted to Aristotle's logic, with the third and fourth years given over to the three philosophies, with natural philosophy predominating. The distribution of texts according to terms was as follows:[16]

Third Year	Winter: Lent: Spring:	*Physica* *De generatione* or *De anima* or *De coelo* or *Meteora* or *Ethica*
Fourth Year	Winter: Lent: Spring:	*Physica* or *Metaphysica* as in third year

The *Physics* was given a pre-eminence as it was the *sine qua non* for everything else in Aristotelian natural philosophy.

This Cambridge undergraduate lecture series was modified in 1488 when a new statute directed that the first two years be given to humane letters (the 'Terence lecture'), with the third year devoted to logic and the fourth to 'libros philosophiae', specified as 'naturalia . . . seu metaphysicalia'.[17] At almost the same time the bachelor's course was changed with the institution of a salaried lecturer in 'mathematicalis'. Thus the quadrivium shared the three years between the B.A. and the inception for the M.A. with the more traditional obligation of hearing 'in scholis libros Aristotelis in philosophia'.[18] The graces granted by Cambridge to graduating students reflect this declining emphasis on undergraduate philosophy at the beginning of the sixteenth century. It was not uncommon for students to record four years spent 'in humanitate ac logica' or ' in logica et Terencia', whereas incepting masters still pursued studies 'tam metafisicalia quam philosophica', or more often, 'cum ordinariis philosophicis ac mathematicalibus'.[19]

At Oxford the study of philosophy in the fifteenth century followed the same lines. Although the 1409 statute for the B.A. says nothing of natural philosophy,[20] the mid-fifteenth century graces provide many examples of undergraduates who were required to hear lectures on natural philosophy; on the *De anima I-II*, *Meteora I-III*, *De celo et mundo I-IV*, Burley's *De potentiis animae*, or other works of Aristotle.[21] The early sixteenth-century graces follow the same pattern regarding natural philosophy, and even specify Canonicus' commentary on the *Physics* once.[22]

Thus, in spite of the statutory differences between Oxford and Cambridge, they seem to have been similar in practice through most of the fifteenth century. Philosophy, especially natural philosophy, was studied by bachelors and advanced undergraduates. The universities diverge at the end of the century, when philosophy at Cambridge was given a smaller place at the undergraduate level in response to the rising popularity of mathematics and the humanities. Oxford seems to have been more conservative in its allotment of time for those fields, and philosophy retained a larger share of the curriculum.

I. Natural Philosophy

As is clear from both the statutes and graces, natural philosophy was the most important of the philosophies. In spite of this central position in the faculty of arts, it was the subject of little creative scholarship during the fifteenth century. Other than transcribers and compilers of *tabulae*, only one man at either university wrote a commentary that circulated broadly.

John Sharpe has already been mentioned for his contribution to the realist cause. A Westphalian priest, he was a fellow of Queen's from 1391, Provost in 1403, and an M.A. and B.Th. (1396-97) of Oxford.[23] His surviving works include a typical *Universalia* that uses the arguments of Burley and Wyclif to refute Ockham,[24] as well as *Questio de anima* in four articles and *Questiones super VIII libros physicorum*. Sharpe wrote these latter collections from and for disputations; the last was 'collected in the manner in which they are normally disputed in the philosophical schools of Oxford.'[25] The reliance on authorities in the realist tradition is evident throughout, particularly in the discussion of place and void in *Physics IV*. The text rehearses the opinions of Aquinas, Burley, and Wyclif, and includes refutations of their positions as well.[26] These two works of Sharpe were often copied along with texts texts of Scotus, Burley, Milverley, Alyngton, and other realists.[27]

Other Oxford men who wrote on natural philosophy show similar tastes. John Alward, rector of Exeter College 1416-17, compiled a *tabula* of all notable propositions in Pseudo-Scotus' *Questiones super meteora*.[28] John Saunders, M.A. and fellow of All Souls, 1471-79 copied a collection of Aristotelian physical tracts that included works by Scotus and Johannes Canonicus.[29] Peter Pauli de Nycopia, a Franciscan at Oxford *c.* 1490, transcribed a *Super animam* attributed to Scotus. His co-religious William Vavasour transcribed in the same codex in 1491 Pseudo-Scotus on the *Meteora*, Antonius Andreas' *Super XII libros metaphysicorum*, and tables of disputed questions that included 'Whether air is naturally hot and humid? Whether stars and comets are of a common nature?'[30] The marginalia on the texts recounts the *opiniones* of Galen, Aquinas, Scotus, Henry of Ghent, Peter Aureoli, Burley, and others. Occasionally a polemical stand is taken, as in noting 'The opinion of the Thomists that *ens mobile* is the subject of natural philosophy is false and irrational', a rare instance of dissent on party lines at either Oxford or Cambridge.[31] Thomas Clare, O.S.B. is the only transcriber known to have worked outside this school, copying in 1441 the commentary of the Averroist John of Jandun with the humanist George of Trebizond's translation of the *De anima*.[32]

Cambridge similarly had a contingent of Scotist copyists. William Gedge, M.A. 1482, transcribed Canonicus' commentary on the *Physics*, a copy he passed on the William Worthington, M.A. 1503 and fellow of Godshouse and Clare.[33] Thomas Penketh, B.Th. Oxford and D.Th. Cambridge by 1468, went to Padua to teach metaphysics and theology, and there edited Scotus' *Opera omnia* (Padua 1474 and Venice 1477).[34] Many other Cambridge men owned works of natural philosophy, either by Duns Scotus or his follower Johannes Canonicus.[35]

This does mean that other schools of thought were not represented as there are many examples of works by Albertus Magnus, Thomas Aquinas, and others that were owned or used in the schools throughout this century and the early years of the next.[36] This was especially true at Cambridge. It should be noted that the popular commentary on the *Physics* by Walter Burley, although the work of a realist, was clearly not the work of a pupil of Duns Scotus. It relies heavily on the opinions of Averroes, Avicenna, Albertus Magnus, and Grosseteste, and has more in common with the commentary of Aquinas than that of any of the Scotists.[37] Burley also wrote a *De potentiis animae* that relies on the same authorities, excepting Grosseteste.[38] The popularity of Burley's works at both universities shows that a plurality of philosophical positions within the realist tradition peacefully co-existed.

Manuscripts used in the schools indicate that students were first introduced to natural philosophy through short elementary tracts that were included in collections of introductory logical works. Many of these circulated anonymously, including one attributed to Thomas Walsingham that was printed in all of the editions of the popular *Libellus sophistarum ad usum Oxoniensium* and *ad usum Canta-brigiensium* that were published in England between 1497 and

1530.[39] This *Introductorium naturalium* is a short and very compact collection of about fifty paragraphs and four diagrams explaining the essentials of Aristotelian physics (nature and motion), the predictables, number, speech ('nota quod oracio dicitur tripliciter; in voce, in mente, in scripto'), bodies (simple and mixed), mathematics (fractions), the four elements, and the four kinds of cause. The basic facts are all stated simply, and the inter-relationship of the *Organon* and natural philosophy is clear.

After being exposed to the rudiments of natural philosophy in his first two years, the undergraduate moved on to more sophisticated works, but still studied them along with logic. A good example of this from Oxford is a collection owned by William Kyrkgarth (*c.* 1440); along with Burley's *De potentiis animae*, it has short works on the *logica vetus* and *nova* by the late fourteenth-century masters John Tartys, William Milverley, and Roger Whelpdale, as well as Burley's exposition of Porphyry.[40] A similar but larger collection was owned by the Benedictine William Exton, B.Th. by 1434. Again there are short works on the *logica vetus*, along with Burley's *Super libros posteriorum*, *De potentiis animae*, John Sharpe's *Questio de anima*, Sacrobosco's *De sphera*, and the *Theorica planetarum* attributed to Gerard of Cremona.[41] Both of these codices were well used in fifteenth-century Oxford, and there are others like them.[42]

Merton College, Oxford, with its strong scientific tradition and broad documentation allows for a more detailed investigation of philosophical concerns among more advanced students. Its members included Thomas Juster, fellow from *c.* 1415 until at least 1432, whose act *apud Augustinenses* (a disputation required of bachelors) survives. His questions dealt with the nature and motions of spheres, from the standpoint of Aristotelian physics.[43] Johann Reynbold, a Hessian from the University of Erfurt *c.* 1430, moved to Oxford where he became a fellow of Merton and a prolific transcriber of Scotist texts, often in the employ of Bishop William Gray. Reynbold was active in Oxford from 1451 until at least 1465.[44]

From the beginning of the sixteenth century numerous disputed questions of bachelors were entered into the Merton *Registers*. They were usually concerned with Aristotelian natural philosophy, and to a lesser extent with metaphysics and moral philosophy. Often the three questions disputed by each fellow would cover several areas. Many of these *questiones* are Scotist, often covering material from the *Physics* and *De celo*, and some could have been taken directly from the texts of Andreas or Canonicus. A representative sample of these *questiones* on natural philosophy and metaphysics includes:

Whether heavenly matter is of the same kind as the matter of inferior [bodies]. (denied)[45]

Whether the intellect, united to the body, understands the universal before the singular.[46]

Whether the intellective soul is incorruptible. (denied)[47]

Whether separated substances are able to be understood according to the most perfect notion of them.[48]

Whether the substantial forms of elements remain formally in mixtures. (affirmed)[49]

Whether being and essence are really the same. (affirmed)[50]

Whether things, before their production, have some real being that is called quidditative being.[51]

Whether the conjoined intellect is able to understand separated substances with respect to their quiddity.[52]

Whether it is necessary to posit another intelligence apart from the prime mover, to move a heaven.[53]

Whether the intellective soul immediately informs prime matter. (affirmed)[54]

It is worth noting that the university disputations that survive from the late sixteenth and early seventeenth century have similar Aristotelian content, although without the Scotist terminology.[55]

There are other indications of the popularity of philosophy at Merton, and of the diversity of interpreters present within the realist framework. On 1 March 1491 John Trowell, on his resignation from the office of Vice-Warden (he was joining the Bridgettines at Syon), gave the college Canonicus on the *Physics* and both Aquinas and Andreas on the *Metaphysics*.[56] Two years later, in 1493, two masters of Merton were charged for losing the library's copy of Averroes on the *Physics*.[57]

An examination of the surviving university, college, and personal library catalogues suggests that, in addition to the *Questiones super VIII libros physicorum* of Johannes Canonicus, the most widely circulated natural philosophy texts at Oxford and Cambridge were:

1. Thomas Aquinas, *Super physicam*: This rivalled the popularity of Canonicus' work at Cambridge, although not at Oxford. His commentary on the *De anima* was, however, the most widely known at both universities.

2. Albertus Magnus: His commentaries on the *parva naturalia* were the overwhelming choice at both universities.

3. Averroes: *Super physicam*: This heterodox thinker was present in the libraries of both universities, although he seems to have been less popular later in the century.

4. Walter Burley: *Super physicam* and *De potentiis animae*: They both circulated extensively throughout the century at Oxford and Cambridge.

5. John Sharpe: *Questiones super VIII libros physicorum*: This Oxford work passed through the hands of many masters at Oxford, and was in the libraries of Canterbury College, All Souls, and Merton College at Oxford, and at Cambridge in those of King's College and the University.

6. Giles of Rome: *Super physicam* and *Super animam*: This late thirteenth-century Parisian master of the Augustinian friars seems to have been more widely studied at Cambridge than at Oxford.

7. Thomas Bradwardine, *Proportiones breves*: This short tract by the most influential of the fourteenth-century Merton calculators deals with the mean speed theorem.[58] It was often bound in collections of the *Logica Oxoniensis* and *Cantabrigiensis*, and was printed along with them in the early sixteenth century.[59]

II. Moral Philosophy

Moral philosophy, the second of the three philosophies, was divided following Aristotle into ethics, economics, and politics. A small but important part of the bachelor's preparation for inception, it was equally important at both universities, and it changed little during the fifteenth and early sixteenth century. Besides the texts of Aristotle, attention was also given to Plato, and especially to Boethius' *De consolatione philosophiae*, a non-statutory work that was universally known and accessible. Nearly every library and dozens of masters at both schools owned this text. Moral philosophy also had a bearing on the study of theology, and Aristotelian tracts were sometimes bound with theological and parochial works.[60] Finally, many classical and humanist items, particularly works of Seneca, Ovid, Cicero, Boccaccio, and Petrarch could fall within this branch of philosophy.

The first indications of important humanist development in moral philosophy are found in the decades between 1500 and 1520, and are particularly evident in the sales of the Oxford stationer John Dorne, whose list of 1,851 books sold in 1520 survives.[61] Nine copies of Lefèvre of d'Étaples' exposition on the *Ethics* and seven by John Argyropolus appear.[62] These humanist versions indicate a break with the tradition of the medieval commentators; they by no means disappear, but rather share the stage with these newer versions.

However, apart from Dorne's list and the inventories of a few private libraries, there is little evidence before 1520 to indicate that anything new was being used in the classrooms. The graces only occasionally speak of lectures or disputations 'in morali philosophia'.[63] One of the Oxford graces from the mid-fifteenth century shows that a candidate did hear the requisite three terms in moral philosophy, although only one grace ever mentions even the *Ethics*.[64] Moral philosophy was sometimes disputed by the masters of Merton College, usually using topics taken from the *Ethics*, as for instance:

Whether happiness consists in an act of the will or in an act of the intellect.   (will)[65]

Whether happiness consists in works of virtue.   (denied)[66]

Whether anyone can be called happy in this life.   (denied)[67]

Whether the moral virtues are in the will as in its subject.[68]

Whether the contemplative life is preferable to the active.[69]

As with natural philosophy and metaphysics, these questions are not very different from those disputed at Oxford and Cambridge one hundred years later.[70]

Only a few masters at either university have left evidence of their interest in moral philosophy. At Oxford, the Augustinian friar Thomas Abendon, D.Th. by 1443, compiled a *tabula* of Giles of Rome's *De regimine principum*.[71] As with similar indices for texts in the other philosophies, this was to help the student to find the articles he needed for disputations. John Gold, M.A. and scholar in theology in the 1460's, transcribed Bruni's translations of the *Ethics* and *Politics* and presented them to Magdalen College.[72] Thomas Hill of Winchester and New College, M.A. 1455 and D.Th. 1463, wrote an *Opuscula commutationis inter mercatores*, a tractate on business ethics illustrated by local examples, which survives in a unique copy.[73]

The celebrated fifteenth-century lay scholar William of Worcester edited a *Saiengis of Philosophres* for his patron Sir John Fastolf, which is known only through the presentation copy.[74] Worcester elsewhere referred to Aristotle's *Ethics* and Cicero's *De amicitia* when writing of friendship.[75] Thomas Hoccleve, who is not certain to have attended university, wrote an English *De regimine principum* c. 1410-12.[76] Hoccleve shows a broad knowledge of the subject, citing extensively from Giles of Rome, the pseudo-Aristotle *Secretum secretorum*, Cicero, Vergil, Quintilian, Sallust, and Burley's *Super politicam*, all marshalled into a critique of contemporary society and politics. This work was later transcribed by William Wylflete, M.A., D.Th. of Clare Hall, Cambridge, Chancellor of the university in 1458.[77] As is evident, then, Giles of Rome's *De regimine principum* was the most popular commentary on Aristotle's moral philosophy in England. It was also mentioned in the prologue of an inception disputation at Oxford in 1420, which touched on the foreign policy of Henry V.[78] The use of such contemporary political examples, if rare, was not unknown in the medieval universities.[79]

Cambridge masters had a similar interest in moral philosophy. John Howson of St. Edmund's Hostel transcribed John Dedicus' *Questiones super ethicam* while preparing to take the M.A. in 1467.[80] John Argentein of Eton and King's College, M.A. 1467, showed a knowledge of both the *Ethics* and *Politics* on graduating.[81] Robert Hacumblen, also of Eton and King's College, M.A. 1480, D.Th. 1506-07, copied the *Ethics* along with a brief commentary.[82]

There are many manuscripts in this area of philosophy that were owned or annotated by the fifteenth-century masters of Oxford and Cambridge. Among the more interesting is a text of the *Ethics* in the translation of Bruni, together with the commentary of Aquinas.[83] It was copied by William Reynoldson, M.A. 1457, B.Th.1464, while he was at Michaelhouse, Cambridge.[84] During his own lifetime Reynoldson lent it to John Gunthorpe, the early English humanist,[85] and on his death he left it to Michaelhouse. The codex includes a schema of the three branches of moral philosophy and is marginally annotated in several fifteenth- and sixteenth-century hands, including that of Thomas Cranmer.[86] Copied on slightly irregular parchment in a clear hand with little ornamentation, it is typical school textbook.

Other well-used manuscripts include an Oxford text with Giles of Rome's *De regimine principum* and commentary on the *De anima*, and Aquinas, *Super ethicam*, which was placed in caution by three different men.[87] As was often the case, this was heavily annotated in several hands in the margins of Giles' treatment of the *Ethics* in the *De regimine principum*, but the rest of that text and the other items in the codex are almost spotless. This same pattern of study occurs in the repeatedly used text of Burley on the *Ethics* and *Politics* given to New College by Thomas Chaundler, D.Th. 1455 and sometime Warden and Chancellor of Oxford,[88] and in a copy of Bruni's translations of the *Ethics* and *Politics* transcribed by John Gold of Magdalen College, M.A. 1464.[89] As frequently happens today, the lectures rarely got beyond the first set book; in this case, it was usually the *Ethics*.

The classroom study of moral philosophy does not seem to have changed significantly before the Reformation. As has been mentioned, there was an influx of humanist commentators such as Jacques Lefèvre d'Étaples, but the texts studied were still Aristotle. The initial change was the introduction of better translations, which were as often as not copied with medieval commentaries and annotations.[90] There are also medieval commentaries that were annotated by humanist hands.[91]

Plato was not an influential force at either university, and there were few copies in the libraries of dialogues other than the *Timaeus*. Duke Humphrey gave a copy of Bruni's version of the *Phaedrus* to Oxford in 1439, which he borrowed in 1445.[92] He also gave a copy of Pier Candido Decembrio's translation of *Republic I-V* (dedicated to Duke Humphrey) to King's College, Cambridge.[93] John Doget, a fellow of that college, wrote a commentary on the *Phaedo*, but it survives only in the presentation copy.[94] Platonism was not a challenge to university Aristotelianism during this time.

The most frequently circulated and annotated commentaries on Aristotle were:

1. Giles of Rome, *De regimine principum*: Clearly the most popular commentary at both universities , this was in most of the college libraries and was owned by many masters. It seems to have waned in popularity around 1500, however.

2. Thomas Aquinas, *Super ethicam* and *politicam*: These were equally popular at Oxford and Cambridge, and were the nearest rivals to Giles' commentary.

3. Walter Burley. *Super ethicam* and *politicam*: These shared nearly the same broad circulation in the fifteenth century as those of Aquinas.

4. Johannes Dedicus, *Questiones super ethicam*: A shadowy figure, possibly of Portuguese origin, Dedicus might have studied at Oxford in the late fourteenth century.[95] Although this rather long commentary (the printed edition is 153 pages in highly abbreviated black-letter) never enjoyed the popularity of the texts above, its easy-to-use presentation made it a valued item at both Oxford and Cambridge well into the sixteenth century. John Dorne sold three copies of the 1518 Oxford edition, as opposed to only one of Burley's *Super ethicam* and none of Aquinas or Giles of Rome.[96]

III. Metaphysics

Metaphysics, the third of the philosophies, was a very difficult subject, and was studied almost exclusively by bachelors. Aristotle's

Metaphysics was the primary text, although it was usually studied through *questiones* or commentaries. At Cambridge it was an optional text to be read in the autumn and lent terms of the fourth year, but was required *pro forma* for taking the M.A.[97] At Oxford there is no mention of metaphysics before the bachelor's level, at which point three terms were to be devoted to it.[98] The graces from both schools confirm that metaphysics was the province of advanced students.[99]

As was noted above, the *Questiones super metaphysicam* of the Scotist Antonius Andreas was the overwhelming favourite in this field. Organised for ready adaptation to disputations, it was present in nearly all of the libraries of both universities, and was owned by many masters as well. Andreas was the only metaphysician assigned for lectures at Oriel College between 1515 and 1535.[100] The disputations from Merton show a similar Scotist bent, where the text was found in the library as well.[101]

As with most of the arts studies in fifteenth-century England, the original contribution was minimal: masters seldom went beyond the compiling of *tabulae* and the transcription of texts. Thomas Derham, O.S.B. a monk of Bury St. Edmonds, B.Th. 1426 of Oxford,[102] compiled a *Tabula alphabetica* of Andreas' *Questiones* that circulated in at least three copies at Oxford, one of which shows signs of heavy use.[103] This same text of Andreas was the basis of an *Expositio* written by John Foxholes, O.F.M., B.Th. 1451 and D.Th. of Oxford, lecturer on Scotus at Bologna, and later Archbishop-elect of Armagh.[104] Thomas Appulby of Balliol, M.A. 1515,[105] wrote a *Tabula questionum* for Scotus' *Questiones in metaphysicam*.[106] Similar interests were shown at Cambridge, although not even *tabulae* have survived. John Howson of St.Edmund's Hostel transcribed Andreas' *Questiones* while preparing to take the M.A. in 1467,[107] as did William Gedge of Peterhouse, M.A. 1482, a copy which he bequeathed to William Worthington of Godshouse, M.A. 1503.[108]

A secondary text for the study of metaphysics was the *Liber de causis*, derived from Proclus but thought to be Aristotelian in the Middle Ages. This brief work was included in many collections of Aristotle from the thirteenth and fourteenth centuries. Although it was found in several libraries in fifteenth-century Oxford and Cambridge and was owned by at least a few masters, there was no broad interest in this text. It seems to have been neither transcribed nor commented on by any fifteenth-century masters.

What is striking about most manuscripts of metaphysics is how little evidence of use they bear. A good example is an Oriel codex that was used by several fellows in the fifteenth and sixteenth centuries.[109] It contains Aquinas' commentaries on several texts of natural philosophy, as well as on the *Liber de causis* and *Metaphysics*. The former items are well annotated, while the latter two are not. In addition to Antonius Andreas' *Questiones super metaphysicam*, the *Metaphysics* of Aristotle was studied through the following expositors:

1.Thomas Aquinas, *Super metaphysicam*: A poor second to Andreas at both universities, athough perhaps more read at Cambridge than at Oxford. Aquinas' *De ente et essentia* and *In librum de causis* enjoyed only limited circulation.

2. Averroes, *Super metaphysicam*.

3. Duns Scotus, *Super metaphysicam* and *Formalitates*: The latter (which is of doubtful authenticity) was more widely read than the former, and although it was not only in many fifteenth-century collections, John Dorne sold eight copies of it in Oxford in 1520.[110].

4. Nicholas Bonetus, *Super metaphysicam*: A fourteenth-century bishop of Malta and Franciscan Scotist, his work enjoyed only limited popularity.

*   *   *

The philosophical landscape of Oxford and Cambridge presented a marked contrast with the turbulent continental scene. At Paris the teaching of philosophy broke down on more rigorously sectarian lines, with the controversy between the 'ancients and moderns' (in broad terms, the realist school versus the nominalists) dominating discussions through most of the century. During the English occupation in the first half of the century the nominalists had waned in influence, and in 1452 a commission of reform had insisted on more study of metaphysics and moral philosophy, to counter the narrowing tendency of what was considered to be valid inquiry by the nominalists.[111] The realist school was further strengthened by a royal edict of 1474 which condemned by name the study of Ockham and his followers, and insisted on the utility of Aristotle as understood by Albertus Magnus, Thomas Aquinas, Duns Scotus, and others.[112] There was to be no royal intervention in the curricula of Oxford and Cambridge until 1535.[113]

This injunction was lifted in 1482,[114] and a plurality of philosophical speculation survived well into the sixteenth century, with Parisian masters much more active in writing and publishing than their English counterparts. The Franciscan scholars usually followed Scotus, and included Etienne Pillet ('Brulifer'), who was active in the 1480's. The most prolific Scotist, however, was the secular Pierre Tataret, who between 1494 and 1509 published extensively on logic and Aristotle's natural philosophy, *Ethics*, and

Metaphysics.[115] The school of St. Thomas was revivified in the first decade of the sixteenth century by Pierre Crockart, O.P., who wrote *questiones* on Aristotle's logic, *Physics*, and *De anima*.[116] The nominalist position found its greatest champion in the secular Robert Bricot, who in addition to several works on the *Organon* and terminist logic, wrote a compendium of the *Physics* in 1491, and re-edited it in 1504.[117] This tripartite Parisian approach served as the model for Cardinal Cisneros when he established separate chairs in the theology faculty of his new university at Alcalá in the first years of the sixteenth century. Salamanca followed this lead in establishing nominalism on an equal footing when, in 1508, nominalist chairs were created in theology, philosophy, and logic.[118]

Paris also differed from England in incorporating humanist teaching from the 1460's,[119] which was to have considerable impact by the 1490's with the increasing interest in establishing better texts of Aristotle. Jacques Lefèvre d'Étaples was the central figure in this movement in Paris. He saw the medieval texts of Aristotle as the primary stumbling block to their proper understanding. To rectify that, he published between 1497 and 1518 versions by Leonardo Bruni, John Argyropolus, and Cardinal Bessarion of all the major Aristotelian philosophical texts. He also sought to replace the scholastic commentaries which relied on the *questio* format with more literal commentaries that were based on philological and historical notes. His commentary on the *Ethics* appeared in 1497, and those on the *Politics* and *Economics* in 1506. In addition, Lefèvre produced paraphases of this 'purified Aristotle' as introductory texts for arts students, 'simple, accurate summaries . . . distinguishing essential from less important matter'.[120] Lefèvre, a nominalist in his logical commentaries, was an orthodox interpreter of Aristotle who was most attracted by moral philosophy. These texts and paraphrases were well received in England, as we have seen, but no similar work was done by the English masters.

Padua had yet another approach to philosophy. There the arts faculty was combined with the celebrated medical school, and the former was meant to directly prepare students for the latter. The emphasis was accordingly on logic and then natural philosophy. The chairs in metaphysics were divided between the *via Thomae* and *via Scoti*, and were in the 1490's held by two celebrated advocates of their respective schools, Thomas de Vio, better known as Cardinal Cajetan, and the Franciscan Antonio Trombetta. Padua was marked by two important philosophical controversies in the second half of the fifteenth century, over the movement of celestial bodies, and over the immortality of souls. This second centred on the allegedly 'Averroist' teaching of Nicoleto Vernia, the *ordinarius* in natural philosophy during the 1480's. The doctrine was condemned by the bishop of Padua in 1498, but discussion continued among the philosophers.[121] This question of the immortality of individual souls was not a point of controversy in England.

The German universities seem to have shared the separate *viae* approach that was found elsewhere on the continent. When the faculty of arts in Freiburg was founded in 1460, it was patterned on the Vienna statutes of 1389, and taught from the nominalist position. However, following ducal intervention in 1484, the *via antiqua* was established as well, and the two separate chairs incorporated into the statutes.[122] This pattern was reversed at Tübingen, where originally the realists were dominant, and had separate *viae* in Thomas and Scotus. In 1508 (simultaneously with the Spanish universities), a third chair in nominalism was added.[123]

The study of philosophy in England was not restricted to the faculties of arts of Oxford and Cambridge. The *studia* of the mendicant friars and the monasteries provided instruction to prepare their members for theological studies, although this area has received little scholarly attention for the fifteenth century.[124] The connection of the monks of Canterbury with the early study of humanist literature has been charted, but there is little evidence that their philosophy differed significantly from what was studied in the universities.[125] As was mentioned above, there were lay scholars such as William of Worcester and Thomas Hoccleve who produced minor philosophical works, and the great patron Humphrey, Duke of Gloucester who supported humanist learning and donated texts to both Oxford and Cambridge.[126] These lay efforts were followed in the early sixteenth century by an interest in the new learning and the Erasmian critique of education among an influential circle in London.[127] But this movement was directed towards renewing the trivium studies to serve scriptural studies and preaching, and its influence on the Aristotelianism of the universities was primarily through the introduction of better translations.

As we have seen, philosophy, and especially natural philosophy, occupied a central position in the faculties of arts of fifteenth century Oxford and Cambridge. By both statute and practice it dominated the study of advanced undergraduates and bachelors. This role changed at Cambridge at the end of the century, when humane letters and mathematics were more fully incorporated into the curriculum of every graduate in arts.

Late medieval English university philosophy was in the realist tradition and the student prepared for it by the logic he studied in his first years. When he studied philosophy proper, it was usually through *questiones* that provided knowledge readily adaptable to disputations (something that the newer humanist paraphrases and commentaries did not). The most popular philosophy texts at Oxford and Cambridge were the *questiones* of the Catalonians Johannes Canonicus and Antonius Andreas, followers of Duns Scotus. However, dozens of other commentaries on Aristotle were known as well, and there was a rich diversity of opinions entertained within the realist fold.

123 Napoleon Blvd
South Bend, Indiana 46617 U. S. A.

REFERENCES

1.   The most useful studies are J. A. Weisheipl, 'The Curriculum of the Faculty of Arts at Oxford in the Early Fourteenth Century', *Mediaeval Studies* 23 (1964), 143-185, and 'Developments in the Arts Curriculum at Oxford in the Early Fourteenth Century', *Mediaeval Studies* 28 (1966), 151-175; and J. M. Fletcher, 'The Teaching of Arts at Oxford, 1400-1520,' *Paedogogica Historica* 7 (1967), 417-454.

2.   Most private collections are itemised in A. B. Emden, *A Biographical Register of the University of Oxford to A. D. 1500.* 3 vols. (Oxford. 1957-59) (*BRUO*), and *A Biographical Register of the University of Cambridge to 1500* (Cambridge, 1963) (*BRUC*). Use has been made of computer printouts of this material provided by Mr. T. H. Aston of the History of the University of Oxford project.

Other library catalogues include H. Bradshaw, 'Two Lists of Books in the University Library,' *Cambridge Antiquarian Society (CAS) Proceedings* 13 (1863), 239-278; G. E. Corrie, 'Catalogue of Trinity Hall,' *CAS Report* 11 (1861), 73-78, and 'Books Presented to Pembroke College,' *CAS Proceedings* 10 (1860), 11-23; J. O. Halliwell-Phillipps, 'Catalogue of Corpus Christi, College, Cambridge'. *CAS*, quarto series 14 (1847), 15-20; R. W. Hunt, 'Inventories of Clare College Library', *Transactions of the Cambridge Bibliographical Society (TCBS)* 1 (1949-53), 105-125; M. R. James' catalogues of manuscripts for Clare, Corpus Christi, King's, and Pembroke College, and Peterhouse, published by the Cambridge University Press between 1895 and 1912 all contain late medieval library catalogues; H. M. Bannister, 'A Short Notice of Some Manuscripts of the Cambridge Friars, now in the Vatican Library', in A. G. Little, et. al. (ed.), *Collectanea Franciscana* (British Society of Franciscan Studies, 5, Aberdeen, 1914, repr. Ridgewood, N. J., 1965), 124-140; F. J. Norton, 'The Library of Brian Rowe', *TCBS* 2 (1958), 339-351; C. E. Sayle, 'King's Hall Library', *CAS Report* 72 (1923), 54-76; W. G. Searle, 'A Catalogue of the Library of Queen's College, 1472', *CAS* quarto series 16 (1862), 165-193; M. H. Smith, 'Some Humanist Libraries in Early Tudor Cambridge', *Sixteenth Century Journal* 5 (1974), 15-34.

Library catalogues for Oxford include L. E. Boyle and R. H. Rouse, 'A Fifteenth-Century List of the Books of Edmund Norton', *Speculum* 50 (1975), 284-288; H. H. E. Craster, 'Index to Duke Humphrey's Gifts', *Bodleian Quarterly Review (BQR)* 1 (1914-16), 131-135; J. M. Fletcher, 'A Fifteenth-Century Benefaction to Magdalen College Library', *Bodleian Library Record* 9 (1973-79), 169-172; E. F. Jacob, 'An Early Book List of All Souls College', *Bulletin of the John Rylands Library* 16 (1932) , 469-481; N. R. Ker, *Records of All Souls College Library* (Oxford, 1871); A. F. Leach, 'Wykeham's Books at New College', *Collectanea III*, (Oxford Historical Society 32,

Oxford, 1896), 213-244; W. A. Pantin, ed. *Canterbury College Oxford* (Oxford Historical Society New Series 6 Oxford, 1947), 96-123; F. M. Powicke, *The Medieval Books of Merton College* (Oxford, 1931); R. W. Weiss, 'The Earliest Catalogues of Lincoln College', *BQR* 8 (1935-38), 343-359.

3.　See below pp. 37-39.

4.　This work survives in some thirty manuscripts, ten of which are in English libraries. There are also seven early printed editions, the earliest being that of Padua in 1475. It was printed at St. Albans in 1481. See C. Lohr, 'Medieval Latin Aristotle Commentaries, Authors: Jacobus-Johannes Juff', *Traditio* 26 (1970), 183-184.

5.　This work survives in some forty manuscripts, thirteen of which are in English libraries. There are also seven early printed at editions, the earliest being that of Bologna in 1471. It was printed at London in 1480, and is also included among the *Opera omnia* of Duns Scotus, edited by L. Wadding (Lyons, 1639) 5. 440-725, 6. 1-600. See C. Lohr, 'Medieval Latin Aristotle Commentaries, Authors A-F', *Traditio* 23 (1967), 364-365.

6.　J. Weisheipl, 'John Canonicus', *New Catholic Encyclopedia* (New York, 1967), 7, 1038; Andreas' agreement with Scotus was complete on the last two books of the *Metaphysics*, which he did not bother to comment on, 'Notandum quod in 13° et in 14° libris . . . secutus sum doctrinam . . . magistri Johannis duns . . . ' Gonville and Caius College MS. 368, f. 228^r.

7.　E. g. Oxford, Magdalen College MS. 38, fols. 10^v-13^v, owned by William Kirkgarth in the mid-fifteenth century, includes a *Tractatus de fallaciis pro parte respondentis* and *pro parte opponentis*. The humanist commentaries, on the other hand, eschewed this approach for more liberal notes. See E. F. Rice, 'Humanist Aristotelianism in France', in *Humanism in France*, ed. A. H. T. Levi (Manchester, 1970), pp. 136-139.

8.　*BRUO* 3. 1455.

9.　*BRUO* 3. 1680.

10.　*BRUO* 1. 30-31.

11.　*BRUO* 2. 1284.

12.　*BRUO* 1. 416.

13.　Examples of these tracts that were owned and annotated by fifteenth-century university masters include London, Lambeth Palace MS. 393; Oxford, Corpus Christi College MSS. 103 & 116; Oxford, New College MS. 289; Magdalen College MS. 92; British Library, Royal MS. 12.B.xix.

14.　J. A. Weisheipl, 'Ockham and Some Mertonians', *Mediaeval Studies* 30 (1968), 197. See also *William Heytesbury on Insoluble Sentences: Chapter One of his Rules for Solving Sophisms*, trans. P. V. Spade (Medieval Sources in Translation 21, Toronto, 1979), and C. Wilson, *William Heytesbury, Medieval Logic, and the Rise of Mathematical Physics* (University of Wisconsin Publications in Medieval Science 3, Madison, Wis., 1956).

15.　M. B. Hackett, *The Original Statutes of Cambridge* (Cambridge, 1970), 277.

16.　Hackett, p. 299.

17.　*Documents Relating to the University and Colleges of Cambridge* (London, 1852), I, 361, no. 87; pp. 384-385, no. 140.

18.　*Docs.* pp. 360-361, no. 86.

19.　*Grace Book Γ*, ed. W. G. Searle (Cambridge, 1908), 12, 49, 72, and 104 (1502-13). This change is the subject of my 'Professorships and Academic Reform in Cambridge: 1488-1520', *The Sixteenth Century Journal* 14 (1983), 215-227.

20.　S. Gibson, *Statuta antiqua universitatis Oxoniensis* (Oxford, 1931), p. 200.

21.   E. g. *Register of Congregation 1448-1463*, ed. W. A. Pantin and W. T. Mitchell (Oxford Historical Society New Series 22, Oxford, 1972), 76, 153, and 247-249 (1451-53).

22.   Oxford University Archives, Register G, fol. 21^{ri} (1505).

23.   *BRUO* 3. 1680.

24.   London, Lambeth Palace MS 393, fol. 50^v; See C. Lohr, 'Medieval Latin Aristotle Commentaries, Authors: Johannes de Kanthi-Myngodus', *Traditio* 27 (1971), 279-280.

25.   Oxford, Balliol College, MS. 93, fol. 91^v,'superficialiter collecte modo quo in scolis philosophicis Oxoniae disputari consuerant'.

26.   Balliol MS. 93, fols. 65^r-67^r. The best survey of this question is E. Grant, *Much Ado About Nothing* (Cambridge, 1981). John Sharpe's commentary, however, is not mentioned.

27.   E. g. Balliol MS, 93; Oriel MS, 35; Oxford, Bodleian Library, Rawlinson MS. C. 677.

28.   Oriel MS. 26, which is also used by William Gryffyth, M. A. 1512. The work is spurious. See C. Lohr, 'Medieval Latin Aristotle Commentaries', *Traditio* 26 (1970), 195.

29.   Oxford, Bodleian Library, Digby MS. 44.

30.   Corpus Christi College, Oxford, MS. 227, fol. 176^v, 'Ultrum aer sit naturaliter calidus et humidus. Utrum stella comata [sic] sit de natura commune'. The attribution of the *De anima* to Scotus is 'doubtful'; see C. Lohr, 'Medieval Latin Aristotle Commentaries', *Traditio* 26 (1970), 193.

31.   Fol. 52^r, 'Opinio thomistarum ponencium quod ens mobile sit subjectum philosophie naturalis est falsa et irrationalis'.

32.   Cambridge University Library Add MS. 6190. For Trebizond's works on natural philosophy, see J. Monfasani, *George of Trebizond* (Leiden, 1976), pp. 55-61, and esp. p. 56, n. 128.

33.   *BRUC*, p. 652.

34.   *BRUC*, p. 448; *BRUO* 3. 1457.

35.   E. g. Gonville & Caius MS. 368 and Peterhouse MS. 188.

36.   E. g. Oriel MS. 48; Corpus Christi College, Oxford MS. 225; Lambeth Palace MS. 97; Gonville & Caius MSS. 414 & 507.

37.   Weisheipl, 'Ockham and Some Mertonians', p. 181.

38.   M. J. Kitchel, 'The "De potentiis animae" of Walter Burley', *Mediaeval Studies* 33 (1971), 85-113.

39.   Seven editions of the Oxford version were printed in England before 1530, and four of the Cambridge by 1524. See *A Short-Title Catalogue of Books Printed in England, Scotland, & Ireland and of English Books Printed Abroad 1475-1640*. First compiled by A. W. Pollard and G. R. Redgrave. Second edition, revised and enlarged, begun by W. A. Jackson and F. S. Ferguson. Completed by K. F. Pantzer, (London, 1976), II, nos. 15574.5-15578.7; See also E. J. Ashworth, 'The "Libelli Sophistarum" and the Use of Medieval Logic Texts at Oxford and Cambridge in the Early Sixteenth Century', *Vivarium* 17 (1979), 134-158; L. M. de Rijk, 'Logica Cantabrigiensis', *Révue Internationale de Philosophie* 29 (1975), 297-315; L. M. de Rijk, 'Logica Oxoniensis', *Medioevo* 3 (1977), 121-164.

40.   Magdalen MS. 47.

41.   Rawlinson MS. C. 677.

42.   E. g. Royal MS. 12.B.xix; New College MS. 289; Lambeth Palace MS. 675.

43.   *BRUO* 2. 1025; Magdalen MS. 38. fols. 37ᵛ-38ʳ.

44.   *BRUO* 3. 1569; For a discussion of his codices see L. Meier, 'Die Skotusausgabe des Johann Reinbold von Zierenberg', *Scriptorium* 7 (1953), 89-114.

45.   *Registrum Annalium Collegii Mertonensis, 1483-1521*, ed. H. E. Salter (Oxford Historical Society 76, Oxford, 1923), 442 (1513), 'Utrum materia celi sit eiusdem racionis cum materia istorum inferiorum'. (non)

46.   Ibid., p. 476 (1518), 'An intellectus corpori unitus prius origine intelligat universale quam singulare'.

47.   Ibid., p. 487 (1519), 'Utrum anima intellectiva sit incorruptibilis'. (neg.)

48.   *Registrum Annalium Collegii Mertonensis, 1521-1567*, ed. J. M. Fletcher (Oxford Historical Society New Series 23, Oxford, 1974), 21 (1525), 'Utrum substantie separate possunt a nobis intelligi secundum perfectissimam rationem earum'.

49.   *Registrum Mertonensis, 1483-1521*, p. 442 (1513), 'Utrum forme substantiales elementorum manent formaliter in mixto . . . sic.'

50.   Ibid., 'Utrum . . . esse et essencia sunt idem realiter . . . sic'.

51.   Ibid., p. 481 (1519), 'An res ante sui productionem habeant aliquod esse reale quod appelletur esse quidditativum'. (neg.)

52.   Ibid., 'Utrum intellectus conjunctus potest intelligere substantias separatas quoad quidditatem earum'.

53.   Ibid., 'Utrum preter primum motorem necesse est ponere aliam inteligenciam ad movendum celum'.

54.   Ibid., p. 487 (1519), 'Utrum anima intellectiva immediate informat materiam primam'. (aff.)

55.   *Register of the University of Oxford*, 2.1 (1571-1622), ed. A. Clark (Oxford Historical Society 2, Oxford, 1887), 170-179. For Cambridge examples see the *questiones* printed on broadsides in the 1580's, *Short Title Catalogue*, no. 4474.

56.   *Registrum Mertonensis, 1483-1521*, pp. 143-144.

57.   Ibid., p. 179; See also F. M. Powicke, *The Medieval Books of Merton*, pp. 218-219, nos. 1092-1094.

58.   The *Proportiones breves* is the *Tractatus de Proportionibus* without the *Proemium* and the last of the four chapters. See *Thomas Bradwardine, His Tractatus de Proportionibus*, ed. H. L. Crosby (Madison, Wisconsin, 1955), 184, n. 46.

59.   See above p. 10, n. 39.

60.   E. g. Royal MS. 6.B.v; Gregory, *Homilia*, Giles of Rome, *De regimine principum*, etc. This fifteenth-century codex shows signs of frequent use.

61.   F. Madan, 'The Day Book of John Dorne', in *Collectanea I*, ed. C. R. L. Fletcher (Oxford Historical Society 5, Oxford, 1885), 71-177.

62.   Of the nine editions of Lefèvre d'Étaples' exposition, eight included the commentary of his student and collaborator Josse Clichtove, D.Th. Paris 1506. See ibid., pp. 80 (92), 82 (135), 84 (206), 93 (422), 99 (600), 107 (851), 114 (1052), 125 (1390), and 106 (808). For Lefèvre d'Étaples see Rice, 'Humanist Aristotelianism in France', and *The Prefatory Epistles of Jacques Lefèvre d'Étaples*, ed. E. F. Rice (New York, 1972).
        The seven editions of John Argyropolus include five without commentary, pp. 78 (23 and 26), 80 (91), 139 (1822), and two with commentary. Of these, one is anonymous, p. 118 (1162), and one has the commentary of Gilbert Crab, p. 124 (1353).

63.   E. g. Register G, fol. 177ʳ (1513).

64.   *Register of Congregation*, pp. 41 (1449) & 121 (1452).

65.   *Registrum Mertonensis 1483-1521*, 443 (1514), 'Utrum felicitas consistit in actu voluntatis vel in actu intellectus'. (voluntatis).

66.   Ibid., 'Utrum felicitas consistit in operibus virtutis'. (non)

68.   *Registrum Mertonensis 1521-1567*, p. 31 (1527), 'Utrum virtutes morales sint in voluntate ut in substantivo'.

69.   Ibid., 'Utrum vita contemplativa sit activa preferenda'.

70.   *Register of the University of Oxford* 2.1, pp. 170-179.

71.   *BRUO* 1. 3; All Souls MS. 92

72.   *BRUO* 2. 780-781; Magdalen MS. 49

73.   *BRUO* 2. 935; New College MS. 115, fols. 184^r-200^r.

74.   *BRUO* 3. 2086-2087; Cambridge University Library , MS Gg.i.34, part 2.

75.   *The Paston Letters*, ed. N. Davis (Oxford, 1976), II, 203.

76.   T. Hoccleve, *De regimine principum*, ed. T. Wright, (The Roxburghe Club 79, London, 1860)

77.   *BRUC* p. 657; Corpus Christi College, Cambridge, MS. 496.

78.   Magdalen MS. 38, fol. 17^v, & Gibson, *Statuta antiqua*, p. 644,'. . . qui mortiferis minis architenensium suorum totam Galliam precipitat in ruinam iuxta famosissimum consilium Egidii de regimine principum plerisque capitulis in ultima parte libri'.

79.   Current affairs were also present in a legal disputation in the same manuscript, where the hereditary rights to the thrones of England, Scotland, and France are discussed (fol. 36^r).
    William Worcester searched London and Cambridge libraries for examples from antiquity and recent history to support his position on the French wars in his *Boke of Noblesse* (K. B. McFarlane, 'William Worcester: A Preliminary Survey', in *Studies Presented to Sir Hilary Jenkinson*, ed. J. C. Davies (London, 1957), 213).

80.   *BRUC*, p. 318; Gonville & Caius MS. 369.

81.   See my 'John Argentein and Learning in Medieval Cambridge', forthcoming in *Humanistica Lovaniensia* 33 (1984).

82.   *BRUC*, p. 278; King's College MS 11.

83.   Royal MS. 9.E.i; The Bruni translation of the *Ethics* was printed in Oxford in 1479. See *STC* no. 752.

84.   *BRUC* p. 479.

85.   *BRUC* pp. 275-277.

86.   Royal MS 9.E.i, fol. 1^v; Cranmer's signature on fol. 2^r.

87.   Bodleian Library, Hatton MS. 15 (s. c. 4121); Magdalen MS. 178, a copy of Aquinas on the *Ethics*, was similarly placed in caution many times (1478-82), although it shows less sign of wear.

88.   *BRUO* 1. 398-399.

89.   *BRUO* 2. 780-781; New College MS. 242 & Magdalen MS. 49.

90.   E. g. Magdalen MS. 49; Lincoln College MS. 21; Royal MS. 9.E.i.

91.   E. g. New College MS. 242, fol. 136^v; Magdalen MS. 189, fol. 1^v.

92.   *Epistolae Academicae*, p. 181 (1439) & p. 246 (1445); See *BRUO* 2. 983-985, with a list of manuscripts given to Oxford and bibliography on Duke Humphrey's contacts with Pier Candido Decembrio and other Italian humanist scholars.

93.   British Library, MS. Harley 1705.

94.   *BRUC* p. 191; British Library, MS. Add. 10344 (*BRUC* has '10334').

95.   *Ex info*. Dr Jeremy Catto of Oriel College; see also *BRUO* 1. 555.

96. *Collectanea I*, pp. 84 (196), 88 (311), 117 (1123), and 134 (1667); see also Balliol MS. 93, fols. 149^r-195^r; All Souls MS. 84. fols. 1^r-240^r; and Gonville & Caius Ms. 369, fols, 143^r-243^r; Copies were used as cautions at Cambridge 1483-1484 and 1489, *Grace Book A*, ed. S. M. Leathes (Luard Memorial Series 1, Cambridge, 1897), 178, and *Grace Book B, Part I*, ed. M. Bateson (Luard Memorial series 2, Cambridge, 1903), 13.

97. Hackett, pp. 277 & 299.

98. Gibson, *Statuta antiqua*, pp. 200 (1409) & 235 (1431).

99. E. g. *Grace Book Γ* p. 72 (1508-09); *Register of Congregation*, pp. 41-42 (1449).

100. *The Dean's Register of Oriel College, 1446-1661* ed., G. C. Richards & H. E. Salter (Oxford Historical Society 84, Oxford, 1926), 38, 40, 44, 87, 94 and 101.

101. *Registrum Mertonensis, 1483-1521*, pp. 143-144 (1491).

102. *BRUO* 1. 572-573.

103. Oriel MS. 26 fols. 1^r-10^v; also All Souls MS. 85, and New College MS. 239. fols, 193^v-211^v.

104. *BRUO* 2. 270; A. G. Little, *The Grey Friars in Oxford* (Oxford Historical Society 20, Oxford, 1892), 261-262.

105. A. B. Emden, *A Biographical Register of the University of Oxford A. D. 1501 to 1540* (Oxford, 1974), 10.

106. Balliol MS. 291, fols. 229^r-230^r.

107. *BRUC*, p. 318.

108. *BRUC*, pp. 255 & 652; Gonville & Caius MS. 369.

109. Oriel MS. 48, fols. ii^r-iii^r; also Oriel MS. 35. fols, 135^r ff.

110. *Collectanea I*. Four are in a Parisian edition, pp. 101 (665), 104 (761), 116 (1111) amd 118 (1186); and four are in a version edited by Antonio Trombetta (Venice, 1514), pp. 96 (517), 114 (1041), 127 (1430), and 130 (1517),

111. A. Renaudet, *Préréforme et Humanisme à Paris* (Paris, 1916), pp. 78-80, citing H. Denifle and E. Chatelain, *Chartularium universitatis Parisiensis* (Paris, 1889-1897), 145, IV, p. 729.

112. Renaudet, p. 92, citing C. E. Du Boulay, *Historia Universitatis Parisiensis* (Paris, 1665-1673), 143, V, p. 706.

113. C. H. Cooper. *Annals of Cambridge* (Cambridge, 1842), i, 374-376.

114. Renaudet, p. 94.

115. Renaudet, pp. 94, 247, 367 and 463.

116. Renaudet, p. 469.

117. Renaudet, pp. 96-97 and 263.

118. M. Bataillion, *Erasme et l'Espagne* (Paris, 1937), pp. 17-18.

119. Renaudet, p. 117.

120. This material is taken from Rice, 'Humanist Aristotelianism in France', pp. 133-136.

121. See C. B. Schmitt, 'Thomas Linacre and Italy' in *Essays on the Life and Work of Thomas Linacre*, ed. F. Maddison, M. Pelling, and C. Webster (Oxford, 1977), pp. 46-53. from which this discussion is taken. This article includes extensive bibliographical notes on Padua in the fifteenth century.

122. H. Ott and J. M. Fletcher *The Medieval Statutes of the University of Freiburg in Breisgau* (Notre Dame, U. S. A., 1964), pp. 19-20 and 73.

123. J. M. Fletcher 'Change and Resistance to Change: A Consideration of the Development of English and German Universities during the Sixteenth Century', *History of Universities* 1 (1981), 4.

124. For an example from Evesham monastery around 1530, see *The Letter Book of Robert Joseph*, ed. H. Aveling and W. A. Pantin (Oxford Historical Society New Series 19, Oxford, 1971).

125. See R. Weiss *Humanism in England*, 3rd, ed., (Oxford, 1967) ch. 8. and generally for the early impact of Italianate learning in England.

126. See above n. 92, and A. Sammut, *Umfredo duca di Gloucester e gli umanisti italiani* (Padua, 1980).

127. J. K. McConica, *English Humanism and Reformation Politics* (Oxford, 1965), esp. pp. 44-75.

RENAISSANCE COMMENTARIES ON AVICENNA'S *CANON*, BOOK I, PART I, AND THE TEACHING OF MEDICAL *THEORIA* IN THE ITALIAN UNIVERSITIES[1]

Nancy G. Siraisi

As is well known, sections of the *Canon* of Avicenna (d.1037) had a place in the medical curriculum of various Western European universities for several hundred years. Translated into Latin in the circle of Gerard of Cremona before 1187, the work appears to have entered university curricula some time during the second half of the thirteenth century.[2] In the Italian schools, to which the present study will be confined, portions of the *Canon* continued to be used as textbooks until well into the eighteenth century; at Bologna, *Canon* I.1 was finally removed from a nominal place in the curriculum in 1800.[3] The survival of Avicenna in university medical curricula of the Renaissance and early modern periods, despite the vigorous criticisms of Arab authorities and Latin scholastic medicine that began to emerge from medical humanist circles in the 1490s, despite the improved knowledge of anatomy and botany of the age of Vesalius and Fuchs in the middle years of the sixteenth century, and even despite the radically revised physiology of the seventeenth century, has often been decried as a prime example of academic inertia. George Sarton, indeed, once characterized the reprinting of part of the *Canon* in the mid-seventeenth century as 'an intellectual scandal'; his judgement was no harsher than that of Scipione Maffei writing in the early years of the eighteenth century.[4] Such judgements, indeed, seem unavoidable as far as the later seventeenth and the eighteenth centuries are concerned.

In the sixteenth and early seventeenth centuries, however, *Canon* I.1 still served as a useful manual of a not yet outmoded Galenic physiology, while *Canon* IV.I performed a similar service for the subject of fevers.[5] In that period, the publication of successive new Latin editions of the *Canon* and of fresh commentaries on these, and occasionally other, sections of the work should not be assumed to constitute in itself evidence either of unthinking conservatism or of deliberate rejection of novelty. Rather, these editions and commentaries represent a range of different responses to Avicenna's work. Furthermore, some of them contain strikingly innovative material which mingles, sometimes uneasily, with more traditional elements. Closer investigation of the content of these productions, of their place in the entire tradition of Latin commentary on the *Canon*, and of the intellectual situation and apparent goals of the commentators is therefore likely to add to understanding the climate of thought in the Italian university faculties of medicine in an age when these institutions provided a milieu of great significance for the history of the life sciences. Accordingly, the present essay offers a few preliminary comments on the treatment of *Canon* I.1, a portion of Avicenna's work normally used as a text book of theoria, the branch of the curriculum that introduced the neophyte medical student to fundamental principles of medical thought. But first let us establish the scope of Italian academic medical interest in the *Canon* of Avicenna during the late fifteenth, sixteenth and early seventeenth centuries.

In the first place, we are confronted by a stream of new Latin editions of the text issuing from Italian (usually Venetian) presses. These editions embody the work of at least eight Italian learned physicians (two of them working as a team) who, one after another, devoted their energies to improving upon the Gerard of Cremona version. Some of these editions are elaborate productions, replete with such tools to aid the serious scholar as a vocabulary of Arabic technical terms, indices of various kinds, and marginal cross-references to relevant works of Galen and other classical medical and philosophical authorities. Moreover, some twenty new commentaries, most based on one or other of the new Latin versions, on various parts of the *Canon* were published in Italy during the same period, and a number of these commentaries went into two or more editions (only one of the commentators also worked on an edition of the text).[6] Other similar commentaries remain in manuscript.[7] Furthermore, Latin translations of two of the principal commentaries on parts of the *Canon* by medieval Arabic writers were published for the first time.[8] In addition, a number of other productions purported to present or examine Avicenna's views on particular topics or contained excerpts from, or defenses of his work.[9] One might add that the production of new text versions and commentaries was not for lack of existing ones. During the first fifty years of printing more than twenty editions of all or part of the unaltered Gerard of Cremona version of the text of the *Canon* appeared, as well as editions of all the major Latin commentaries on the *Canon* produced in the fourteenth and fifteenth centuries.[10]

Only after about the 1620s does the interest among circles connected with the Italian universities in publishing new work on the *Canon* appear to taper off. Thereafter, although respect for academic tradition and appreciation of Avicenna's role in the history of medicine ensured that parts of the *Canon* long remained the subject of university lectures, the practice of editing those lectures for publication in the form of printed commentaries became a thing of the past, presumably because neither commentary as a mode of scientific discourse, nor a special interest in Avicenna were any longer likely to add much lustre to the reputation of professor of medicine.[11]

The output of Latin commentaries on the *Canon* during the sixteenth century, taken in conjunction with the related attempts to present an improved Latin text of the *Canon*, can be viewed as part of a larger and more general effort to re-examine traditional authorities in philosophy and medicine in the light of a fuller understanding of original texts and languages. In short, in the Italian universities Renaissance interest in the medical writings of Avicenna had much in common with Renaissance Aristotelianism and Renaissance Galenism.[12] In all three cases, there is obvious and important continuity with an antecedent scholastic tradition; but at the same time the reality and significance of change is also undeniable. Moreover, the sixteenth-century interest in Avicenna was intimately associated with contemporary Galenism. It was widely recognized that Avicenna's physiological and pharmaceutical system and medical knowledge were in great part derived from Galen. One possible response to this realization is expressed in Benedetto Rinio's remark (1555) to the effect that 'Avicenna cannot be condemned while Galen is praised'.[13] Another is exemplified by the critical re-examination of Avicenna's adequacy as an interpreter of Galen undertaken by G. B. Da Monte (d.1551), in his commentary on *Canon* I.1, to which we will return later.

While the parallel with, and influence of Renaissance Galenism — and to a lesser extent of various contemporary trends in philosophy — appears to be of considerable significance in the sixteenth-century interpretations of the *Canon*, the approach to the medical writings of Avicenna was, obviously, also affected by factors that did not apply to the study of Galen or other Greek authors. In the first place, even though the ability to deal with Greek texts in the original language was probably far from universal among academically educated Italian physicians during the sixteenth century, knowledge of Greek was certainly more widely disseminated and more readily obtainable than knowledge of Arabic.[14] Whereas one can probably assume some degree of first hand familiarity with Greek texts on the part of most sixteenth-century authors of academic works on medical theory (though not on the part of all their readers), no such assumption can safely be made for Arabic, even in the case of commentators on the

Canon. Indeed, G. B. Da Monte, probably the best mind among them, several times proclaimed his ignorance of that language.[15] Secondly, as we shall see, Avicenna along with the entire Arabic contribution to medicine was subjected to vigorous attack in the early years of the century, at a time when Galen was much admired and seldom challenged. Indeed, the main thrust of much of the criticism directed against Arabic medical writers was that they had misrepresented their Greek sources.

One possibility raised by such attacks was that Avicenna had in turn been misrepresented by his twelfth-century Latin translator or misinterpreted by his fourteenth and fifteenth-century Latin commentators. The attacks themselves thus probably helped to stimulate the repeated efforts to revise (or at least improve the presentation of) the Latin text of the *Canon*, and to provide a new body of commentary that would take these efforts and other recent intellectual developments into account. In Italy, this kind of reaction seems to have been stronger and more widespread in the case of Avicenna than in that of most other Arabic medical authors (although there were, of course, sixteenth-century printings of and commentaries upon other medical works of Arabic origin),[16] perhaps because of the greater importance of portions of the *Canon* as teaching texts.

Canon I.1, the focus of the present essay, contains a discussion of the nature of medical science and an overview of the fundamental principles of Galenic physiology, set in the context of a chiefly Aristotelian natural philosophy.[17] Hence, it offered the lecturer on medical *theoria* a better opportunity to consider both physiology as a whole and the relationship of medicine to natural philosophy than most other traditional textbooks afforded. For example, neither of the other two books which, with *Canon* I.1, made up a three year sequence of assigned texts in *theoria* in the Paduan curriculum, namely the *Aphorisms* attributed to Hippocrates and the Galenic *Microtechne* (*Tegni, Ars parva*) contain the kind of systematically ordered general survey found in *Canon* I.1.[18]

Commentaries on *Canon* I.1 written in the Italian universities during the sixteenth century reflect the relationship between medicine and natural philosophy at a time when both were beginning to be exposed to powerful and indeed revolutionary forces of change, but both still relied heavily upon a book oriented, classicizing, and scholastic approach to nature. At the same time, these commentaries also represented the continuation of a regional tradition of medical learning that stretched back to the thirteenth century. Although the manuscript tradition of the medieval Latin text of the *Canon* and its commentaries is complex, fragmented, and as yet very incompletely explored, it is clear both that major and venerated figures in north Italian scholastic medicine of the fourteenth and fifteenth centuries owed much of their reputations to commentaries on the *Canon* — one thinks, for example, of Gentile da Foligno, Giacomo da Forlì, and Ugo Benzi — and that most of the major commentators on this work were in fact Italian.[19] Earlier generations had indeed proudly hailed the pioneers of scholastic medical commentary in the north Italian schools as important innovators, who deserved to be placed alongside the Italian 'restorers' of the other arts and sciences.[20]

Hence, in assessing the sixteenth-century commentaries on *Canon* I.1 it is necessary not only to consider them in the light of the intellectual and scientific movements of their own day, but also to place them in the context of the older tradition of Latin scholastic medicine. The latter goal involves attention both to the history of commentary production in general, and to such aspects of the commentaries themselves as the rhetorical stance adopted by the commentators toward their fourteenth- and fifteenth-century predecessors, the extent of actual knowledge of earlier commentaries that is displayed, and the evidence for any substantial shifts in the manner, matter, and purposes of commentary. In the course of such an investigation we may be able to trace developments in the teaching of *theoria*, as aspect of Renaissance medical education that has, as a rule, aroused less interest among historians than more practically oriented or scientifically innovative parts of the curriculum, but which is nonetheless significant as the means by which basic assumptions about the life sciences were transmitted to medical students. The remainder of the present essay will therefore be devoted firstly to a few general remarks concerning the history of the production of commentaries on the *Canon*, and especially *Canon* I.1, in Italy between the fourteenth and the early sixteenth century, and then to a sampling along the lines indicated above of a group of commentaries associated with the University of Padua and written between about 1540 and 1580. These are interim results, representing the first stage of an investigation on which much further work remains to be done.

The uses made of the *Canon* in the schools of the West were from the beginning shaped by the fact that the work is less an integrated *summa* of the whole of medicine than a collection of treatises and reference works on a variety of topics. Consequently, the practice of assigning various portions of the work as textbooks for different branches of the curriculum, noted above in the sixteenth and seventeenth centuries, extends back into the earliest period in which the *Canon* was used in the universities. The precise portions of the *Canon* allocated to the different parts of the curriculum of course varied from university to university and no doubt from time to time. Overall, it seems likely that the widest use made of the *Canon* was in the teaching of the academic discipline known as *medicina practica* for which at various times and places Book I, Part 4 (on general therapy), Book II (on simples), most of Book III (on diseases or different parts of the body), and all or part of Book IV (on diseases affecting the whole organism) were used.[21] Book I was assigned for the branch of the curriculum referred to in Bolognese university statutes of the fifteenth century as *medicina* and in Paduan statutes and other university documents as *theoria* or the obligation of *theorici*, but it appears seldom to have been taught in its entirety. Of its four parts, *Canon* I.4 was, as just noted, apparently often used in teaching *practica*, and *Canon* I.3 seems to have been little studied.[22] The portions of Book I from which *theoria* was taught were, for the most part, parts 1 and 2, and, judging from the commentary tradition, often part 1 alone. Furthermore, at Bologna, and it would appear in other medical faculties, *Canon* I.1 was by the early fourteenth century adapted for its role as a textbook from which basic principles of *theoria* were taught by the omission of a rather substantial section on anatomy, perhaps on the grounds that anatomical detail was more appropriately conveyed in a course on *practica*.[23] Consequently, the tradition of commentary on *Canon* I.1 as it developed in Italy was usually based on a text abbreviated in this way.

Commentaries were written on the sections prescribed for study (practical as well as theoretical); in addition, individual masters seem often freely to have selected short passages for treatment in the form of a *lectio* or as the basis for a *quaestio*. Some of these short pieces also appear as part of longer commentaries. It is not always possible to tell in any given instance whether a short work is an excerpt from a longer commentary or an originally independent item that was subsequently incorporated into a longer work. Furthermore, other works were based on parts of the *Canon* without actually taking the shape of a formal commentary thereon.[24]

Commentaries, therefore, are normally on portions — long or short — but not the whole of the work. The only Latin commentator known to the present writer who seems to have made a conscientious effort to expound the whole of the *Canon* was Gentile da Foligno (d. 1348), and even his endeavour probably owes some of its apparent completeness and continuity to his early sixteenth-century editors.[25] While most parts of the *Canon* attracted Latin commentary at some time or other, the sections most frequently the subject of exposition were, naturally enough, those most widely used in university curricula. Thus, at least eighteen commentaries on the section in Book IV on fevers were written before 1500, but so far as is known only one on Book V, which seems not to have been used as an academic textbook. In the same period, the number of commentaries on Book I, Part 1, or Book I, Parts 1 and 2, falls somewhere in the middle between these two extremes.

The authors of substantial *Canon* commentaries who achieved lasting reputation in the Italian schools for their work on Avicenna were a relatively small group. They include Antonio da Parma (fl. 1310), Dino del Garbo (d. 1327), Gentile da Foligno, Dino's son Tommaso (d. 1370), Marsilio Santasofia (d. 1405), Giacomo (Jacopo) da Forlì (d. 1414), Ugo Benzi (d. 1439), Giovanni Arcolano (d. 1458), Jacques Despars (d. 1458), Leonardo da Bertipaglia (d. 1448) and Gian Matteo Ferrari da Grado (d. 1472). Of these, only Antonio, Gentile, Marsilio, Giacomo, Ugo, and Jacques Despars seem to have written on *Canon* I.1.[26] Other authors who were often cited for their views on topics treated in *Canon* I.1, but who did not actually write commentaries on that work, include the very philosophically oriented learned physicians Pietro d'Abano (d. ca. 1316), Turisanus (Pietro Torrigiano de'Torrigiani, d. ca. 1319) and Tommaso Del Garbo.[27] One may note again that the provenance of all these authors, with the solitary though important exception of the Frenchman Jacques Despars, lies in the north Italian universities. Although a regional tradition of scholarship and perhaps a certain element of *campanilismo* was no doubt in part responsible for the frequency with which the authors named were cited by their successors in the Italian schools and for the subsequent selection of their works for publication by Renaissance Italian printers, it nonetheless appears that in the fourteenth and first half of the fifteenth century the tradition of commentary on the *Canon* was more flourishing and more diverse in the schools of northern Italy than at Montpellier or any other western European centre of medical education.

As is apparent from the foregoing, the major expositions of the Gerard of Cremona translation of the *Canon* were produced in a relatively short time span, extending from the early fourteenth to about the third quarter of the fifteenth century. The few commentaries, mostly brief, that were produced before 1300 seem to have achieved little lasting influence; and the composition of major *Canon* commentaries appears to have tapered off after about 1460. In particular, we may note for present purposes, that the last two commentators of enduring repute who knew only the unrevised Gerard of Cremona text of *Canon* I.1 were Ugo Benzi of Siena and Jacques Despars, who, as just remarked, died in 1439 and 1458 respectively.

However, if the production of major new commentaries on the *Canon* diminished, those already in existence probably achieved wider circulation than ever before between the 1470s and the 1520s. In that period, as noted earlier, Venetian and other north Italian presses issued and re-issued rather numerous editions of fourteenth- and early fifteenth-century commentaries on the *Canon* (and, of course, of other scholastic medical works). All of the commentaries just mentioned, with the exception of that of Antonio da Parma, appeared in print, some of them several times. We may take the single, but doubtless not uncharacteristic, example of Ugo Benzi, chosen because the printing history of his works has already been the subject of thorough investigation by a modern scholar: between 1478 and 1524, Ugo's commentary on *Canon*, Book I, Parts 1 and 2, appeared in five editions; his commentary on Book I, Part 4 (general therapy) was printed eleven, perhaps twelve times; and his commentary on Book IV, Part 1 (fevers) five times. All of these editions were from Italian presses. Thereafter, with the exception of excerpts in Lockwood's study from which the foregoing data are taken, none of Ugo's Latin commentaries was ever printed again.[28] In short, mid sixteenth-century commentators on the *Canon* had excellent opportunities for access to the works of a handful of fairly distant predecessors whose names were synonymous with the early achievements of Italian university medical learning; but the lectures of more recent teachers of the *Canon*, who flourished in the fifty years or so centring on 1500 seem to have been much less frequently regarded as worth preserving.[29]

The editions of the fourteenth- and early fifteenth-century commentaries appeared in precisely the period in which medical learning was becoming permeated by a medical humanism centred upon the direct study of the works of Galen and other Greek medical authors. The new Latin translations of Galen and other writers from the Greek, so prized by humanist physicians even though many of the texts had been available in medieval Latin versions for centuries, were mostly completed in the years 1484-1531; the long and eagerly awaited first printed edition of Galen's *Opera* in Greek issued from the Aldine press in 1525. However one may rate the actual importance of this intellectual movement for the development of medicine, there can be no doubt that those involved perceived it as an innovation of profound significance. Few learned physicians remained untouched by medical humanism, although levels of humanistic accomplishment and interest varied widely.[30]

Associated with medical humanism, as already noted, was a vein of vigorous criticism of Arabic medical authorities in general and Avicenna in particular. By the 1520s, criticism of the Arabs had become a commonplace of advanced medical thought throughout Europe. Controversies over the issue erupted at the University of Montpellier in the 1520s and 1530s, and the subject also sparked acrimonious publications or debate at Paris (Brissot, 1525), Basel (Paracelsus, supposedly, 1527), and Strasbourg (Laurent Fries, 1530), and doubtless elsewhere as well.[31] Yet the original fount of such criticisms was among learned humanist physicians associated with the Italian schools. The doyen of the critics was no doubt Leoniceno, who had published animadversions on Avicenna as early as the 1490s.[32] Without attempting to trace here the emergence of this strain of thought in Italy, or its course among Giovanni Manardi and other disciples of Leoniceno, we may merely note that the attack on Avicenna was still being energetically promoted as an essential ingredient of the reform of medical learning in 1533, when there appeared at Venice a collection of treatises entitled *A Little Work of the New Florentine Academy Against Avicenna and the Recent Physicians, Who, Having Neglected the Discipline of Galen, Cultivate the Barbarians.*[33] The first treatise in this collection is attributed to Bassiano Landi who later in 1551, became first ordinary professor of medical theory at Padua. The young Landi, admittedly under the cloak of anonymity, expressed the hope that 'just volumes about Avicenna's errors will soon issue from our academy', and described the famous Italian commentators on the *Canon* of the fourteenth and fifteenth centuries as men of great ingenuity who had been misled by following the Arabs.[34]

Meanwhile, however, efforts to secure an improved Latin text of the *Canon* had already begun before the end of the fifteenth century. The motives that led two learned physicians in the service of the Venetian Republic, first Girolamo Ramusio (d. 1486) and later Andrea Alpago (d. 1522) to use the opportunity provided by residence in the Middle East to undertake this task are not altogether clear. Most likely a mixture of academic and practical interests was involved in each case. Neither man achieved the retranslation of the *Canon* in its entirety, but Alpago produced an emended and revised version of the Gerard of Cremona text. The Paduan College of Philosophers and Physicians, pursuing the modernization of medical teaching according to its own lights, gave Alpago's version its official endorsement;[35] with the publication of the work in 1527 a new phase in the history of Latin commentary on the *Canon* could begin.

Thus, despite the doubtless more or less continuous history of the practice of lecturing on the *Canon* in the Italian universities since before 1300, despite (as we shall see) considerable continuity in the topics discussed, and despite general availability of the older commentaries, a real chronological and intellectual separation existed between the sixteenth-century commentators and their best known predecessors. Furthermore, our group of sixteenth-century writers lived in a milieu of medical science that was in important respects different from that of the fourteenth and fifteenth centuries, since advances in anatomy, botany, and the systematization of clinical teaching began to make their appearance in the north Italian universities (notably Padua) well before the mid-sixteenth century.[36]

The works on which I shall draw for some illustrative examples of the new phase of commentary on *Canon* I.1 provide a reasonably representative, though not complete overview of the content of university teaching of the work during a forty-year period. That all are associated with Padua reflects Padua's high level of activity and productivity in every aspect of medical education but not any uniquely Paduan curricular or, as far as one can tell, intellectual characteristics. The chief common characteristics of four of the five authors are possession of a chair in medical *theoria* at Padua (carrying with it the obligation to lecture on *Canon* I.1) and the attainment of a general reputation sufficient to ensure, for three of those four, posthumous publication of their works. None of these men appears to have been especially noted either for attachment to Avicenna or to traditionalism in general.

The earliest commentary that will be discussed is that of Giambattista Da Monte, presumably composed while he held the first ordinary chair in medical theory, and probably written between 1543 and 1546. Among the authors, Da Monte stands out as a man of unusually able and flexible intellect who managed to take part in a good many of the more innovative movements in medicine of his day. Da Monte is remembered for his efforts to revitalize the teaching of *practica*, exemplified by his role in the founding of the Paduan botanic garden and his habit of giving students clinical instruction in a hospital,[37] for his writings on scientific method;[38] and for his contributions to Renaissance Galenism as editor-in-chief of the celebrated edition of Galen's *Opera* in new Latin dress published by Giunta in 1541-1542.[39] Despite the latter position, Da Monte also acquired some contemporary reputation as a critic of Galen on a few issues.[40] In addition, Da Monte was one of the very few sixteenth century authors to comment on more than one section of Avicenna's *Canon*; he also produced commentaries on *Canon* I.2 and I.4.

The commentary of Oddo Oddi, in his day a celebrated Galenist, who was appointed to the second ordinary chair in medical theory in 1535 and transferred to the first position in *practica* (just vacated by Da Monte in favour of *theoria*) in 1543, was left uncompleted at Oddo's death in 1558.[41] The work was finished by his son Marco Oddi, who became professor of theory (extraordinary) in 1578,[42] and

published in 1575.[43] Also published posthumously was the
commentary of Bernardino Paterno, who held the first ordinary chair
in medical theory from 1563 until 1592, although a manuscript of his
lectures on *Canon* I.1. bears the date 1578.[44] It seems unlikely that
Paterno's lectures in fact varied very much over the course of a
professorship more marked by length than by accomplishment. All
three commentaries presumably embody the material of classroom
teaching, although with an undetermined degree of subsequent
editing. Da Monte's commentary is, for example, divided into
lectiones; frequent use of the second person plural and repetition to
drive points home confirm the classroom origin of the work.

   Finally, Andrea Graziolo, a former pupil of Oddo Oddi, published
in 1580 a revised version of the complete text of *Canon* I.1,
accompanied by explanatory *scholia*. Graziolo's *scholia*, while not
necessarily emanating from classroom lectures in the same way as the
other works discussed, are sufficiently full to be classified as a
commentry for present purposes. In his preface, Graziolo stated that
had undertaken his edition of *Canon* I.1. at the urging of Oddo Oddi
and had been persuaded to complete it by Paterno (along with
Fracastoro).[45]

   Although the attitudes to Avicenna as a medical authority and to
his earlier interpreters expressed in the prefaces of these works are not
always consistently maintained throughout the respective
expositions, the introductory remarks provide some useful clues to
the general orientation of the author in each case. All the authors
made it clear that they valued Avicenna primarily as an interpreter of
Galen, and all had as a fairly important goal the keying of Avicenna's
remarks to specific passages in the works of Galen and other medical
or philosophical authors so that their readers could make direct
comparisons. In addition, Da Monte, Oddi, and Graziolo all
explicitly weighed Avicenna's merits.

   Da Monte, after demoting Avicenna from his traditional place as
'prince of physicians' with the remark that the expression should be
used only in the sense that in medicine Hippocrates was the emperor,
Galen the king, and Avicenna the prince, nonetheless defended the
utility of the *Canon* as 'real and not imaginary', since Avicenna was,
as it were, Galen's vicar. This utility he placed chiefly in Avicenna's
capacity to assemble and organize material from a wide variety of
sources.[46] The general tone of his preface is one of modified but
genuine respect for Avicenna. Oddo, or perhaps Marco Oddi was
much more openly and sharply critical of Avicenna in his preface,
accusing him of introducing confusion and obscurity into Galen's
own clear thought.[47] By contrast, however, Graziolo's preface finds
no fault with Avicenna. Rather, Graziolo stressed Avicenna's

historic role as a transmitter of Greek medicine and dismissed as
outmoded those who would abandon the study of the *Canon*.
According to Graziolo, the revival of letters (dated by the arrival in
Italy of learned Greek refugees from the Ottoman conquests and the
invention of printing) had led to the humanistic transformation of
medicine, which had recently been 'recalled to its sources', 'purified',
and 'restored to light'. However, in the intellectual night that
preceded this happy state of affairs, the Arabs had cultivated and
indeed advanced mathematics, judicial astrology, and medicine.
Among the Arab medical authors, Avicenna was outstanding, so that
the restoration of the Greek works had not led to the discarding of
Avicenna by the learned, 'as some used to think' would be the case,
but rather to the equal celebration and frequent study of the *Canon* by
men of good judgement. Graziolo's preface goes on to dismiss
Avicenna's critics as ignorant of the teachings of Hippocrates and
Galen and malevolent, and to assert that Avicenna had improved on
Galen.[48] Graziolo attached importance to elegance of expression and
was therefore unable to indulge in the kind of outright attack on
humanism in medicine found in Girolamo Cardano's preface to a set
of lectures on *Canon* I.1 that he gave at Pavia in 1561 and again at
Bologna in 1563. Cardano pointed out that Avicenna had known
works of Galen that had subsequently been lost. Stressing the
scientific achievements of the Arabs, he further declared that
emphasis on classical elegance of expression and contempt for the
Arabs had led to neglect of intellectually demanding disciplines and
produced physicians who were 'even further from Galen in discipline
than from the Arabs in words'.[49]

Our authors laid varying degrees of emphasis upon the idea that
apparent obscurities and inadequacies in the *Canon* were due to
faulty translation. None of them seems to have been in a position to
study the Arabic text; indeed, Da Monte, as already noted, explicitly
disavowed any knowledge of the Arabic language. Da Monte based
his commentary upon Alpago's text and was apparently reasonably
satisfied with it. On the whole, although he occasionally referred to
the superior rendering of a particular passage by Alpago as compared
with Gerard of Cremona, or the meaning of particular Arabic
words,[50] he evinced very little interest in appraising the degree of
accuracy with which Avicenna's thought had been conveyed to the
West. As one might expect, given his own familiarity with the
problems of translating Galen, he was somewhat more sensitive to
the possibility that Avicenna might not have understood a Galenic
text correctly because of problems in translation. On several
occasions he quoted a word or two in Greek to demonstrate
Avicenna's misunderstanding, but even these instances are not

especially numerous. The question of the form in which the Galenic texts were known to Avicenna is never raised. In the main, however, Da Monte seems to have taken for granted both the adequacy of Avicenna's attitude to Avicenna's apparent differences with Galen is summed up in the remark 'I would not say that Avicenna does not understand Galen, but rather that he speaks from his own opinion against Galen'.[51] Oddo Oddi, however, devoted much attention throughout his work to comparing three Latin versions of *Canon* I.1, namely Alpago's revision, the translation from a Hebrew version published in about 1540 by the Jewish physician Jacob Mantino,[52] and the *versio antiquior*, not always to the disadvantage of the latter.[53] Much the most emphatic denunciation of Gerard's translation was provided by Graziolo, who claimed that his own revision of the text was based at least in part upon the hitherto unpublished version produced by Ramusio in the late fifteenth century. Graziolo ascribed much of the bad repute into which the *Canon* had fallen to the faults of Gerard's translation. Avicenna himself, Graziolo maintained, had been an eloquent and most polished author who had had the misfortune to fall into the hands of a translator who 'obscured his opinions, did not understand many things and defiled everything barbarously'.[54]

Da Monte, Oddo or Marco Oddi, and Graziolo each incorporated into his preface in one form or another the claim that his was a modern approach to Avicenna, distinctly different from and superior to that of earlier Latin commentators. Da Monte promised his readers that he would not discuss 'useless' and 'vain' questions;[55] the Oddi were even more explicit, avowing 'we will not examine questions in the manner of the Latin commentators, which leaves the audience bored and uncomprehending';[56] and Graziolo's references to the sorry state of medicine in the West before the fall of Constantinople and the rise of printing have already been noted. Throughout their works, moreover, Paterno and Graziolo as a rule avoided citation by name of fourteenth- and fifteenth-century medical authors. Da Monte and the Oddi cited their predecessors relatively freely, although usually only to disagree: Da Monte made mention of the opinion on various topics of Pietro d'Abano, Gentile da Foligno, and Jacobus (either Giacomo da Forlì or Jacques Despars), while Oddo Oddi seems to have read the *Conciliator* of Pietro d'Abano and the *Summa medicinalis* of Tommaso del Garbo and Marco Oddi the *Plusquam commentum* of Turisanus with some thoroughness.[57]

The claim to modernity is to a degree borne out in the presentation of the commentaries, although some of the changes are perhaps more apparent than real. The sixteenth-century commentators under discussion did to some extent discard or modify the typical structure of the scholastic *quaestio*, with its list of arguments pro and contra, objections, and resolution, but they did not necessarily stop breaking their material up into *quaestiones*. Thus, for example, the format of the 1557 edition of Da Monte's commentary on *Canon* I.1 (the choice, of course, of his posthumous editor or publisher), with its italic type, octavo page size, and alphabetically arranged subject index, conveys the impression of a self-consciously modern work. Yet a reading of the subject index reveals elements of a register of *quaestiones*, such as often accompanied fourteenth- or fifteenth-century scholastic commentaries both in manuscript and subsequently in incunabular or early sixteenth century folio editions. Over fifty of the entries in the index to Da Monte's work are in fact the titles of *quaestiones* beginning *An* or *Utrum*. Furthermore, there was much continuity in the topics discussed, as may be seen from a comparison of these entries with the titles of forty-six *quaestiones* on *Canon* I.1 written by Giacomo da Forlì before 1414.[58] It seems likely that the editor of Da Monte's work selected for listing in this traditional manner the more traditional topics taken up; furthermore the main subject matter — that is, the elements, the humours, *complexio* or *temperamentum*, the members, and the virtues — of Da Monte's as of Giacomo's exposition is of course dictated by *Canon* I.1 itself. Nonetheless, the repetition of topics is very striking. Thus, on the subject of *complexio*, both Giacomo and Da Monte inquired into the nature of *complexio* 'equal in weight' and whether it can be found in man; both attempted to determine whether woman is always colder than man in *complexio*; Giacomo asked whether *spiritus* is the hottest component of the human body, Da Monte whether blood is hotter than *spiritus*. These are, of course, traditional *quaestio* topics, by no means found only in these two authors or in commentaries on the *Canon*. Indeed, probably at least half of the questions listed in Da Monte's index had earlier been taken up in one form or another by medical authors going back to Taddeo Alderotti and his pupils at the turn of the thirteenth/fourteenth centuries, and in some instances beyond.[59] When one looks at the whole list of the topics of Giacomo's and Da Monte's questions, the chief difference in the concerns of the two writers seems to be that Giacomo was somewhat more interested in the *complexio* of individual parts of the body, and Da Monte in the elements, *spiritus* and the humours.

While such a comparison is a salutary reminder of the strength of academic medical tradition, it is also somewhat misleading. Shifting philosophical interests, access to philosophical and medical works of antiquity unknown to or ignored by fourteenth- and fifteenth-century medical authors, and contemporary investigations in anatomy and, later, physiology did not necessarily induce sixteenth-century commentators on *Canon* I.1 to abandon long discussed topics, but rather spurred their re-examination and perception in somewhat different focus. Such re-examination, far from being confined to lectures on long used textbooks, was, of course, characteristic of much Renaissance medical thought. Some well known examples are the treatments by medical authors of the subject of scientific method, and their discussion of the relative merits of the Aristotelian and Galenic positions on the functions of heart and brain, both topics discussed since the thirteenth century in the Latin west.[60] While the impact of the writings on the former topic is debated, and the history of those on the latter is not yet fully explored, it is clear that for sixteenth-century physicians both subjects were living issues that were neither exhausted nor delimited by a long history of earlier exposition.

Furthermore, on turning to the body of the commentaries themselves, one finds that Da Monte and the others habitually modified significant features of traditional commentary and habitually introduced new material. Characteristic of the fourteenth- and fifteenth-century commentaries on the *Canon* is respect for Avicenna as an independent authority and a willingness to place his views on a par with those of Galen when the two differed or appeared to differ. In these works, too, an important goal appears to have been to acquaint the reader with the views of leading professors in the Italian schools from the time of Taddeo Alderotti (d. 1295) to that of the writer. Thus, Gentile da Foligno referred repeatedly to the opinions on *Canon* I.1 of Antonio da Parma, and Giacomo da Forlì to those of Dinus and Mundinus (Dino del Garbo and, probably, Mondino de' Liuzzi, d. 1326), as well as to those of Gentile himself.[61]

In the sixteenth-century commentaries, by contrast, overt references to the views of earlier Latin commentators play a very minor role in comparison with the importance attached to Greek authors; Avicenna is, as noted, usually subordinated to Galen; and in the commentaries of Da Monte and Marco Oddi Avicenna is subjected to sharp criticism. These points may be illustrated with reference to passages in Da Monte's work.

Thus, Da Monte engaged in a lengthy discussion of medicinal qualities and of how these are brought from potentiality (when the medicine is outside the body) to actuality (when it is ingested).[62] In particular, if as Galen says, medicines are activated by the heat of the human body, how does this work in the case of medicines of predominantly cold complexion? This topic, under the title 'the reduction of medicine to act' (an expression Da Monte did not use), was a favourite in the late thirteenth- and fourteenth-century Italian medical schools. Tommaso del Garbo devoted a treatise to it and

Gentile da Foligno discussed it in a *quaestio* in which he reviewed the opinions on the subject of eleven Italian medical authors, beginning with Taddeo Alderotti.[63] One could read Da Monte's discusion without realizing that the subject had ever been raised by anyone other than Galen, Avicenna himself, and Averroes.[64]

But the principal feature that marks off Da Monte's commentary on *Canon* I.1 from most earlier ones is the author's attitude to Avicenna as a medical authority. Da Monte made it clear to his readers from the beginning that his primary goal was not to expound Avicenna's views but to weigh them critically. Reappraisal does not, of course, necessarily imply rejection, and initially, as already noted, Da Monte adopted an attitude of modified respect for Avicenna. In the first part of the commentary the moderate tone found in the preface is on the whole maintained fairly consistently. Although Avicenna is disagreed with on a number of specific issues, he is praised for his ability to organize a comprehensive account of medicine, and also for his skill in the compositive method, proceeding from the general to the particular.[65] Da Monte's expression of admiration for Avicenna's capacity to organize the material in Book I of the *Canon* was certainly not pro forma, since he introduced somewhat similar remarks into his preface to the Giunta Galen.[66] Moreover, remarks are scattered throughout Da Monte's commentary on *Canon* I.1 which strengthens the impression of a certain detachment in regard to the competing schools of medical opinion. He observed, for instance, that Manardi was wrong to claim that the Arabs had not understood Greek views on *pituita*, since the opinion Manardi reprehended could be found in an unnamed Greek source.[67] In another passage, defending a position of Aristotle against Galen, he characterized Galen as malign and his arguments on the point at issue as frivolous.[68]

Despite the parade of moderation, as one proceeds through the commentary one becomes aware that Avicenna's opinions and interpretations are being subjected to increasingly acerbic criticism. This is especially the case as regards humours. The section of his commentary devoted to this topic reveals that Da Monte considered Avicenna's views on almost every aspect of the subject to be thoroughly misleading. Thus, of Avicenna's assertion that good humours all become part of the body as it is nourished, he protested; 'Is not milk a humour that is good and intended by nature? But into what part of the body are these absorbed, since they are excretions? For since they are excreted they are not produced on account of the nourishment of the body, but are useful excretions with other purposes . . . And Gentile da Foligno and the others saw these difficulties, but they so admired Avicenna that they didn't dare to carp. But Plato is a friend and Socrates is a friend; but a better friend is truth'.[69] On the same general topic, we subsequently learn that Gentile da Foligno defended Avicenna by telling a lie; that some of Avicenna's views on various kind of humidity in the body are 'totally false'; and that 'Avicenna is far both from Galen and from the truth of the thing itself'. The passage ends with the exhortation: 'And so you have the classification and opinion of Galen, which is very true, and that of Avicenna, of which you have seen how much it is in error. And if anyone subsequently prefers to eat acorns rather than bread, he should choose what he prefers. For he has acorns and he has bread'.[70] In another passage, Da Monte jocularly distinguished between Avicenna's venial and his mortal sins in misinterpreting Galen.[71] Still later, summarising his lecture on Avicenna's views on the humour *pituita* (phlegm), he declared: 'Now you have seen all the distinctions of *pituita* that are taught by Avicenna, and you have heard them faithfully expounded by us; but I don't think any one of you is of such divine ingenuity that he can say he has learned anything from Avicenna'.[72]

After perusing Da Monte's diatribe against Avicenna's views on humours, the reader feels disposed to echo a rhetorical question posed by Da Monte himself at the beginning of the section on bile: 'Someone may say here "Why are you expounding a book that you attack so vigorously?"' Da Monte's own response to this question was as follows: 'In the first place, I am not attacking the whole book, but only those things in it that seem to me reprehensible; besides, I am not doing anything new. For Galen never wrote better commentaries than those on books that he reprehended'.[73] Da Monte and, to a lesser extent, Marco Oddi seem indeed to have been consciously experimenting with the production of commentaries incorporating substantial elements of criticism of the work commented upon. For Marco Oddi a recent exemplar may have been Matteo degli Corti, who is referred to so frequently by name in the commentary of Oddo Oddi as to give rise to the supposition that he was perhaps that author's teacher. Corti's own commentary (published in 1550) on the *Anatomia* of Mondino de' Liuzzi (d. 1326) amounts to a diatribe against Mondino for his failure to understand, or in some instances agree with, Galen.[74] Such an approach certainly constitutes a radical revision of the goals of commentary as they had been understood by the medical authors of the fourteenth and fifteenth centuries. Those authors had been, essentially, engaged in recording and contributing to modern scientific debate on an authoritative work. For Da Monte, the commentary became to a significant extent a tool for detaching students from faith in Avicenna as an independent authority, and teaching them to analyse his adequacy as an interpreter of Galen. But

Da Monte was, of course, correct in asserting that he was 'not attacking the whole book'. Indeed, it is arguable that his ingenuity in modernizing and finding fresh pedagogical uses for commentary on the *Canon* contributed importantly to the survival of the text in the curriculum. It should further be noted that attacks on Avicenna are by no means a salient feature either of Paterno's commentary or of Graziolo's *scholia*, so that it cannot be maintained that criticism became the prevailing mode of commentary as a result of Da Monte's efforts.

We may conclude with a single somewhat more detailed example of the approach of this group of commentators to traditional lines of medico-philosophical investigation. One could choose such an example from the treatments in the commentaries under discussion of the major topics of scientific method and of the differences between the physiological views of Aristotle and Galen. For instance, Da Monte, author of a well known work on method, naturally introduced his views on resolution and composition into his lectures on *Canon* I.1;[75] Paterno, supporting his arguments with reference to observations during the vivisection of animals, defended Galen's position on the association of brain and nervous system against both Aristotle and what he considered to be the distortions of Aristotle's views transmitted by Averroes.[76] However, since the Renaissance treatment of these particular topics has, as noted above, already been the subject of a good deal of historical investigation, it seems preferable to turn to another, perhaps somewhat less explored area. Accordingly there follows a brief review of the treatment of a central issue relating to the theory of *complexio*, or to use the term preferred by sixteenth-century writers, *temperatura*, first by Giacomo da Forlì in the years around 1400, and then by Da Monte, Oddi, Graziolo, and Paterno.

Analysis of the Hippocratic-Galenic idea of *complexio* (*krasis*), that is the notion of a particular balance of the primary qualities of hot, wet, cold, and dry as a defining characteristic of all categories of living beings, occupied a very large place in the intellectual enterprise of learned physicians between the thirteenth and the fifteenth centuries. Since each plant and animal species, each individual human being, each component of the human body, and each compounded medicine was supposed to have its own distinct *complexio*, and since *complexio* in human beings was also thought of as subject to change as a result of such factors as the passage of time or the onset of disease, the scope for exploration of the logical and therapeutic implications of the whole cluster of concepts was really limited only by the ingenuity of the investigator. But for the philosophically inclined physician of that period the fundamental problem was to provide a definition of *complexio* that would relate it satisfactorily to the Aristotelian concepts of form and matter, essence and accident on the one hand, and to the in some respects parallel discussions of the elements in a mixture on the other. Accordingly, medical authors of the thirteenth through the fifteenth centuries considered such questions as how *complexio* was to be distinguished from substantial form and whether and in what way the elementary qualities survived in a perfected *complexio*.[77] Avicenna's first chapter on *complexio*, which in the Gerard of Cremona version of *Canon* I.1 begins '*complexio est qualitas*' provided a locus classicus for these discussions, although they are also to be found in many other places.

Giacomo da Forlì's inquiry as to whether Avicenna had been in correct in calling *complexio* a quality is relatively straightforward and perhaps betrays a certain impatience with a century of debate. Giacomo began by pointing out that it was hard to see how *complexio* could be a single quality in itself when it was by definition supposed to be a balance of qualities. He concluded 'it probably can be held that *complexio* is not any quality distinct from the whole aggregate of the primary qualities'. Since he also rejected the possibility that *complexio* might be either matter, or substantial form, or a composite, or nature, this conclusion seems to amount to a rather effective denial of the real existence of *complexio* (though not of that of the primary qualities in the body). Giacomo immediately backed away from this radical position with the assertion that is is more probable and more consonant with reason to suppose that *complexio* is a quality distinct from the primary qualities yet somehow containing them in its active virtue.[78]

Unlike Giacomo da Forlì, Da Monte, writing well over a hundred years later, showed no sign in his commentary on the same text of thinking that discussions of the definition of *temperatura*, as he preferred to term it, had exhausted their fruitfulness. On the contrary, he declared that Avicenna's definition contained 'very beautiful difficulties badly handled by the moderns'. He perhaps anticipated some resistance to the exploration of these difficulties on the part of his audience of medical students, since he also found it necessary explicitly to assure them that proper understanding of the nature of *temperatura* was highly relevant to therapy. In any case, Da Monte evidently thought it part of his pedagogical duty to ensure that his students gave some consideration to general philosophical or scientific issues in the course of their medical studies; thus, for example, he found occasion in the same passage to inform them of the nature of the theories of Democritus and the atomists.[79]

Da Monte's goal was a re-examination of the traditional problem of the relationship between *temperatura* and substantial form. This issue he declared to be of great importance, although so difficult that great men get stuck in it.[80] Da Monte, correctly on the whole, attributed the view that *temperatura* and substantial form are distinct to 'the Arabs and more recent Latin writers', while maintaining that Hippocrates, Galen, 'and perhaps even Aristotle' had held *temperatura* and substantial form to be identical — a somewhat hypothetical judgement as regards Hippocrates as well as Aristotle.[81] After reviewing arguments in favour of each of the two positions, Da Monte concluded that from the standpoint of theology it was necessary to adopt the position of the Arabs; speaking as a philosopher, however, he endorsed the view attributed to Hippocrates and Galen and maintained the identity of *temperatura* and substantial form.[82] The latter position was, of course, unacceptable to faith because the substantial form in man was held to be the rational soul. Hence, the assertion that substantial form in man is to be identified with a balance of the physical qualities of hot, wet, cold, and dry presumably implied a mortalist and materialist position as regards the soul. As befitted one who was at one time a pupil of Pomponazzi, Da Monte was re-examining the problem of *complexio* and substantial form in the light of recent and still current interest in the question of the immortality of the soul.[83]

Despite his awareness of contemporary issues in philosophy and despite his wholesale repudiation of the philosophical validity of views ascribed to the Arabs and Latin writers who followed them, Da Monte's exposition falls within a largely traditional framework;. His 'moderns' and 'more recent writers' are Latin scholastics; the only one named in this passage is Albertus Magnus, although as already noted citations elsewhere in the commentary suggest that Da Monte had also read quite widely in Italian scholastic medical authors. Da Monte's thoroughgoing medical humanism here found expression only in defending views believed to be Galen's against the Latin tradition.

Almost every aspect of Da Monte's approach was abandoned by both Oddo Oddi and Graziolo, whose treatments of the same passages, as one might expect from master and pupil, somewhat resemble one another.[84] These authors ignored the earlier discussions of substantial form, and made no mention of any Latins who wrote before 1500. Instead, they concentrated on the issue of the nature of the mixture of the primary qualities that constituted *temperatura*. In so doing they were concerned not to attack Avicenna's views but to explain and endorse them in the light of material about physics derived from current trends in philosophy. Both authors reviewed Avicenna's definition of *temperatura* in the light of the *De mixtione* of Alexander of Aphrodisias. The latter author was influential during the sixteenth century both as an interpreter of Aristotle and as a source of information about Stoic physics, which he attacked in *De mixtione*.[85] This treatise was first published in an Aldine edition of the Greek text in 1527, and received three separate Latin translations, two of them by physicians, between about 1540 and 1553; in all, five editions were published by 1559.[86] Thus Oddo Oddi who, as already noted died in 1558, was drawing upon a work that had only recently become available and that aroused much contemporary interest.

In the discussions of Avicenna's definition of complexion by Oddo Oddi and Graziolo the topic of the soul, so important to Da Monte, is never explicitly raised (conceivably it may be implicitly present, since Alexander of Aphrodisias was a well known source of mortalist ideas). An explicit objective of Graziolo's *scholium* is, however, to defend Avicenna against the attacks of Jean Fernel, who is named along with Leonhart Fuchs.[87] Despite his notoriety as one of the most radical of the medical *moderni* of his age, Fernel taught a physiology that was in many ways quite conservative. He certainly did not discard the idea of *temperamentum* or *temperatura*, although he seems to have given more emphasis to the notion of innate heat. But in his best known work, published in 1542 and reissued in 1554, he poured scorn on the notion that a fifth quality, *temperamentum*, could emerge from a mixture of the primary four, and hence on Avicenna's definition *'temperatura est qualitas'*.[88] (We have see that Fernel's point had, essentially, already been made by Giacomo da Forlì about 1400, although Giacomo was not prepared to insist upon it.) Thus, Graziolo identified his 'modern' opponents as contemporaries, whereas Da Monte had placed his in the fairly distant past. We may note in passing, moreover, that attempts to evaluate the work of contemporaries — Fernel in physiology and Vesalius in anatomy — are also a feature of Marco's portion of the Oddi commentary.[89]

Paterno's commentary on the same passage may be thought to represent a somewhat lower level of teaching medical *theoria*.[90] In it, most of the arguments just surveyed are vaguely alluded to without explication. The main intention seems to be to defend Avicenna, but the grounds on which he had been criticized are not really made clear. No very definite, let alone controversial, stands are taken by the author. The principal information that the reader comes away with is that *complexio* is a mixture of qualities not of particles. Paterno's lack of interest in complexion theory is not, of course, necessarily to his discredit, although it must be admitted that much of the rest of his commentary does not seem to be of much higher quality than this passage.

Judging by the commentaries here briefly surveyed, professors who taught *theoria* from Book I, Part 1, of the *Canon* of Avicenna at Padua in the years 1540-1580 distanced themselves in various ways from the earlier Italian tradition of academic medical learning. They were highly responsive to intellectual movements of their own day — particularly to the whole cluster of ideas and attitudes designated medical humanism — and aware, if not always approving, of new work in physiology and anatomy. In different ways, Da Monte, Oddo and Marco Oddi, and Graziolo were all dissatisfied with the traditional teaching of *Canon* I.1 and laboured to increase its worth as a text. Whatever the faults of these authors, they were none of them, even the rather uninspired Paterno, prisoners of an uncritical dependence upon traditional Arab authorities. Their conviction that *Canon* I.1 was worth salvaging probably sprang less from attachment to any particular views of Avicenna than from a general belief that philosophy had a part to play in medical education. What they shared with their fourteenth- and fifteenth-century predecessors was the assumption that a university medical student should have a background in natural philosophy and that it was appropriate that his specifically medical training should begin with a broad survey of physiological generalities with due attention to their philosophical implications and some introduction to current controversy. But the tensions inherent in the approach of these authors to the *Canon* and the ambiguities of their relationship with their late medieval and early Renaissance predecessors perhaps suggest that such conventional categories as 'scholastic medicine' and 'humanistic medicine' need, at least in this instance, to be re-examined.

Department of History
Hunter College and City University of New York Graduate School
New York, New York, U. S. A.

REFERENCES

1.   Earlier versions of parts of this paper were given at seminars at the Department of the History of Science, Harvard University, the Department of the History and Philosophy of Science, Princeton University, and the Johns Hopkins Institute of the History of Medicine, at which I benefited greatly from the discussion. I am grateful to all those who took part. Grants from the PSC-CUNY Research Foundation, the National Endowment for the Humanities, and the J. S. Guggenheim Memorial Foundation aided the larger research project of which this article presents partial results.

In the following notes and appendices, punctuation has been modernized and abbreviations silently expanded in titles of and quotations from Latin works published before 1700.

2.   The earliest surviving Latin academic commentaries on parts of the work appear to be those attributed to Johannes de Sancto Amando (ca.1280) (Lynn Thorndike and Pearl Kibre, *A Catalogue of Incipits of Mediaeval Scientific Writings in Latin*, 2nd edition, Cambridge, Mass., 1963, col.361) and Taddeo Alderotti (d. 1295) (N.G. Siraisi, *Taddeo Alderotti and His Pupils*, Princeton, 1981, pp. 416-417). The *Canon* was, however, intensively studied by Albertus Magnus and others earlier in the thirteenth century. 'Avicenna', meaning no doubt the *Canon*, was prescribed for study in the medical curriculum at Montpellier in 1309; see *Cartulaire de l'Université de Montpellier*, I (Montpellier, 1890), 219-221, no. 25. Medical masters at Montpellier were studying the *Canon* from about the middle of the thirteenth century; see Luis Garcia Ballester, 'Arnau de Vilanova (c.1240-1311) y la reforma de los estudios médicos en Montpellier (1309): El Hipócrates latino y la introducción del nuevo Galeno', *Dynamis* 2 (1982), 103-104.

3.   See Umberto Dallari, ed., *I rotuli dei lettori legisti e artisti dello studio bolognese* (Bologna, 1889-1919), III, 2, 326. In 1721 the use of *Canon* I.1 as a text in *theoria* has been abandoned in favour of Galen, *De methodo medendi* (ibid., III, 1, 260, 282), but in 1737 the study of the *Canon* was reintroduced (ibid. III, 2, 5) and retained until the end of the century. I am grateful to Professor Herbert Matsen for drawing my attention to this.

4.   George Sarton, 'Query No. 134 — Was any attempt made by the editors of the late Latin editions of Avicenna's *Canon* to modernize it'? *Isis*, 43 (1952), 54, and Biagio Brugi, ed., 'Un parere di Scripione Maffei', *Atti del R. Istituto Veneto di Scienze, Lettere ed Arti*, 69 (1909-10), part 2, 578.

5.   On the use of this portion of the work in the sixteenth century, see Iain M. Lonie, 'Fever Pathology in the Sixteenth Century: Tradition and Innovation', in *Theories of Fever from Antiquity to the Enlightenment*, ed., W.F. Bynum and V. Nutton, *Medical History*, Supplement No. 1, 1981, pp. 19-44.

6.   For the editions and commentaries referred to, see Appendices I and II. The extensive printing history of Arabic medical works in Latin in the sixteenth and early seventeenth century is noted in Owsei Temkin, *Galenism* (Ithaca, 1973), pp. 127-128.

7.   I hope to publish a list of these manuscripts at some future date.

8.   *Avicennae philosophi praeclarissimi . . . Libellus de removendis nocumentis, quae accidunt in regimine sanitatis . . . Syrasi philosophi, ac medici excellentissimi expositiones super secundam, et tertiam, et partem quartae fen primi Canonis Avicennae. Ebenfis philosophi, ac medici excellentissimi expositio super quintum Canonem Avicennae . . . Ab Andrea Alpago bellunensi . . . ex Arabico in latinum versa . . .* (Venice, 1547). I have consulted the copy at the New York Academy of Medicine. On the translator, see Francesca Lucchetta, *Il medico e filosofo bellunese Andrea Alpago († 1522) traduttore di Avicenna* (Padua, 1964). Ibn al-Nafis, celebrated for his discussion of the lesser circulation of the blood (not in the present work, however) flourished at Damascus and d. 1288-89; al-Shirazi, who drew on the former's work, d. 1311.

9.   For example, *Contradictiones, dubia, et paradoxa, in libros Hippocratis, Celsi, Galeni, Aetii, Aginetae, Avicenna cum eorundem conciliationibus. Nicolao Rorario . . . auctore* (Venice, 1566), consulted at the New York Academy of Medicine, and *Ioannis Planerii . . . Febrium omnium simplicium divisio, et compositio ex Galeno et Avicenna excerpta et in arbores, ut facilius intelligatur redacta* (Venice, 1574), consulted at the British Library. The *arbores* are elaborate tables.

10.   See A. C. Klebs, *Incunabula scientifica et medica* (Bruges, 1938), p. 44, no. 80.1-2; pp. 68-69, no. 131.1-14; p. 123, no. 336.1-3; p. 139, no. 394.1; pp. 152-153, nos. 448.1-2, 451.1, 452.1; pp. 183-184, nos. 548.1-3, 550.1-3; pp. 326-327, nos. 997.1-4, 998.1-2, 999.1.

11.   A few commentaries were still being printed in the late seventeenth century. That of Giovanni Arcolano (d. 1458) on *Canon* IV.1 (fevers) was reissued at Padua in 1685 as *De febribus Ioannis Arculani in Avicennae IV Canonis fen primam dilucida atque optima exposition nunc denuo accuratissime expurgata* . . . ; the late sixteenth century commentary of Pietro Salio Diverso on *Canon* III was published as *De morbis particularibus* at Padua in 1673 (both consulted at the British Library).

12.   On Renaissance Aristotelianism, see Charles B. Schmitt, *Aristotle and the Renaissance* (Cambridge, Mass., 1983), and the other studies by this author. For an evaluation of the relationship of philosophy and science in the Italian universities of the period, see idem, 'Philosophy and Science in Sixteenth Century Italian Universities', in *The Renaissance: Essays in Interpretation* (London, 1982), pp. 297-336. Much current work on Renaissance Galenism is summarized in Richard J. Durling, 'Linacre and Medical Humanism', in *Linacre Studies: Essays on the Life and Work of Thomas Linacre c.1460-1524)*, ed. Francis Maddison, Margaret Pelling, and Charles Webster (Oxford, 1977), pp. 77-106, and Vivian Nutton, 'John Caius and the Linacre Tradition', *Medical History*, 33 (1979), 373-389; see also Owsei Temkin, *Galenism* (Ithaca, 1973), pp. 125-174, and Andrew Wear, 'Galen in the Renaissance', in *Galen: Problems and Prospects*, ed. Vivian Nutton (London, 1981), pp. 229-262. Helpful analyses of various trends in Italian university milieux are contained in Cesare Vasoli, 'La cultura dei secoli XIV-XVI', in *Atti del primo convegno internazionale di ricognizione delle fonti per la storia della scienza italiana: I secoli XIV-XVI* (Pisa, 1966), ed. Carlo Maccagni (Florence,1967), pp. 31-78, and following discussion, pp. 78-105, and Paola Zambelli, 'Scienza, filosofia, religione nella Toscana di Cosimo I', in *Florence and Venice: Comparisons and Relations*. Vol. II: *Cinquecento* (Florence, 1980), 3-52.

13.   ' . . . non igitur vituperari potest Avicenna, Galenus autem commendari', *Canon*, ed. Rinio (Venice, 1555), preface [iv^r]. (For full bibliographical citations of this and other sixteenth-century Latin editions of the *Canon* referred to, see Appendix I.)

14.   For a survey of the state of Arabic studies in western Europe in the sixteenth century, see Karl H. Dannenfeldt, 'The Renaissance Humanists and the Knowledge of Arabic', and Johann Fück, *Die arabischen Studien in Europa bis in den Anfang des 20.Jahrhunderts* (Leipzig, 1955), pp. 35-58. A few scholars made great efforts to study the language, often inspired by missionary or polemical goals. Among physicians, knowledge of Arabic appears to have been exceptional; the famous printing of the *Canon* in Arabic by the Medici press (Rome, 1593) was undertaken as part of a missionary project, was supervised by a scholar who was not a physician (G. B. Raimondi), and was intended for distribution in the Middle East (see J. R. Jones, 'The Arabic and Persian Studies of Giovan Battista Raimondi, ca. 1536-1614', (M. Phil. dissertation, The Warburg Institute, 1981), and G. E. Saltini, 'Della stamperia orientale medicea e di Giovan Battista Raimondi', *Giornale storico degli archivi toscani*, 4 [1860], 257-308). The physicans who contributed to Arabic studies, alluded to by Temkin, *Galenism*, p. 128, belonged, with the notable exceptions of Ramusio and Alpago (see below) chiefly to the seventeenth century and to northern Europe. As far as routine teaching of medicine in the Italian universities went, the remark of Pietro Castelli probably sums up the situation: the *medicus* 'sermone latino non possit carere . . . sine magna turpitudine, Graeco non sine turpitudine solum . . . Sed equidem illum quoque mirum in modum commendarem, qui Arabici peritus esset sermonis . . . verum scientiam laudo, non requiro'. *Petri Castelli Romani . . . Optimus medicus . . .* (Messina, 1637), in *Hermanii Conringii In universam artem medicam singulasque ejus partes introductio . . .* (Helmstadt, 1687; consulted at the British Library), part 2, separately paginated, pp. 28-29. I owe this reference to Dr. Charles B. Schmitt, who also drew my attention to the work of Jones. I am grateful to Mr Jones for corresponding with me on this subject.

15.   '. . . nescio litteras Arabes', and 'sive modo ita stet littera Arabica sive non, ego id nescio quoniam ignarus sum', Da Monte, comm. *Canon* I.2 (Venice, 1557) pp. 93, 247 (for full bibliographical references to this and other sixteenth-century commentaries on the *Canon* cited, see Appendix II). Da Monte's awareness that lack of Arabic is a deficiency marks him off from most other Latin commentators on the *Canon*.

16.   I have attempted no systematic survey of Latin editions by other Arabic medical authors. Probably the only ones who received anywhere near the same amount of attention as Avicenna were Rasis and Mesue, whose works were valued entirely for the teaching of *practica*. R. J. Durling, *A Catalogue of Sixteenth-Century Printed Books in the National Library of Medicine* (Bethesda, 1967), lists eleven Latin editions of works or collections of works attributed to Rasis printed in the first three-quarters of the sixteenth century (nos. 3311-3317, 326, 528-529, 331-332, 1101, 1105, 4013). Furthermore, at least seven fourteenth- or fifteenth-century commentaries on Rasis were printed after 1500, that of Arcolano many times (ibid., nos. 247-253, 1747, 2054-2055, 2587-2589, 4293). There are also a few sixteenth-century commentaries on Rasis, including one by G. B. Da Monte, namely *Io. Baptistae Montani Veronensis in nonum librum Rhasis ad Almansorem . . .* (Venice, 1554, consulted at the New York Academy of Medicine). For Mesue, see Durling, *Catalogue*, nos. 3121-3151. Printings of works of other Arabic medical authors seem less frequent, and other Arabic medical works had not traditionally attracted commentary to anything like the same extent as those of Avicenna and Rasis. Furthermore, printings of most other works of Arabic medical authors seem to have tapered off long before editions of the *Canon*.

17.   The six *doctrinae* or subsections, of Fen (Part) 1 of Book I of the *Canon* deal with 1) the definitions and subject of medicine; 2) the elements; 3) complexions; 4) the humours; 5) the members; 6) virtues and operations. The use of the term 'physiology' for most of this material is not anachronistic; Jean Fernel divided his *Physiologiae libri VII*, somewhat similarly, into 1) parts of the body; 2) the elements; 3) temperaments (or complexions); 4) *spiritus* and innate heat; 5) faculties of the soul; 6) functions and humours; 7) procreation of man. Originally published under the title *De naturali parte medicinae* in 1542, the *Physiologiae libri* were published under the latter title as part of *Io. Fernelii Ambiani Medicina . . .* (Paris, 1554, consulted at the New York Academy of Medicine). I am grateful to Professor Jerome Bylebyl for pointing out this parallel in content and organization to me.

18.   The *Aphorisms* range over a variety of subjects and are only loosely organized; the *Microtechne* covers definitions of health and disease, signs, and causes. The latter work did, however, offer opportunity for the discussion of scientific method, as is well known (see Edwards, note 60, below), and of much general physiology, as P.-G. Ottosson, *Scholastic Medicine and Philosophy: A Study of Commentaries on Galen's Tegni (ca. 1300-1450)* (Naples, 1984) has recently pointed out.

19.   There is, as yet, no complete specialized catalogue of Latin manuscripts of the *Canon* or its commentaries, although Thorndike and Kibre provides a helpful starting point. Forthcoming studies by Ilona Opelt and Danielle Jacquart should fill these lacunae (information from private communications). In the following pages, assertions about the number and authorship of commentaries written before 1500 are based on Thorndike and Kibre unless otherwise indicated.

20.   See, for example, the biography of Taddeo Alderotti (d. 1295) in Filippo Villani's *Liber de civitatis Florentiae famosis civibus . . .* , ed. C. G. Galletti (Florence, 1847), pp. 26-27. Villani, who wrote in 1381/82 and revised his work in 1395/96, took up the idea of the modern revitalization of poetry and, to some extent, art in Italy and extended it to medicine and law.

21.   The statutes of the University of Arts and Medicine of Bologna of 1405, for example, provide for a four year cycle of lectures on *practica* for which Book III of the *Canon* was the only assigned textbook; *Statuti delle università e dei collegi dello studio bolognese*, ed. Carlo Malagola (Bologna, 1888), pp. 276-277. Other portions of the *Canon* assigned *pro secunda lectione*, namely Book II, and Book IV.1-2, also seem to relate to *practica* (ibid., p. 274-276). The title of Dino del Garbo's (d. 1327) commentary on *Canon* 1.4, namely *Dyni florentini super quarta fen primi Avicennae preclarissima commentaria que dilucidatorium totius practice generalis scientie nuncupatur* . . . (Venice, 1514) certainly suggests that this portion of the work may have been used in the teaching of *practica*. The provision of a separate professorship of *practica* had already begun at Bologna by 1324; see Siraisi, *Taddeo*, p. 21, and bibliography there cited.

22.   At Bologna in 1405, Book I was assigned with the omission of a few sections of Fen 1 and 2 and of most of Fen 3 (Malagola, pp. 274-276); at Padua the statutes insisted that 'totum primum Canonis' be read (*Statuta Almae Universitatis D. D. Philosophorum et Medicorum Cognomento Artistarum Patavini* [Padua, 1607], 2.16, p.80, reprinting a statute of 1465), but the apparent dearth of commentaries on *Canon* I.3 suggests that this was seldom done. *Canon* I.2 was only intermittently the subject of lectures at Padua.

23.   All of *doctrina* 5 but the introductory chapter *De membris* is omitted from the commentary on *Canon* I.1 by Antonio da Parma (fl. 1310), who probably taught medicine at Bologna; see MS Vat.lat. 4452, fols. 1ʳ-47ᵛ. Gentile da Foligno (d. 1348) remarked unfavourably on the practice of omitting commentary on the bulk of the section on anatomy, but nonetheless followed it; see *Primus Avicennae Canon cum argutissima Gentilis expositione* (Pavia, 1510; consulted at the New York Academy of Medicine), fol. 54ᵛ. The Bologna statutes of 1405 endorsed the practice (Malagola, p. 274; in this as in other instances the earliest surviving statutory evidence long postdates the origins of the usage). It may be noted that the omitted portion concerned the anatomy of bones, muscles, nerves, arteries and veins, while, for a variety of reasons, anatomical interests at Bologna in the age of Mondino de' Liuzzi were chiefly concerned with the internal organs.

24.   For example, the reflections on specific form included by Taddeo Alderotti in his questions on *Canon* I.2.2.15 are also found, abbreviated, in his commentary on the medical *Isagoge* of Johannitius (Siraisi, *Taddeo*, pp. 243-244). The celebrated *Conciliator differentiarum philosophorum et precipue medicorum* (Venice, 1496 and other early editions) of Pietro d'Abano certainly owes much, including part of its organization, to Book I of the *Canon*.

25.   No manuscript appears to survive, for example, of a complete commentary by Gentile on *Canon* III, although there are manuscripts of commentaries by him on various subsections of that part of the work (see Thorndike and Kibre 265, 543, 735, 1009, 1506, 1701). It seems likely that *Tertius Canonis Avicenne cum dilucidissimis expositionibus Gentile fulginate* . . . , 3 vols. (Venice, [ca. 1505, according to the catalogue of the Wellcome Historical Medical Library]), was put together from these or others similar to them.

26.   Biographies of Marsilio Santasofia and Giacomo da Forlì are included in *Monumenti della Università di Padova (1318-1405)*, ed. Andrea Gloria (Padua, 1888), I, 390-395, 437-439; on Gentile, see Fausto Bonora and George Kern, 'Does Anyone Really Know the Life of Gentile da Foligno?' *Medicina nei secoli* 9 (1972), 29-53; on Antonio da Parma and Dino del Garbo, Siraisi, *Taddeo*, pp. xx, 55-64; on Tommaso del Garbo, A. Corsini, 'Nuovo contributo di notizie intorno alla vita di maestro Tommaso del Garbo', *Rivista di storia delle scienze mediche e naturali* 16 (1925), 268-278; on Ugo Benzi, Dean P. Lockwood, *Ugo Benzi: Medieval Philosopher and*

Physician (Chicago, 1951); on Jacques Despars, Danielle Jacquart, 'Le regard d'un médecin sur son temps: Jacques Despars (130?-1458), *'Bibliothèque de l'École des Chartes* 138 (1980), 35-86; on Leonardo da Bertipaglia, T. Pesenti Marangon, '"Professores chirugie", "medici e ciroici" e "barbitonsores" a Padova nell'età di Leonardo Buffi da Bertipaglia († dopo il 1448)', *Quaderni per la storia dell' Università di Padova* 11 (1978), 1-38; on G. M. Ferrari da Grado, H. M. Ferrari da Grado, *Une chaire de médecine au XV siècle: Un professeur a l'université de Pavie de 1432 à 1472* (Paris, 1899); the death date supplied for Giovanni Arcolano comes from Juliana H. Cotton, *Name-List Medical Register of the Italian Renaissance, 1350-1550* (Oxford, 1976).

27.   Like the *Conciliator* of the Pietro d'Abano, the *Plusquam commentum in Microtegni Galieni* (Venice, 1512) of Turisanus, and the *Summa medicinalis* (Venice, 1506) of Tommaso del Garbo (I indicate the editions at the New York Academy of Medicine) are comprehensive general introductions to medical theory reflecting much study of the *Canon* on the part of their authors.

28.   Lockwood, pp. 382-398.

29.   There are, of course, exceptions to this generalization, for example the work of Pietro Antonio Rustico, *Qui atrocem horres pestem pestilentemque times febrem . . .* (Pavia, 1521), and the commentary of Leonardo Legio on *Canon* II.1.1.29 (Venice, 1523), but these are minor works, not cited by later commentators. No doubt, too, the difficulties of the universities of Bologna and Padua in the disturbed times of the early sixteenth century reduced the output, not just the preservation, of academic discourses of all kinds. Discussions of the *Canon* continued, however; Professor Herbert Matsen has kindly drawn my attention to a series of student disputations on questions derived from *Canon* I.1 preserved in the Archivio di Stato di Bologna, dating from various years between 1496 and 1524.

30.   On these developments, see Durling, 'Linacre', pp. 76-84, Nutton, 'Caius', p. 374-377, and Vivian Nutton, 'Medicine in the Age of Montaigne', in *Montaigne and His Age*, ed. K. Cameron (Exeter, 1981), pp. 15-17. Medical humanism is evaluated positively in Walter Pagel, 'Medical Humanism — A Historical Necessity in the Era of the Renaissance', in *Linacre Studies*, ed. Maddison et al., pp. 375-386.

31.   On the opposition to the Arabs, see Felix Klein-Franke, *Die klassische Antike in der Tradition des Islam* (Darmstadt, 1980), pp. 17-66; E. Wickersheimer, 'Laurent Fries et la querelle de l'arabisme en médecine (1530), *'Les Cahiers de Tunisie*, 9 (1955), 56-103; Gerhard Baader, 'Medizinisches Reformdenken und Arabismus im Deutschland des 16 Jahrhunderts', *Sudhoffs Archiv: Zeitschrift für Wissenschaftsgeschichte*, 43 (1979), 261-296; for Montpellier, Roland Antonioli, *Rabelais et la Médecine*, Études Rabelaisiennes XII, Travaux d'Humanisme et de Renaissance 143 (Geneva, 1976), Chapter 3.

32.   Leoniceno's *De Plinii et plurium aliorum medicorum in medicina erroribus* contains numerous attacks on Avicenna as well as on Pliny. I have consulted this in *Nicolai Leoniceni . . . Opuscula . . .* (Basel, 1532; at the New York Academy of Medicine), but the work was first published in 1492. Leoniceno, a professor at Ferrara and one of the most noted Renaissance translators of Galen, aimed his criticisms of Avicenna at specific instances of what he believed to be misrepresentation of botanical and anatomical terms by the latter author, e.g. Book I, chapter 29 (*Opuscula*, 1532, fols. 9ʳ⁻ᵛ): 'Error Avicennae, multas herbas figura et natura diversas uno capite confundentis'. On Leoniceno's work, and the fairly widespread debate over it in humanist medical, and botanical circles, see Charles G. Nauert, Jr. 'Humanists, Scientists, and Pliny: Changing Approaches to a Classical Author', *The American Historical Review*, 84 (1979), 72-85; on Leoniceno's intellectual position in general, Daniela Mugnai Carrara, 'Profilo di Nicolo Leoniceno', *Interpres*, 2 (1978), 169-212.

As Gerhard Baader has suggested in the article cited in the preceding note, more generalized criticism of the Arabs involve, to some extent, the internalization within sections of the medical profession of a hostility to Arabic medical and natural philosophical learning that among non-medical Italian humanists goes back to Petrarch. Suspicion of medical learning is, however, only one strain in Italian humanist thought; others were appreciative of it (see N. G. Siraisi, 'The Physicians's Task: Medical Reputations in Humanist Collective Biographies', forthcoming).

33.   *Novae academiae Florentinae opuscula adversus Avicennam et medicos neotericos qui Galeni disciplina neglecta, barbaros colunt* . . . (Venice, 1533; at the New York Academy of Medicine). Landi's treatise is entitled *Barbaromastix*; on his academic career at Padua, see Bartolo Bertolaso, 'Ricerche d'archivio su alcuni aspetti dell'insegnamento medico presso la Università di Padova nel Cinque- e Seicento', *Acta medicae historiae patavina*, 6 (1959-60), 23. Manardi's criticisms of Avicenna are expressed in his *Epistolae medicinales in quibus multa recentiorum errata et antiquorum decreta reserantur* . . . (Ferrara, 1521; at the New York Academy of Medicine). The first letter, a general justification of the whole work, refers to the *Canon* as containing 'densam caliginem, infinitum ambagum chaos' (fol. 1ᵛ); the passage goes on to mention a forthcoming commentary which is expected to point out many more hitherto unnoticed errors. The *Epistolae medicinales*, of which the first edition is cited above, were reissued Paris, 1528, Basel, 1540, and Venice, 1542, the later editions being greatly expanded (all those mentioned are at the New York Academy of Medicine).

34.   '. . . spero ut ex nostra academia de Avicennae erratis iusta volumina prodeant', (*Barbaromastix*, fol. 10ᵛ); and 'quos proculdubio ingenio superant: De latinis loquor, Gentile, Iacobo, Ugone caeterisque quamplurimis, quorum errata ex malis ducibus quos sectati sunt, ortum habuere . . . ' (ibid., fol. 9ᵛ).

35.   On Ramusio, Alpago, and the official endorsement of the Alpago version, see Lucchetta, *Alpago*; Marie-Thérèse d'Alverny, 'Les traductions d'Avicenne (Moyen Age et Renaissance)', *Problemi attuali di scienza e di cultura*, Accademia Nazionale de Lincei, Quaderno No. 40 (Rome, 1955), 84-87; and idem, 'Avicenne et les médecins de Venise', *Medioevo e Rinascimento: Studi in onore di Bruno Nardi* (Florence, 1955) 178-197. Alpago did translate other works of Avicenna (Lucchetta, *Alpago*, pp. 57, 64) and two Arabic commentaries on the *Canon* (see note 8 above), but for Book I at any rate editions of his version of the *Canon* indicate that he merely emended the Gerard of Cremona text. Alpago also compiled an Arabo-Latin technical vocabulary, published in various editions of the *Canon* (see Appendix I). No study in detail of the merits or defects of either the Gerard version of the *Canon* or of Alpago's revisions has so far been published. On Gerard's translating techniques, see, however, Ilona Opelt, 'Zur Übersetzungstechnik des Gerhard von Cremona', *Glotta*, 38 (1960), 135-154. I am grateful to Dr. Charles Burnett for this reference.

36.   See Jerome J. Bylebyl, 'The School of Padua: Humanistic Medicine in the Sixteenth Century', in *Health, Medicine, and Mortality in the Sixteenth*, ed. Charles Webster (Cambridge, 1979), pp. 335-370.

37.   For Da Monte's career, see G. Cervetto, *Di Giambattista Da Monte e della medicina italiana nel secolo XVI* (Verona, 1839), and G. Facciolati, *Fasti gymnasii patavini* (Padua, 1757), II, 331, 343, 386; also Bylebyl, 'School of Padua', pp. 346-349, 361. Da Monte held the first ordinary professorship in *practica* from 1540, and moved to *theoria* in 1543. He seems not to have been teaching at Padua after 1546, although he held a professorial chair until his death in 1551 (Facciolati, II, 343).

38.   See William P. D. Wightman, '*Quid sit methodus*? "Method" in Sixteenth Century Medical Teaching and Discovery', *Journal of the History of Medicine and Allied Sciences*, 19 (1964), 360-376.

39.   Bylebyl, 'School of Padua', p. 346.   The Giunta edition of Galen's *opera* went into at least eight editions in the sixteenth and early seventeenth century. I have consulted *Galeni Opera ex sexta Iuntarum editione* . . . (Venice, 1586; at the New York Academy of Medicine), in which Da Monte's preface, explaining his responsibility for the ordering of the works of Galen in the sequence adopted for this edition, appears at I, sig. [A8^r]-B2^r.

40.   Girolamo Capodivacca (d. 1589), professor of *practica* at Padua, several times took Da Monte to task for differing with Galen; see *Hieronymi Capivacci* . . . *Opera omnia* . . . (Frankfurt, 1603; at the Wellcome Library), pp. 421, 425, 435.

41.   For Oddo Oddi's career, writings, and reputation, see I. P. Tomasini, *Patavini illustrium virorum elogia iconibus exornata* (Padua, 30), pp. 46-49; N. C. Papadopoli, *Historia gymnasii patavini*, I (Venice, 1726), 313, giving the date of death as 1558; Facciolati, II, 343, giving the date of death as 1563, and 348, giving it as 1559; Bertolaso, 'Ricerche d'archivio', p. 23-24.

42.   Ibid., p. 26.

43.   Marco Oddi's dedicatory epistle explains the circumstances; see comm. *Canon* I.1 (Venice, 1575), sig. [A3^v]-[A4^r]. Oddi's work ends on p. 372 (in the middle of *doctrina* 5, on the members), and the rest is by Marco, who may also have supplied the preface, or parts of it.

44.   For Paterno's career, writings, and reputation, see Tomasini, *Elogia*, pp. 151-153; Papadopoli, I,34; Facciolati, II, 343; Bertolaso, 'Ricerche d'archivio', p. 23. The manuscript is Wellcome 602.

45.   Graziolo, ed. *Canon* I.1 (Venice, 1580), sig. [b3^v]-[b4^r]. Bertolaso, 'Ricerche d'archivio', does not list Graziolo as a Paduan professor.

46.   Da Monte, comm. *Canon* I.1 (Venice, 1557), pp. 2-5; at p.5, 'haec utilitas non est imaginosa, sed vera. Videtis enim, tot praeclaros medicos fuisse versatos duntaxat in doctrina Avicennae sine Galeni lectione. Neque equidem possum comparare Avicennam cum aliquo Graeco alio, quam cum Galeno; fuit nam verus Galeni vicarius'.

47.   Degli Oddi, comm. *Canon* I.1 (Venice, 1575), pp. 1, 7-9.

48.   Graziolo, ed. *Canon* I (Venice, 1580), b^r-c^v. Graziolo's preface is discussed in d'Alverny, 'Avicenne et les médecins de Venise', pp. 183-184. At [b3^r]: 'Ubi vero . . . Hippocratis, Galeni, caeterorumque opera suo nitori restituta in lucem prodiere, non (ut quorundam erat opinio) excussus est ex eruditorum manibus Avicenna, sed pariter celebratus'.

49.   'Garrulos in sermone, ambitiosos in conversatione, infelices in medendo, magis re alienos a Galeni disciplina quam verbis ab Arabum doctrina . . . ' Cardano, comm. *Canon* I.1 in his *Opera*, IX (Lyon, 1663), p. 459. For the dates and places of Cardano's lectures on *Canon* I.1, ibid. pp. 455, 458.

50.   For examples, see Da Monte, comm. *Canon* I.1 (Venice, 1557): 'appellant Arabes sal alchali illud sal, quod nunc appellatur alumen catile, et est frequens Venetiis. Arabes confundant alchali et chachile' (p. 376 — but see note 15 above); and '*In corpore generatur*. Vult dicere quod in hepate generatur, et ita erit clarior textus; et ita emendavit Andreas de Alpago' (p. 410). Such remarks are, however, rare.

51.   ' . . . quidem non dixerim Avicennam non intelligere Galenum, sed potius loqui ex propria intentione contra Galenum' (ibid., p. 335).

52.   On Mantino's translations of *Canon* I.1 and I.4, see Moritz Steinschneider, *Die hebraeischen Übersetzungen des Mittelalters und die Juden als Dolmetscher* (Berlin, 1893; repr. Graz, 1956), p. 685; for the several partial translations of the *Canon* into

Hebrew in the late Middle Ages, and the printing of the work in Hebrew at Naples in 1491/92, ibid. pp. 683-684. On Mantino's career, see D. Kaufman, 'Jacob Mantino. Un page d'histoire de la Renaissance', *Revue des études juives* 27 (1893), 30-60, 207-238. Mantino's translations of these sections of the *Canon* (first published ca. 1540 and 1530, respectively) were made in a deliberate effort to improve on Alpago and with school use in mind; see Mantino's dedicatory epistle to Doge Andrea Gritti in the Paris, 1532, edition of his translation of *Canon* I.4, fol. 1 (consulted at the National Library of Medicine).

53.   In the Oddi commentary the text is printed in both the 'translatio Bellunensis' (i. e. Alpago) and the 'translatio Mantini'; on p. 3 it is announced that the commentary mostly follows the Alpago version.

54.   'Hanc vero barbariem quid est, quod aliqui Avicennae scriptis obijciant, cum interpretis, non authoris culpa contracta sit? Ut enim nihil de Avicennae eloquentia, qui Arabice scripsit, decernere possimus, credendum tamen est, virum sublimi ingenio, politissimisque disciplinis ornatum, hac etiam in parte, quantum ferat idioma illud, non fuisse infelicem. Sed mala quadam forte nactus est latinum interpretem, quales habuit aetas illa, qui proculdubio multas per se illustres sententias obscuravit, multa non intellexit, omnia barbarie foedavit', Graziolo, ed. *Canon* I (Venice, 1580), [b3^r]. These remarks certainly suggest that Graziolo did not himself know Arabic. In his commentary on *Canon* I.2, Da Monte, too, had asserted that Avicenna was regarded as a polished and elegant literary author in the Arabic world, citing an Imperial ambassador as his source of information (Venice, 1557, pp. 35, 93).

55.   'Quaestiones igitur omnes vanas praetermittam. Vanas dico; quoniam quaestiones quae pertinent ad rem non sunt praetermittandae . . . Tractabo autem sicut docuerunt et Aristoteles et sui boni expositores, et Averroes, et Galenus, solvendo scilicet difficultates per naturam rerum, et non per ambagam implicationem'. Da Monte, comm. *Canon* I.1 (Venice, 1557), p. 2. Da Monte is presumably objecting to some of the typical features of scholastic medical commentary as it had developed in the hands of such authors as Giacomo da Forlì and Ugo Benzi; see Ottosson, *Scholastic Medicine*, pp. 57, 59-60.

56.   'Non tamen quaestiones expositorum latinorum more examinabimus, quid adeo perplexo et longo stylo eas pertractant, ut auditores saepe defaticari, tandem quid sentiant minime percipiant', Degli Oddi, comm. *Canon* I.1 (Venice, 1575), p. 2.

57.   I hope shortly to make a more detailed study of the actual extent of the commentators' knowledge of some of the works referred to.

58.   *Iacobi Forliviensis medici singularis expositio et quaestiones in primum canonem Avicennae* . . . (Venice, 1547); at the New York Academy of Medicine. The *quaestiones* occupy fols. 188^r-225^v.

59.   On the history of medical question literature, see Brian Lawn, *The Salernitan Questions* (Oxford, 1963), translated, with additions as *I quesiti salernitani* (n. p., 1969), and idem, *The Prose Salernitan Questions* (London, 1979); also Siraisi, *Taddeo*, chapter 8 and appendix I.

60.   See William F. Edwards, 'Niccolo Leoniceno and the Origins of Humanist Discussion of Method', in *Philosophy and Humanism: Renaissance Essays in Honor of Paul Oskar Kristeller*, ed. Edward P. Mahoney (New York, 1976), pp. 283-305, and Charles B. Schmitt, 'Towards a Reassessment of Renaissance Aristotelianism', *History of Science* 11 (1973), 159-193. An extensive earlier literature is cited in these studies. Also, J. Roger, 'La situation d'Aristote chez les anatomistes padouans', in *Platon et Aristote à la Renaissance*, XVIe Colloque International de Tours (Paris, 1976), pp. 217-224.

61.   See, for example, Giacomo's *Expositio et quaestiones* on *Canon* I.1 (Venice,

1547), fols. 3^r, 219^v-220^v, and *Primus Avicennae Canonis cum argutissima Gentilis expositione* (Pavia, 1510; at the New York Academy of Medicine), fol. 13^v.

62.   Da Monte, comm. *Canon* I.1 (Venice, 1557), pp. 164-186. It is worth noting that although Da Monte's commentary on *Canon* I.1 appears in both its editions in a volume much less massive than, say, that of Gentile da Foligno on the same portion of the *Canon* in the Pavia edition of 1510, the difference in length between the two works is not in fact very great. A rough estimate of the number of words involved suggest that Da Monte's commentary was as a whole something like eighty percent of the length of Gentile's, and Da Monte's treatment of individual topics was sometimes just as or even more prolix than that of his scholastic predecessor.

63.   Tommaso's treatise is printed with his *Summa medicinalis* (Venice, 1506); *Questiones et tractatus extravagantes clarissimi Domini Gentilis de Fulgineo . . .* (Venice, 1520), q. 46, fols. 63^r-65^v.

64.   Da Monte's references to Averroes are frequent and mostly respectful in tone; see for example, note 55 above.

65.   Da Monte, comm. *Canon* I.1 (Venice, 1557), p. 12. In line with the views on method that he expressed elsewhere (see note 38 above), Da Monte distinguished between methodology appropriate for teaching and methodology appropriate for scientific investigation, and praised the *Canon* chiefly for the former: 'respondendum est ad quaesitum, quo ordine sit usus Avicennae. Utitur nam compositivo, qui est aptior addocendum, nam resolutivus magis est aptus ad inveniedum quam ad docendum, et ita non convenit rudis et incipientibus discere'.

66.   See note 39 above.

67.   Da Monte, comm. *Canon* I.1 (Venice, 1557), p. 480. Da Monte had studied at Ferrara under Leoniceno (ibid., p. 253), and was a friend of Manardi, who addressed *Epistolae medicinales* 11.1 (Basel, 1540, pp. 299-302) to him.

68.   Ibid., p. 605.

69.   'Praetera lac nonne est humor bonus et intentus a natura? Semen etiam, nonne est humor bonus, intentus a natura? Sub quo igitur membro continebuntur ista, quae sunt excrementa? Nam, quae excernuntur extra non sunt propter nutrimentum corporis, sed sunt excrementa utilia propter alius usus. Et ita divisio mala est, neque potest excusari. Et viderunt Gentilis et alii has difficultates, sed ita admirabantur Avicennam ut non auderent carpere. Verumtamen amicus Plato, et amicus Socrates, magis tamen amica veritas'. Ibid., p. 327.

70.   Ibid., pp. 330, 332; 'Et ita habetis divisionem et sententiam Galeni, quae est verissima, et illam quae est Avicennae, quae quantum peccet vidistis. Et, si quis velit postea magis vesci glandibus quam pane, eligat quod vult. Habet enim panem, et habet glandes'. Ibid., p. 336.

71.   Ibid., 364.

72.   'Iam vidistis omnes differentias pituitae quae docentur ab Avicenna, et audivistis eas a nobis fideliter declaratas; sed non arbitror quemquam ex vobis esse tam divini ingenii ut possit dicere se ab Avicenna aliquid didicisse. Audiatis modo (ut discatis veras divisiones pituita) in quibus erraverit Avicenna . . . ', ibid., p.384.

73.   'Hic dicet quis: Cur exponis tu librum quem vituperas? Primum quidem ego non vitupero librum totum, sed ea tantum quae mihi videntur reprehendenda. Praeterea non facio rem novem. Nam Galenus nullibi facit meliores commentationes quam in libros quos repraehendit, sicut in librum *Prorrheticorum* et in librum *De natura humana*'. Ibid., p. 409.

74.   An Italian translation of this commentary is contained in Aldo Scapini, *L'archiatro mediceo e pontificio Matteo Corti (secolo XVI) e il suo commento all'Anatomia di Mondino di Liuzzi*, Scientia Veterum no. 142 (Pisa, 1970). Corti (*ca.*

1475-1544) taught at Pavia, Pisa, Padua, and Bologna, and served as physician to Pope Clement VII. For biographical data, see Lynn Thorndike, *History of Magic and Experimental Science* V (New York, 1941), 325-326 and references there cited. Girolamo Cardano referred approvingly to Corti's efforts to learn Arabic in extreme old age (Cardano, *Opera*, 1663, IX, 459).

75.   Da Monte, comm. *Canon* I.1 (Venice, 1557), pp. 8-12.

76.   Paterno, comm. *Canon* I.1 (Venice, 1596), fols. 147^v-150^r.

77.   See, for example, the questions of Taddeo Alderotti and Turisanus listed in Siraisi, *Taddeo*, p. 319. An account of the sources and medieval and early Renaissance development of complexion theory is to be found in Ottosson, *Scholastic medicine and Philosophy*, pp. 129-154.

78.   *Expositio et quaestiones* on *Canon* I.1 (Venice, 1547), fol. 190^{r-v}; at fol. 190^r: 'probabiliter teneri potest complexionem non est qualitatem aliquam distinctam a toto aggregato ex primis qualitatibus taliter refractis. Patet, quia quascunque operationes attribuimus complexioni si esset simplex qualitas attribuere possumus huic toto aggregato'.

79.   'In hac definitione sunt pulcherrimae difficultates, male a modernis tractatae', Da Monte, comm. *Canon* I.1 (Venice, 1557), p. 116. The entire discussion occupies pp. 114-127.

80.   'Et in hac quaestione haerent maximi viri, et attinet valde ad medicos', ibid., p. 122.

81.   'Duae sunt opiniones summorum virorum. Prima est Arabum et Latinorum recentiorum, qui credunt nullo modo formam substantialem esse temperaturam, sed temperaturam primam solum dispositionem ad formam substantialem. In qua sententia fuit Avicenna in libro *De anima*, parte prima, cap. primo, et Albertus secundo *De generatione*, tract. secundo, cap. 15. In parte autem opposita sunt Hippocrates et Galenus et fortassis etiam Aristoteles, qui volunt nihil aliud esse formam substantialem quam temperaturam eductam ex materia. Habet unaquaeque harum opinionum suas rationes. Ego recitabo fideliter eas quae potissimae mihi videtur, deinde indicabo quid sit tenendum in ista quaestione', ibid., p. 123.

82.   'Quid circa eas sit determinandum, si me rogetis, possum respondere dupliciter secundem duplicem formam, quam possum induere. Si enim velim esse philosophus, et stare in principiis philosophiae, non autem fidei, non possum non Hippocrati et Galeno assentire. At si formam theologicam velim induere (quod certe debemus facere) dicendum est opinionem Arabum esse veram. Sed hoc, ut est re ipsa verum, ita credi debet sine ulla demonstratione, nam nihil peius est quam quaerere demonstrationibus probare quod fide tenendum est. Quia potius sunt agendae gratiae Deo qui intellectum nostrum illuminavit, ut ea sciret, quae nullo medio naturali percipi possunt; et rogandus Dominus ut augeat credulitatem in nobis. Et certe in hoc Scotus valde egregie se gessit, qui, cum tenuisset animam in via naturali, et peripatetica, mortalem esse, in quarto libro *Sententiarum*, quaest. 41 vel 43, poeta conversus ad Dominum, egit illi gratias quod id cognovisset illuminatione divina esse verissimum, quod naturaliter falsum videbatur.

Lectio XVI
Sed, quia nunc in scholis profitemur nos philosophos et medicos; ideo ex principiis philosophiae defendamus opinionem Galeni et Hippocratis'. Ibid., pp. 126-127.

83.   For some account of this issue at Bologna, and Padua, see Bruno Nardi, *Saggi sull'Aristotelismo padovano dal secolo XVI al XVI* (Florence, 1958), pp. 313 to end. Da Monte quotes a remark of Pomponazzi's in comm. *Canon* I.1 (Venice, 1557), p. 409; that he was his student is asserted by Cervetto, p. 8.

84.   Degli Oddi, comm. *Canon* I.1 (Venice, 1575), pp. 99-100; Graziolo, ed. *Canon* I (Venice, 1580), fols. 13^v-14^r.

85. The text of *De mixtione* with an English translation and extensive introductory material is available in Robert B. Todd, *Alexander of Aphrodisias on Stoic Physics* (Leiden, 1976). The scope of Renaissance interest in Alexander is well illustrated in F. Edward Cranz, 'The Prefaces to the Greek Editions and Latin Translations of Alexander of Aphrodisias', *Proceedings of the American Philosophical Society*, 102 (1958), 510-546.

86. F. E. Cranz, 'Alexander Aphrodisiensis', *Catalogus translationum et commentariorum*, I (Washington, D.C., 1960), 81, 113-114.

87. Fuchs was a principal opponent of Arab medicine in Germany; see the article by Baader cited in note 31 above.

88. Fernel, *Medicina* (Paris, 1554).

89. For example, Degli Oddi, comm. *Canon* I.1 (Venice, 1575), pp. 384-391, contains a lengthy discussion, and repudiation, of Fernel's views on the motion of the heart and arteries (in this passage Fernel is credited with holding that the dilation of the heart and arteries is not synchronous). A laudatory reference to Vesalius — 'Vesalius, lumen totium artis anatomicae' — appears, however, in Da Monte, comm. *Canon* I.2 (Venice, 1557), p. 46.

90. Paterno, comm. *Canon* I.1 (Venice, 1596), fols. 27^r-29^r. He does not cite Alexander of Aphrodisias, or any of the Latin scholastics; among contemporaries, he alludes only to Da Monte's views on the passage under discussion. Marginal references cite works of Aristotle and Galen and Plato's *Phaedrus*, but no detailed exposition of passages in them is undertaken in the text.

Appendices

Latin Editions of the *Canon* published after 1500 and Editions of Latin Commentaries on the *Canon* written in Italy after 1500.

No complete bibliography of Latin manuscripts and editions of and commentaries on the *Canon* has yet appeared. Two older bibliographies, Felix Willy Eckleben, *Die abendländischen Avicenna-Kommentare* (Leipzig dissertation, 1921) and Saïd Naficy, *Bibliographie des principaux travaux européens sur Avicenne* (Teheran, 1953), are a useful starting point, but both include only printed works and are incomplete. General bibliographies, namely Thorndike and Kibre, *Catalogue of Incipits*, Klebs, *Incunabula scientifica et medica*, and the *Index aureliensis*, yield information for limited categories and time periods. The following preliminary checklists are intended merely to illustrate certain aspects of European interest in the *Canon* during the sixteenth and seventeenth centuries. Not only are the lists doubtless incomplete in themselves, but the categories of works listed do not constitute a complete overview even of this restricted portion of the Latin *fortuna* of the *Canon*. In the first place, as is noted in the introduction to Appendix

II, some commentaries were written after 1500 outside Italy. Furthermore, substantial numbers of works could be added in three categories other than editions of the text and of commentaries written after 1500. These other categories, for which I hope to provide checklists at a later date, are 1) surviving manuscripts of commentaries written after 1500 (including a number that remained unpublished); 2) works in which the *Canon*, or part of it, or Avicenna as a medical author, is discussed but which do not take the form of either text editions or commentaries; and 3) sixteenth- and seventeenth-century printings of commentaries written before 1500. Some works in the third category are, however, included in the present Appendix I because they are found in volumes identified by the *Index aureliensis*, part I, vol. II, 448-454, s.v. Avicenna, and/or the title page of the work itself as primarily editions of the text of the *Canon*. Conversely, it should be noted that some other editions in the third category, not listed in Appendix I because their primary identification in the *Index aureliensis* or on their title pages is as the work of early commentators, in fact include portions of the text.

Of the various library catalogues consulted, special mention must ae made of Richard J. Durling, *A Catalogue of Sixteenth Century Printed Books in the National Library of Medicine* (Bethesda, Md., 1967), and *A Catalogue of Printed Books in the Wellcome Historical Medical Library* I. *Books Printed Before 1641* (London, 1962, and II and III. *Books Printed from 1641 to 1850* (London, 1966, 1976), A-L.

I indicate only the libraries where I consulted the works, locations being abbreviated as follows:

BL   British Library, London
NLM   National Library of Medicine, History of Medicine Division, Bethesda, Md,
NYAM   New York Academy of Medicine, Rare Book Room
WL   Wellcome Historical Medical Library, London

I am most grateful for all the help I received at these libraries. Works included in the *Index aureliensis* bear the notation IA; the latter indicates European, but seldom American, locations. An asterisk indicates works I have not had the opportunity to examine personally.

Appendix I: Latin Editions of the *Canon* published after 1500.

These publications appear to fall into six main categories: 1) the complete Gerard of Cremona text without commentary or intentional alteration; 2) major subdivisions of the *Canon*, in Gerard's version, accompanied by the expositions of one or more of the fourteenth- or fifteenth-century commentators, sometimes in multivolume series (portion of the text appear in more editions of these commentaries than are listed here; see the introductory note to the appendices for criteria of selection); 3) short sections of the *Canon* prescribed in the schools, in Gerard's version, published presumably for the benefit of students, either alone or in compilations such as the *Articella*; 4) rearrangements and abbreviations of Gerard of Cremona's text in the form of aphorism, maxims, and so on; 5) the complete *Canon* with textual revisions and apparatus by Alpago and other sixteenth-century medical scholars; 6) retranslations of parts of the work either from the Arabic or, in the case of Mantino and Cinqarbres (Quinquarboreus), from the Hebrew. Categories 1, 2 and 4 predominated in the output of printings of the *Canon* in the early sixteenth century, but subsequently diminished greatly; works in category 5 began to appear in the 1520s and continued to do so until the first decade of the seventeenth century. Works in category 6, with the two exceptions named, mostly represent the interest in the *Canon* of a handful of seventeenth-century Arabists in northern Europe. Works in category 3 seem to appear mostly in the first half of the sixteenth century and after 1610. In addition, portions of the text are also printed with some of the commentaries listed in Appendix II. For printings of the *Canon* in Latin before 1500, see Klebs, pp. 68-69, where fourteen editions are listed, and GW, III, nos. 3314-3127. As already noted, the *Canon* was also printed in Hebrew (Naples, 1491/92) and Arabic (Rome, 1593). Editions listed here are the complete text unless otherwise noted.

Tertius Canonis Avicenne cum dilucidissimis expositionibus Gentile Fulginate nec non Jacobo de Partibus parisiensis (Venice: Bernardinus Benalius ca. 1505). Book III, in three large folio volumes. Gerard text, copious commentary. WL; IA 110.580.

Liber Canonis Avicenne revisus et ab omni errore mendaque purgatus summaque cum diligentia impressus (Venice: Bonetus Locatellus for heirs of Octavianus Scotus, 1505). Gerard translation. NLM; IA 110.581.

[Articella.] *In hoc volumine parvo in quantitate, maximo virtute, continentur infrascripti codices . . . Textus duarum primarum fen primi Avicenne in theorica. Textus fen quarte primi, et prime quarti in practica* (Pavia: Bartholomeus de Morandis for Jacobus de Burgofranco, 1506). *Canon* I.1-2,4, and IV.1 (Gerard translation) as part of an expanded *articella* that includes a humanistic translation of the Hippocratic *Aphorisms*. The introduction of *Canon* excerpts into the *articella* seems to be a novelty. Dedicatory letter by Pietro Antonio Rustico, professor of *theorica medicina* at the *studium* of Pavia. WL. 'Nova impressio' of foregoing item (Venice: Petrus Bergomensus de Quarengis, 1507). NLM; IA 109.132.

Liber canonis Avicenne revisus et ab omni errore mendaque purgatus summaque cum diligentia impressus (Venice: Paganinus de Paganinis, 1507; facsimile, Hildesheim, 1964). Gerard translation. IA 110.582.

Flores Avicenne (Lyon: Claudius Davost, 1508). Drastic abbreviation with the goal of producing memorizable aphorisms, according to the preface by Michael de Capella, *artium et medicine magister*. NLM; IA 110.583.

Primus Avicenne Canonis cum argutissima Gentilis expositione . . .(Pavia: Jacobus de Burgofranco, 1510). Actually includes Books I and II, separately foliated. Gerard translation, copious commentary. NYAM. I am unclear as to whether this is to be equated with IA 110.585. Part of a four volume set with the next entry.

**Tertius Canonis Avicenne cum amplissima Gentilis Fulginatis expositione* (Pavia: Jacobus de Burgofranco for Aloysius de Castello Comensis and Bartholomeus de Morandis, 1511) IA 110.586. NLM has *two more volumes (Books IV and V) of this set with Gentile's commentary, Pavia; Jacobus de Burgofranco, 1511-1512 (Durling, *Catalogue*, no. 379).

Flores Avicenne collecti super quinque Canonibus quos edidit in medicina, nec non super decem et novem libris de animalibus cum Canticis eiusdem ad longum positis (Lyon: Gilbertus de Villiers for Bartholomeus Trot, 1514). Reprint of 1508 edition, with additions as indicated. NLM; IA 110.588.

Articella nuperrime impressa cum quamplurimis tractatibus pristine impressioni superadditis . . . (Lyon: Johannes de la Place, for Bartholomeus Trot, 1515). NYAM; IA 109.135. Includes *Canon* I.1-2, I.4,IV.1,V.3-5 (surgery).

Soli Deo. Memoriale medicorum canonice practicantium a Rustico medicine cultore ordinatum . . . (Pavia: Bernardinus de Garaldis, 1517). The first two sets of *canones* are based on *Canon* I.4 and IV.1 respectively. The text is broken down and abbreviated into short, memorizable axioms for the benefit (according to Pietro Antonio Rustico's letter of dediciation) of students at Pavia. NYAM.

Articella nuperrime impressa . . . (Lyon, 1519; reprint of 1515 collection). NLM; IA 109.136.

*Textus principis Avicenne ordinem alphabeti in sententia reportatus cum quibusdam additionibus et concordantiis Galieni et quorundum aliorum . . . (Bordeaux; Gaspard Philippe, 1520). IA 110.589.

Primus Avicenne Canonis. Avicenne medicorum principis Canonum liber una cum lucidissima Gentilis Fulginatis expositione . . . (Venice: heirs of Octavianus Scotus, 1520). Actually Books I and II, separately foliated. Gerard translation, extensive commentary, register of Gentile's *quaestiones.* WL; IA 110.591 (where, however, heading of *tabula* is given).

Quartus Canonis Avicenne cum preclara Gentilis fulginatis expositione . . . *Quintus etiam Canonis cum eiusdem Gentilis fulginatis, lucidissima expositione* . . . (Venice: heirs of Octavianus Scotus, 1520). Books IV and V, with two other partial commentaries besides that of Gentile. Gerard translation. Register of commentator's questions. WL; IA 110.592 (where, however, heading of *tabula* is given).

Liber Canonis totius medicine ab Avicenna arabum doctissimo excussus, a Gerardo Cremonensi ab arabica lingua in latinam reductus. Et a Petro Antonio Rustico Placentino in philosophia non mediocriter erudito ad limam ex omni parte ab erroribus et omni barbarie castigatus; necnon a domino Symphoriano Camperio lugdunensi fecundis annotationibus terminisque arabicis et eorum expositionibus nuper illustratus; una cum eius vita a domino Francisco Calphurnio non minus vere quam eleganter excerpta (Lyon: Jacobus Myt, 1522). This edition contains the promised 'castigations' by Symphorien Champier, Arabo-Latin glossary, and life of Avicenna; however, it is difficult to see what Rustico's contribution was, as any alterations he may have made to the text are not distinguished typographically. Comparison of *Canon* I.1.4.1 (on humours) in this edition with that in the edition of Venice, 1507, suggests that in this section at least Rustico presented the unaltered Gerard of Cremona text. NYAM; IA 110.592.

Tertius Canonis Avicenne cum amplissima Gentilis Fulginatis expositione . . . *Secunda pars Gentilis super tertio Avicenne* . . . (Venice: heirs of Octavianus Scotus, 1522). Continuously foliated two volume set. Book III, with other partial commentaries besides those of Gentile. Gerard translation. WL; Vol. II: IA 110.594.

Praesens maximus codex est totius scientiae medicinae principis Aboali Abinsene cum expositionibus omnium . . . interpretum ejus. . . (Venice: Philippus Pincius for L. A. Junta, 1523). Five volume set; the complete *Canon* (Gerard translation) and a roundup of commentators including Gentile da Foligno, Jacques Despars, Dino del Garbo, Taddeo Alderotti and Ugo Benzi. NLM; IA 110.595.

Habes humane lector Gabrielis de Tarrega Burgdalensis civitatis medici regentis et ordinarii opera brevissima theoricam et prathicam (sic) *medicinales scientie . . .* A collection of treatises of which the third is *Textus Avicenne per ordinem alphabeti in sententia per eundum reportatus. Cum quibusdam additionibus et concordàntiis Galieni et quorundum aliorum antiquorum* (Bordeaux: Johannes Guyart, 1524?). BL. It is possible that this work is to be identified with 1A 110.589 (see above). The *Textus Avicennae* is undated but other treatises in the collection have colophons with the dates 1520 and 1524 respectively.

Articella nuperrime impressa . . . (Lyon, 1525; reprint of 1515 and 1519 collection). NLM; IA 109.138.

Principis Avicenna libri Canonis, necnon De medicinis cordialibus et Cantica ab Andrea Bellunensi ex antiquis arabum originalibus ingenti labore summaque diligentia correcti atque in integrum restituti, una cum interpretatione nominum arabicorum, quae partim mendosa partim incognita lectores antea morabantur. Opus plane aurem ac omni ex parte absolutum (Venice: L. A. Junta, 1527). This, the first publication of Andrea Alpago's work on Avicenna's medical writings was edited by Paolo Alpago, nephew of Andrea. Gerard text, with Alpago's suggested emendations in the margin. Two prefatory epistles by the younger Alpago. Privileges from the Pope, the King of France and the Venetian Senate granting Paolo copyright over the printing of Andrea Alpago's *castigationes et expositiones* for the next ten years. NYAM; IA 110.598.

Flores Avicennae . . . (Lyon: Gilbertus de Villiers for Bartholomeus Trot, 1528). Reprint of 1514 edition. WL; IA 110.589.

Avicennae quarta fen primi libri de universali ratione medendi: nunc primum M. Iacobi Mantini medici hebrei opera latinitate donata (Venice: L. A. Junta, 1530). *Canon* I.4. Dedicatory letter to Doge Andrea Gritti explains Mantino's plan to translate other parts of the

Canon used in the schools from the Hebrew, in order to improve upon Alpago's revision of the text. NLM; IA 110.600.

Avicennae arabis medicorum ob succinctam brevitatis copiam facile principis quarta fen primi de universale ratione medendi, nunc primum M. Iacobi Mantini medici hebraei latinitate donata, et in studiosorum utilitatem ab phisicae studiosis quibusdam germanis typis tradita (Ettlingen: Valentinus Kobian, 1531). *Canon* I.4. Bound with *Galeni pergameni dissectionis venarum arteriarumque commentarium* . . . *Antonio Fortolo Ioseriensi interprete* (Basel, 1529) and other works. Biblioteca Nazionale, Rome; IA 110.601.

Avicennae arabis medicorum ob succinctam brevitatis copiam facile princeps quarta fen primi de universali ratione medendi. Interprete Iacob Mantino medico hebreo (Paris: Claudius Chevallonius, 1532). *Canon* I.4. NLM; IA 110.602.

Avicennae arabis inter omnes medicos cum ex stemmate, tum ob succinctam brevitatis copiam, facile principis quarta fen primi de universali ratione medendi per M. Iacob Mantinum medicum hebreum latinitate donata, denuo Germanis typis nuper multo emendatior in lucem edita (The Hague: Valentinus Kobian, 1532). *Canon* I.4 NLM; IA 110.603.

Articella nuperrime impressa . . . (Lyon: Johannes Moylin, 1534). Reprint of the same collection as the Lyons editions of 1515, 1519 and 1525. WL; IA 109.140.

. . . *Caput illud aureum Avicennae 29 tertii fen primae tractatus primi de canonibus universalibus curationis dolorum capitis, nuper ab eximio artium et medicinae doctore Iacobo Mantino hebraeo latinitate donatum ante hac non excussa.* Printed with *Methodus universae artis medicae . . . Cornelio a Baersdorp gosersi autore* (Bruges, 1538), at sig. Vii^r-[Vv^v]. *Canon* III.1.1.29. Dedicatory letter from Mantino to Hadrianus Brant of Germany. BL.

Avicennae primi libri fen prima nunc primum per Magistrum Iacobum Mantimam (sic) *Medicum hebreum ex hebraico in latinum translata* (n. p.,n. d; WL catalogue suggests Venice, ca. 1540). *Canon* I.1. *WL; IA 110.604.*

Avicennae liber Canonis, De medicinis cordialibus, et Cantica cum castigationibus Andreae Alpagi Bellunensis philosophi ac medici clarissimi, una cum eiusdem nominum arabicorum interpretatione.

Quibus recens quamplurimae accesserunt ab eodem ex multis arabum codicibus excerptae huiusmodi asterisco* notatae. Cum privilegiis Summi Pontificis, Francorum Regis, et Senatus Veneti (Venice: Junta, 1544). Paolo Alpago's second edition of his uncle's work, with more new readings in the margins of the text and additional items in the glossary. The volume also contains a second glossary entitled *Antiqua expositio Arabicorum nominum*, and a life of Avicenna by Nicolò Massa. The second part of the volume (containing the glossaries and biography) is separately paginated. Decorated title page, and illustrations following fol. 16ᵛ of the second section. NLM; IA 110.606.

*Primi libri fen prima nunc primum per Iacobum Mantinum ex hebraico in latinam translata et diligentius nuper emendata (Padua: Bernardius Bindonus and Jacobus Fabrianus, 1547). *Canon* I.1. IA 110.608.

Prima primi Canonis Avicennae sectio, Michaele Hieronymo Ledesma Valentino medico et interprete et enarratore. (Valencia: Ioanne Mey of Flanders, 1547). Date from title page; on fol. 118ʳ is the date 1548. *Canon* I.1 in Ledesma's own translation from the Arabic, with his commentary. Ledesma's objectives, translation techniques, and cultural context are discussed in Luis Garcia Ballester, *Historia social de la medicina en la Espana. I La minoria musulmana y morisca* (Madrid, 1976), pp. 77-97.

Prima fen quarti Canonis Avicennae de febribus ... (Paris, Vaenundantur a Ponceto le Preux bibliopola universitatis addicto, 1549). Gerard of Cremona version. *Canon* IV.1. NLM; IA 110.610.

*Quarta fen primi: de universali ratione medendi. Interprete Iacob Mantino medico hebreo (Paris: apud M. Iuvenem, 1555). *Canon* I.4. IA 110.611.

Avicennae liber Canonis, De medicinis cordialibus, et Cantica, iam olim quidem a Gerardo Carmonensi ex arabico sermone in latinum conversa, postea vero ab Andrea Alpago Bellunensi, philosopho et medico egregio, infinitis pene correctionibus ad veterum exemplarium arabicorum fidem in margine factis, locupletissimoque nominum arabicorum ab ipso interpretatorum indice decorata, nunc autem demum a Benedicto Rinio Veneto, philosopho et medico eminentissimo, eruditissimis accuratissimisque lucubrationibus illustrata. Qui et castigationes ab Alpago factas suis quasque locis aptissime inseruit. Et locos in quibus auctor ipse vel eandem sententiam, eandem ve medicamenti unius compositionem iterat, vel oppositas inter se sententias ponit, vel aliquid denique ab Hippocrate, Aristotele, Dioscoride, Galeno, Paulo, Aetio, Alexandro, Serapione, Rasi, Halyabate, Alfarabio mutuatur diligentissime indicavit. Plurimis etiam arabicis vocibus nunquam antea expositis, latinum nomen invenit. Indicemque latinum medicamentorum simplicium in secundum librum composuit . . . (Venice: Iunta, 1555). The volume also includes Alpago's translations of Avicenna, *De removendis nocumentis* and *De syrupo acetoso*, and Massa's life of Avicenna, as well as epistles by Rinio to the reader and to his sons, to whom the work is dedicated. The latter contains a well thought out defense of Avicenna. The verbose title, or rather blurb, of this work has been quoted at length because it correctly indicates the contents: Rinio inserted Alpago's emendations in the body of the text of the *Canon*, freeing his margins for abundant, learned, and for this reader very helpful, cross-references to Galen and other authors. However, whereas the reader of Paolo Alpago's editions can see at a glance the extent of the older Alpago's emendations of the Gerard text, the reader of Rinio's edition has no way of knowing this, unless by comparison with an edition of the unrevised text. Alpago's glossary and the 'old' glossary are separately foliated at the end of the volume. Bound together is *Index in Avicennae libros nuper Venetiis editos . . . Julio Palamede Adriensi medico auctore* (Venice: Junta, 1557). BL; IA 110.612.

Avicennae medicorum arabum principis liber Canonis, De medicinis cordialibus, et Cantica . . . ab Andrea Alpago Bellunensi . . . correctionibus . . . decorata . . . a Benedicto Rinio . . . lucubrationibus illustrata . . .(Basel: Ioannes Hervagios, 1556). Reprint of foregoing item. The copy at NYAM has a few manuscripts marginalia in Arabic on fol.*5v and elsewhere. On the copy at NLM the imprint date has been altered by hand to 1576 (see Durling, *Catalogue* no. 386). IA 110.613.

Methodus generalis et compendaria ex Hippocratis, Galeni, et Avicennae placitis deprompta ac in ordinem redacta . . . Alfonsi Bertotii Fanensis opera hinc inde collecta: et in communem studiosorum usum in lucem edita . . . (Venice: Ioannes Andrea Valvasorius cognomento Guadagninus, 1556). An outline handbook for students. BL; IA 118.063. NYAM also has subsequent editions of Lyon, 1558, and Geneva, 1588. IA 118.064-065.

Avicennae liber Canonis, De medicinis cordialibus, Cantica, De removendis nocumentis in regimine sanitatis, De syrup acetoso . . . (Venice: Iunta, 1562). The Alpago-Rinio version with fresh emendations by Rinio: 'Novissime autem idem Rinius in hac editione toto volumine summa iterum diligentia per lecto, adhibitis etiam exemplaribus manu Alpagi scriptis (quorum copiam nuper nobis fecerunt eius haeredes) innumeris pene aliis tum castigationibus, tum locorum citationibus praesertim in Canticis illustravit'. This edition contains, in addition to the prefatory matter noted above, a poem in honour of the *Canon* by I. M. Rota. Also present are the two indices of the simples in *Canon* II, one by Andrea Alpago, the other by Rinio, beginning on fol. 85^r; the first consists of transliterated Arabic terms. Palamede's index appears at the end of the volume. NYAM; IA 110.616.

Avicennae principis et philosophi sapientissimi libri in re medica omnes, qui hactenus ad nos pervenere, idest libri Canonis quinque, De viribus cordis, De removendis nocumentis in regimine sanitatis, De sirupo acetoso, et Cantica, omnia novissime post aliorum omnium operam a Ioanne Paulo Mongio Hydruntino, et Ioanne Costaeo Laudensi recognita . . . (Venice: Vincentius Valgrisius, 1564). In addition to a general dedicatory letter by Costeo to Cardinal Ludovico Simoneta, the first four books of the *Canon* are each prefaced by a separate letter of dedication: Book I, Costeo to Bernardino Paterno; Book II, Costeo and Mongio to G. A. Cortusio; Book III: idem to Nicolò Sanmichele; Book IV, Costeo to Francesco Modegnano. Paterno and Sanmichele were professors at Padua, and Modegnano at Pavia. Cortusio was prefect of the Paduan botanic gardens. Costeo's letter to Paterno explains that Costeo and Mongio elected to print the *antiqua versio* since, like Paterno, they believed that it was 'puriorem certe et plerunque meliorem nisi paulo esset obscurior'. However, they placed in the margins readings selected from Alpago and Mantino, as well as fresh emendations of their own. Although Rinio appears not to be named, it seems evident that this edition was intended to supplant his and to be clearer about the origins and extent of variants. Costeo and Mongio placed their cross-references to ancient authors (less prolific than Rinio's) within substantial *annotationes* — really amounting to commentary — at the end of each short section of the text. The edition is accompanied by the two Arabo-Latin glossaries (the 'old' and Alpago's), an index to the text, and an index to the annotations. WL; IA 110.618.

Avicennae medicorum arabum facile principis libri tertii fen secunda, quae latine ex synonymo hebraico . . . Ophan reddi potest, intuitus sive rotundus sermo secundus, qui est de aegritudinibus nervorum, tractatu uno contentus, ad fidem codicis hebraici latinus factus. Interprete Iohanne Quinquarboreo Aurilacensi, literarum hebraicarum et caldaicarum professore regio . . . (Paris: apud M. Iuvenum, 1570). *Canon* III.2, from the Hebrew. Translator's preface indicates the version was made from a manuscript brought from Rome. NLM; IA 110.620.

Avicennae medicorum arabum facile principis libri tertii fen primae tractatus quartus, in quo accurate et cogitate scribit ille de aegritudinibus capitis et noxa multa illarum in functionibus sensus et moderaminis sive partis rectricis, in linguam latinam conversus, et a salebris ac mendis, quibus scatebat, ad fidem codicis hebraici correcti et emendati maxime, in integrum restitutus ac perpurgatus. Interprete Iohanne Quinquarboreo exemplaris hebraici latina conversio . . . (Paris, 1572; bound with a copy of the preceding item). *Canon* III.1.4, from the Hebrew. Includes two prefatory letters by the translator and a letter addressed to Symphorien Champier by Dionisio Coroneo from Rome in 1533, which praises the superior style and accuracy of the Hebrew version of the *Canon* as compared with Alpago's revised Latin text. BL.

Principis Avicennae liber primus de universalibus medicae scientiae praeceptis, Andrea Gratiolo Salodiano interprete. Adiectis utilissimis eiusdem interpretis scholis Hippocratis et Galeni praecipue loca commonstrantibus . . . (Venice: Franciscus Zilettus, 1580). *Canon* I. Version claimed by Graziolo to be based on 'all previous interpreters', especially Alpago; Graziolo also made use of a manuscript of a translation from Arabic into Latin by Girolamo Ramusio, and acknowledged the assistance of Jacob Anselmi, a Jewish physician who owned the *Canon* in Hebrew. Two prefatory epistles. Scholia. NYAM; IA 110.622.

Avicennae liber Canonis, De medicinis cordialibus, Cantica, De removendis nocumentis in regimine sanitatis, De syrupo acetoso . . . (Venice: Junta, 1582). A reprint of the Alpago/Rinio edition of 1562. A short poem in praise of Alpago and Rinio by Filippo Pellenigro has been added. NLM; IA 110.623.

**Libri tertii fen primae tractatus quintus, de aegritudinibus cerebri, ad fidem hebraici exemplaris, latinus factus et passim restitutus ac emendatus. Interprete Iohanne Quinquarboreo* (Paris: Dionysius a Prato, 1586). *Canon* III.1.5. IA 110.625.

Avicennae arabum medicorum principis. Ex Gerardi Cremonensis versione, et Andreae Alpagi Bellunensis castigatione. A Ioanne Costaeo, et Ioanne Paulo Mongio annnotationibus iampridem illustratus. Nunc vero ab eodem Costaeo recognitus, et novis alicubi observationibus adauctus . . . Vita ipsius Avicennae . . . a Nicolae Massa Latine scripta . . . Additis nuper etiam librorum Canonis oeconomiis, necnon tabulis isagogicis in universam medicinam ex arte Humain [sic], *idest Ioannitiis Arabis. Per Fabium Paulinum Utinensem . . .* (Venice: Junta, 1595). A new edition of the Costeo and Mongio version with significant additions; the annotations really were revised by Costeo, a professor at Bologna, as they now contain references to his *Disquisitiones physiologicarum* published at Bologna in 1589 (see appendix II); Fabio Paolino provided an ode in praise of Avicenna and lengthy and elaborate tables outlining both the *Canon* and the brief *Isagoge* of Johannitius. Also included are figures previously used to illustrate the Junta edition of 1544 (see above). NYAM 2 volumes; IA 110.627.

Avicennae . . . ex Gerardi Cremonensis versione, et Andreae Alpagi Bellunensis castigatione. A Ioanne Costaeo et Ioanne Paulo Mongio annotationibus jampridem illustratus. Nunc vero ab eodem Costaeo recognitus et novis alicubi observationibus adauctus . . . (Venice: Junta, 1608). A reprint of the preceding item, with a few minor typographical alterations. NYAM 2 volumes.

Liber secundus de canone Canonis a filio Sina studio sumptibus ac typis Arabicis Petri Kirstenii ph. et. M.D. . . . (Breslau, 1609 according to NLM catalogue; BL catalogue dates 1610). Arabic and Latin texts, Arabo-Latin vocabulary. The author's preface explains that he has chosen not to translate Book I, since this has already been partially restored by Graziolo, no Arabic manuscripts are available, and the printed Arabic edition (Rome, 1593) contains errors. For Book II, he apparently had more than one Arabic manuscript; however, he noted that he also had to hand the Gerard of Cremona Latin text, and the emended editions of Lyon, 1522 (Rustico), Basel, 1556 (Alpago/Rinio), Venice, 1595 (Costeo and Mongio). Of Costeo, he remarked 'mea opinione melius fecisset si ex fontibus arabicis hunc authorem restituere voluisset, quam quod sibi proposuerat eum ex Galeno restituere'. Kirsten also announces plans to proceed with his translation (although he apparently published no more) because 'Praeter utilitates itaque illas non parvas, quas studiosi huius linguae ex hoc nostro labore haurire possunt, haec certe omnes veri medici inde assequi poterunt, ut tamen elegantis et operosae editionis arabicae hujus *Canonis*, Romanae, integritatem agnoscere, et de versionibus hujus authoris, eo melius judicare possint'. Text accompanied by philological scholia. NLM.

Avicennae summi inter medicos nominis fen I, libri 1 Canonis . . .
(Vicenza: apud Orlandum Iadram bibliopolam patavinum, 1611).
Canon I.1, Gerard of Cremona version, abbreviated; bound with
Galen's *Ars*. A brief preface terms *Canon* I.1. Avicenna's *opusculum*
and refers to its usefulness for students. BL.

*Avicennae summi inter Arabes medici fen I, libri Canonis in usum
Gymnasii Patavini . . .* (Padua, 1636). *Canon* I.1, Gerard of Cremona
version, abbreviated by the omission of the anatomy, intended for
student use. Preface by Paolo Frambotto begins 'Prudenti majorum
instituto usque ad nostram memoriam Avicennae dogmata Italiae
gymnasia retinuerunt'. BL.

*Schola medica in qua Hippocratis, Galeni, Avicennaeque medicinae
facile principum pro tyronibus habentur fundamenta . . .* (Venice,
1647). Contains Galen, *Ars* and Hippocrates, *Aphorisms*, tr.
Leoniceno, and *Canon* I.1 in the Gerard of Cremona version,
abbreviated by omission of the anatomy. The preface used in the
edition of Vicenza, 1611 is reprinted. At the end of the volume are
printed the 'Capita sive puncta quae laureandis proponi solent in
celeberrimis collegiis'. BL.

*Avicennae arabum medicorum summi fen I libri I Canonis, Gerardo
Cremonense interprete, in usum Gynmasii Patavini. Nova editio
castigatior.* (Padua: Paulus Frambottus, 1648). Bound with Galen
Ars, Hippocrates, *Aphorisms* and *Prognostics* (tr. Leoniceno). *Canon*
I.1 (Gerard version) is printed in full, not abbreviated. BL.

*Clarissimi et praecellentissimi doctoris Abualj Ibn-Tsina qui hactenus
perperam dictus est Avicennae Canon medicinae, interprete et
scholiaste Vopisco Fortunate Plempio. Tomus 1, librum primum et
secundum Canonis exhibens, atque ex libro quarto tractatum de
febribus* (Louvain: Hieronymus Nempaeus, 1658). Plemp's preface *ad
lectores medicos* explains that he had hoped to print an edition and
translation of the entire *Canon* with Arabic and Latin on facing
pages, but local unavailability of Arabic type, the consideration that
'paucissimos tamen in orbe Christiano' either knew Arabic or might
be expected to know it in future, and the representations of his
publisher had led him to the decision to present only this Latin
translation of *Canon*, Books I and II and IV.1. Plemp's preface also
contains an evaluation — mostly negative — of the previous efforts to
secure a better Latin text of the *Canon*. His scholia are in large part
philological as well as medical. NLM.

Abugalii filii Sinae sive, ut vulgo dicitur, Avicennae philosophorum ac medicorum arabum principis, De morbis mentis tractatus, editus in specimen normae medicorum universae ex arabico in latinum de integro conversae et a barborum inscitia spurcitiaque vindicatae. Interprete Petro Vatterio . . . (Paris, 1659). Excerpts from *Canon* III.1. The preface claims that this is a completely new translation and not merely interpolations into an existing one. 'Hoc ideo dico, quod ex eiusmodi interpolatione magni viri non parvam nec sane immeritam laudem consecuti sint, Iacobus Sylvius ex Mesue librorum trium, Vesalius ex nono Rhasis ad Almansorem; vanitatis tamen in hoc cujusdam non absolvendi, qui ex Arabico horum autorum sermone Latinum suum expressisse videri quasi voluerint, que neque aspexerant unquam, neque si aspexissent, ullam eius literam legere potuissent, homines alias quidem doctissimi. . .' NYAM, microfilm.

Avicennae quarti libri Canonis, fen prima de febribus. Nova editio caeteris accuratior . . . (Padua: Matthaeus Cadorinus, 1659). Gerard of Cremona's text of *Canon* IV.1. Presumably for students. Edited by Girolamo Santasofia, holder of first extraordinary chair of medical theory at Padua. His preface stresses the value of the text for physicians. BL.

Georgii Hieronymi Velschii Exercitatio de vena medinensi ad mentem Ebnsinae, sive De dracunculis veterum. Specimen exhibens novae versionis ex Arabico . . . (Augsburg: Theophilus Coebelius, 1674). *Canon* IV.3.21-22. The preface evaluates earlier workers on the text of the *Canon* and quotes a number of opinions about them. Welsch referred to Costeo as 'linguarum orientalium omnium ignarissimus'. NLM.

Appendix II: Editions of Latin Commentaries on the *Canon* Written in Italy after 1500.

The scope of this category depends on how narrowly the term 'commentary' is defined; only formal, academic commentaries presumably based on university lectures are included in the list that follows. The limitation of this list to commentaries written in Italy has resulted in the exclusion of one other major group of commentaries, namely those from the Iberian peninsula. On the uses of the *Canon* in Spain, and on sixteenth-century humanistic commentary on the *Canon* there, see the important article of Luis Garcia Ballester, 'The Circulation and Use of Medical Manuscripts in Arabic in Sixteenth-

Century Spain', *Journal of the Hisory of Arabic Science*, 3 (1979), 183-199. The apparently more reactionary commentaries produced in Iberia in the early seventeenth century seem to have been little studied. Relatively few *Canon* commentaries appear to have been written in northern Europe at any time. The reader is once more reminded that substantial sixteenth-century scholia and notes, amounting in some cases almost to full commentary, are included in some of the editions of the text of the *Canon* listed in Appendix I, above (notably those of Graziolo, Venice, 1580, and Costeo and Mongio, Venice, 1564, 1595), while some of the following commentaries also print portions of the text.

Works are listed chronologically by date of publication; however, second and subsequent editions of the same work are listed immediately after the first edition.

Bartolemeo Corso, *Bartholomei phisici servi Pape apologia. . . cum apta expositione vel clara declaratione illorum Avicenne verborum quorum fuit contentio et altercatio* (Rome, 1519). NLM. Dispute over *Canon* I.3.1.

Pietro Antonio Rustico, *Qui atrocem horres pestem pestilentemque times febrem ecce dicta principis Avicene de pestilentia seu peste . . . ordinata, exposita, discussa a Rustico medicine cultore . . .* Printed with Baverio Baviera, *Consilia Baverii* (Pavia, 1521). Based on portions of *Canon* IV. NYAM.

Idem, *Qui venenosa formidas apostemata et pestiferos paves bubones ecce dicta Avicene aràbis de igne persico pruna vel carbone . . . ordinata, exposita, discussa a Rustico medicine cultore . . .* Printed with preceding item. Based on portions of *Canon* IV. NYAM.

Leonardo Legio, *Propositiones seu flosculi ex Galeni libros per . . . D. Magistrum Leonardum Legium . . . collecte . . . Eiusdem magistri Leonardi ex expositione capituli aurei Avicenne introductorium medicorum . . .* (Venice, 1523). The *Introductorium medicorum* is separately foliated (2ʳ-16ᵛ), and is a commentary on *Canon* III.1.2.29. The author identifies himself as a professor at Pavia. NLM.

Bartolomeo degli Emanuelli, . . . *Adnotationes super dicta Gentilis de Fulgineo dicta ab illo super definitione de febre data ab Avicenna in primo capitulo libri eius quarti in tractatu primo de febribus . . .* (Rome, 1524). A brief commentary on *Canon* IV.1. NLM.

Mariano Santo, *Mariani Sancti Barolitani philosophi ac medici celeberrimi ad communem medicorum chirurgicorum usum commentaria nuper in lucem aedita in Avicennae textum* . . . (Venice, 1543). On *Canon* IV.3.1. Prefatory epistle to Francesco Frigimelica, professor at Padua. WL.

G. B. Da Monte, . . . *De differentiis medicamentorum* . . . (Wittenberg, 1551). This work corresponds to part of Da Monte's commentary on *Canon* I. (see below). NLM.

Giovanni Filippo Ingrassia, . . . *De tumoribus praeter naturam* . . . *occasione sumpta ab Avicennae verbis, arabum medicorum principis, tertia fen, quarti libri, tractatu primo, cuius interim universum primum caput in hoc tomo elucidatur* . . . (Naples, 1553). The author (d. 1580), obtained his M.D. at Padua in 1537 and was subsequently *protomedicus* in Palermo; he was an admirer of Vesalius. On *Canon* IV.3.1. WL.

G. B. Da Monte, . . . *In primam fen libri primi Canonis Avicennae explanatio* . . . (Venice, 1554). On *Canon* I.1, NLM.

Idem, . . . *In primi libri Canonis Avicennae primam fen profundissimi commentaria. Adiecto nuper secundo quod nunquam ante fuerat typis excussum de membris capite* . . . (Venice, 1557). On *Canon* I.1, second edition with an additional chapter. NYAM.

Idem, . . . *In quartam fen primi Canonis Avicenne lectiones* . . . (Venice, 1556). On *Canon* I.4. NLM.

Idem, . . . *In secundam fen primi Canonis Avicennae* . . . (Venice, 1557). *Canon* I.2. NLM.

Antonio Maria Betti, *Antonii Mariae Betti Mutinensis philosophi ac medici doctissimi practicae vespertinae in academia Bononiensi ordinarii interpretis in quartam fen primi Canonis Avicennae commentarium* . . . (Bologna, 1560). On *Canon* I.4. NYAM. IA 118.243.

*Idem, another edition of the same (Bologna, 1562). IA 118.244.

Idem, . . . *In IIII fen primi Canonis Avicennae commentarius* . . . (Bologna, 1591). Another edition of foregoing item. NLM.

Oddo Oddi,. . . *In primam totam fen primi libri Canonis Avicennae dilucidissima et expectatissima expositio* . . . (Venice, 1575). On *Canon* I.1 NYAM.

Idem, . . . *In primam totam fen primi libri Canonis Avicennae dilucidissima expositio. Nunc tertio in lucem edita* . . . (Padua, 1612). BL. I do not know where, or when, the second edition was published.

Angelo Forte, *Da calamitoso errore Avicennae, unde communium medicorum orrenda malitia inter homines cotidie pullulant* (Venice, 1582). an attack on Avicenna's teaching on humours in *Canon* I.1. (and also on university trained physicians, so that it falls somewhat outside the genre of the present list). NLM.

Constantino Luca, . . . *In Avicennae caput de phlebotomia expositio* (Pavia, 1584). Apparently on part of *Canon* I.4. The author was a professor at Pavia. NLM.

Giovanni Costeo, *Disquisitionum physiologicarum* . . . *in primam primi Canonis Avicennae* . . . *libri sex* . . . (Bologna, 1589). On *Canon* I.1. The author, a professor at Bologna, also edited the text of the *Canon* (see Appendix I, above). He died in 1603. NLM.

Bernardino Paterno, *Bernardini Salodiensis philosophi et medici clarissimi, qui in praecipuis Italiae gimnasijs ac demum Patavino totos quinquaginta annos rem medicam ad veterem Hippocratis et Galeni disciplinam summa cum laude interpretatus est, explanationes in primam fen primi Canonis Avicennae* . . . (Venice, 1596). On *Canon* I.1. Paterno died in 1592. NYAM.

Vittorio Trincavella, . . . *Explanationes in primam fen quarti Canonis Avicennae habitae Patavii MDLIIII ac in commentarii formam redactae*, in his *Opera* (2nd edition, Venice, 1599), Vol. III of 3 vols. in 2. The author was a professor at Padua and died in 1563. On *Canon* IV.1. WL.

Alessandro Massaria, *Alexandri Massariae Vicentini medici aetatis nostrae olim in Patavino Antenoris Gymnasio medicinam primo loco profitentis Practica medica* . . . (Tarvisii, 1607). Book 7, *De febribus*, pp. 314-446, is a commentary on *Canon* IV.1; its preface is strongly critical of Avicenna. NYAM. Other editions of Massaria's *Practica medica* were published Venice, 1622 (NYAM), Frankfurt, 1601 (BL), and *Lyon, 1622 (BL *General Catalogue of Printed Books*). Massaria died in 1598.

Girolamo Capodivacca, *Practicae medicinae liber sextus de febribus*, in his *Opera omnia* (Frankfurt, 1603), section IV, 824-912. A commentary on *Canon* IV.1; as already noted, Capodivacca was professor of *medicina practica* at Padua and died in 1589. WL Other editions of his *Opera omnia* were published *Venice, 1597, *Venice, 1598, and *Venice, 1599 (IA 131.679-681).

Giovanni Colle, *Elucidarium anatomicum et chirurgicum, una cum commentariis in quartum librum Avicennae, fen tertiam* . . .(Venice, 1621). On *Canon* IV.3. WL.

Santorio Santorio, . . . *Commentaria in primam fen primi libri Canonis Avicennae* . . . (Venice: apud Iacobum Sarcinam, 1626). Biblioteca Comunale degli Intronati, Siena. I am unclear as to whether this should be regarded as a separate edition from the copy in the British Library, which appears identical as regards title, publisher, place, contents, dedication, and typography, but bears the date 1625. On *Canon* I.1 Santorio, who had been a professor of medical *theoria* at Padua, died in 1636.

Idem, . . . *Commentaria in primam fen primi libri Canonis Avicennae* . . . (Venice, 1646). Another edition of the previous item. NYAM.

Idem, *Sanctorii Sanctorii Iustinopolitani* . . . *Opera* . . . (4 vols., Venice, 1660). Volume III contains the commentary on *Canon* I.1 Biblioteca Nazionale, Rome.

Giovanni Stefani, *Paraphrasis Ioannis Stephani physici et alma Venetorum Medicorum et Philosophorum Collegii Prioris in primam fen libri quarti Avicennae de febribus studiose perpolita* (Venice, 1646). Bibliothèque Nationale, Paris. The author's purpose was to present the solid teaching of *Canon* I.4 in clearer form. His paraphrase actually falls somewhere between a commentary and a revised version of the Latin text. I have been unable to ascertain his death date, but he was still alive in 1653 (see next item). On the college of which Stefani was prior, see Richard Palmer, *The Studio of Venice and its Graduates in the Sixteenth Century* (Padua, 1983).

Idem, . . . *Opera universa, cum medicinae ac philosophiae tum cultioris literaturae studiosis apprime utilia* . . . (Venice, 1653). The paraphrase of *Canon* I.4 occupies pp. 242-296. At pp. 88-233 is found Stefani's *Paraphrasis in novem fen libri III Avicennae continens universos capitis affectus*. The volume is prefaced by complimentary letters to and from the author dated 1653. BL. The handwritten catalogue of printed books of the Biblioteca Lancisiana, Rome, includes another edition of each paraphrase, both published *Venice, 1649.

Sebastiano Scarabicio, . . . *De ortu ignis febriferi historia physica medica ad Avicennae ordinem* . . . (Padua, 1655). Organisation follows *Canon* IV.10. NLM.

Girolamo Cardano, *Commentaria in quatuor primas principis primae sectionis doctrinas, seu floridorum libri duo*, in his *Opera*, IX (Lyon, 1663), 453-567. On *Canon* I.1.1-4. According to the prefatory material of this commentary, Cardano, who is better remembered as a mathematician, lectured on *Canon* I.1 when a professor at Pavia in 1561 and at Bologna in 1564. NYAM.

Pietro Salio Diverso, . . . *In Avicennae librum tertium de morbis particularibus* . . . *annotationes luculentissimae, opus posthumum, nunc primum in lucem editum* (Padua, 1673). The author seems to have flourished in the second half of the sixteenth century. BL.

G. Battista Morgagni, *Commento ad Avicenna* in his *Opera postuma*, ed. Adalberto Pazzini, vols. IV, V, VI (Rome, 1969, 1975, 1981). On *Canon* I.1 Latin commentary with modern Italian translation. This commentary remained in manuscript until the twentieth century.

THE LIMITS OF 'REFORM':SOME ASPECTS
OF THE DEBATE ON UNIVERSITY EDUCATION
DURING THE ENGLISH REVOLUTION

John Twigg

On the question of university reform, the English Revolution flattered to deceive. It is certain that revolutionary governments regarded educational reform as vital; their favourite educational theorist, Samuel Hartlib, wrote that 'this Endeavour alone, or nothing, will be able to work a Reformation in this our Age'.[1] Encouragement was given to reformers such as Hartlib, Dury and Comenius, attempts were made to propagate the Gospel in remote and backward regions, the universities were purged, Trinity College Dublin was reformed, and a new University college was founded at Durham, yet these grand schemes produced little that was deep-rooted and lasting.[2] Certainly the pressures of war and revolution hampered the reformers, and many hopes were dashed at the Restoration, but in this essay I wish to advance the tentative hypothesis that the ostensible 'failure' of revolutionary governments to implement far-reaching change was perhaps in part because the intellectual preconditions for such change were not yet present, and many modern notions of 'reform' may be out of place in the seventeenth century.

Firstly, many contemporaries perceived the universities' role in society in narrowly political terms. This was possibly due in part to the changes in the function of the universities during the sixteenth century, particularly the greater emphasis on a learned clergy, and the influx of the gentry, a process which Curtis describes as the 'Englishing' of the universities: they were brought into a closer relationship with the specifically English cultural and social environment.[3] Oxford and Cambridge products permeated the influential quarters of English society and institutions.

The Duke of Newcastle commented that 'it is a great matter in a state or kingdom, to take care of the education of youth, to breed them so, that they may know first how to obey, and then how to command and order affairs wisely'.[4] This was echoed by two leading authorities on educational theory, writing over a century apart: in

1570, Roger Ascham noted that 'the good or ill bringing up of our children doth as much serve to the good or ill service of God, our prince and our whole country as any one thing doth beside'; in 1678 Christopher Wase observed that 'Now that universities flourish, and schools are in many populous towns erected, from these places of public education especially, persons are sent into all parts of the land engaged in the strictest bonds of allegiance'.[5] These defences of the conservative, not innovative, rôle of education were supported by Henry Burton and John Aubrey, both of whom saw education as a means of maintaining a static social order.[6] The humanist ideals of educational thinkers were compromised by such demands throughout the Tudor and Stuart period, but it is difficult to imagine how it could have been otherwise.[7]

Change and innovation in the universities were therefore considered potentially dangerous instruments of social disintegration; in 1610 the Earl of Northampton complained that too many young men left the universities to 'go up and down breeding new opinions'.[8] This danger was particularly apparent after the Revolution and was expressed most notably in the writings of Clarendon and Hobbes. These are well known and do not require repetition here, except in one respect: both believed that the universities were 'not to be cast away, but to be better disciplined' — in other words, that there were no fundamental weaknesses in the universities as institutions, but only failings in the hearts and minds of the individuals who studied there.[9] This 'personalisation' of the university question was common in contemporary writings; at its worst, it engendered philistinism: the Duke of Newcastle believed that 'wise men rather than learned, should be chosen heads of schools and colleges'; but it is also very important in understanding the attitudes of seventeenth-century reformers, as will appear below.[10]

If significant reform, in anything approaching the modern sense, were to be accomplished at the universities, then a deeper investigation of the role of the university in society was required. Recognition of the need to go beyond the 'political' and 'personal' themes cited above was contained in some contemporary literature, but was for the most part merely implicit. The description of the universities as 'nurseries' or 'fountains' of church and commonwealth was employed so frequently by commentators of all kinds that it became a cliché: contemporaries were aware of the universities' importance, but employed a well-worn expression which avoided the need for deeper analysis.[11] There was some confusion over the question, and certainly no coherent approach or attitude. For example, in 1632 Sir Edward Cecil naively suggested that the universities should teach 'the brave exercise of horsemanship' in order to improve the quality of the nation's cavalry, for 'who may better do it than the Universities, which are ordained for the learning of all manner of virtues?'.[12] Although Cecil misunderstood the nature of contemporary university education, he was suggesting a means for enhancing the relevance of the universities to society, albeit within the narrow context of the dominant social élite.

Such confusion was due in part to the limited impression of university education which contemporaries received. In 1622 John Brinsley wrote that the views of many were distorted by the examples of those who had not used their time at university to good advantage, and returned home 'almost as rude as they went thither'.[13] Such attitudes were encouraged by the élitism of university members, as expressed in Isaac Barrow's description of scholarship as 'a calling which, being duly followed, will most sever us from the vulgar sort of men, and advance us above the common pitch', and by the impression of the luxurious existence enjoyed there, described by William Fleetwood as a life of 'perfect Ease and Liberty', with 'all the Helps, and all the Encouragements that We can want or wish for'.[14] This made the 'personalised' attitude a natural channel for hostility.

The attitudes of the Stuarts, and of the different revolutionary régimes, towards the universities, are made much clearer when understood in this light. Charles I's policy was summed up in a letter from Chancellor Holland to the University of Cambridge in 1635 requiring the university authorities to secure from their members 'a fitting obedience of their superiors at home, as they may not take the liberty to importune his Majestie with needles complaints'.[15]

This emphasis on discipline and, wherever possible, non-intervention, was followed by revolutionary governments. The purges of Oxford and Cambridge in the 1640s were not in essence 'reformist' measures: that of Cambridge in 1644-5 was brutal, but hastily conceived and executed because of the exigencies of the civil war; at Oxford, where there were no such urgent pressures, the parliamentary visitation was muddled and incoherent, with no clear aims or methods.[16] Such purges of the politically and religiously disaffected formed part of the first stage of revolutionary governments' strategy for higher education. The second stage was the promotion of new schemes.[17] Existing beliefs made the first stage easy, but did not provide adequate conceptual framework for the second.

This becomes more apparent when we examine certain features of the university debate during the Revolution. Firstly, there was no truly great intellectual contributor to dominate the debate. Many Puritans regarded Francis Bacon as an intellectual figurehead;

unfortunately, Bacon left no all-embracing scheme for educational reforms behind at this death. The concept of the 'Great Instauration' was of paramount importance for subsequent Puritan thought, but it degenerated easily into a slogan. As Webster has shown, Puritans accorded a near-canonical status to Bacon's works, but the dominant influences were, paradoxically, the vague schemes of the *New Atlantis*, which was left incomplete. The fully-fledged Baconian educational doctrine propounded by Comenius in the 1640s was only a 'somewhat mystical version' of this.[18]

Secondly, although the educational debate took on a new momentum and sense of urgency after 1640, the heady optimism of the early revolutionary years following the collapse of censorship was perhaps more conducive to inchoate and impulsive ideas about reform, rather than coherent and rational planning. There was a 'reform movement' of sorts, but not in any organised sense, and those who called for reform represented a wide variety of opinions. Some well known examples of the different shades of thought illustrate the hypothesis of the limits of 'reform'.

Attacks on the universities were not new; they grew out of traditional English anticlericalism. None of the writers of the 1640s and 1650s could outdo the Elizabethan separatist Henry Barrow in extreme expressions: he had attacked university learning as profane, ungodly, idolatrous, venal and superstitious; he thought university members idle and claimed that the ban on marriage there led to sodomy, concluding that the universities had 'a popish original', and should be abolished. It is significant that a selection of Barrow's writings, entitled *The Pollution of Universitie-Learning* was published in 1642, and his arguments seemed quite up to date.[19] It should also be noted that Barrow's method, based on invective rather than reasoned argument, was common to many writings of this period, which fostered a predominantly negative attitude.

This is particularly evident in the writing of Samuel How, one of the first major contributors to the revolutionary debate. The threat which 'radicals' such as How posed to the existing order came as much from their persons as from their writings: in the 'radical movement' there was a strong leavening of artisans (How was a cobbler) and *déclassés* (such as the New Model Army chaplain Hugh Peters). Not only were How's arguments unoriginal, they were also similar to those of respectable men in society; How would have endorsed Fulke Greville's view: 'What then are all these humane Arts, and lights, but seas of errors? In whose depths who sound, Of truth finde only shadowes, and no ground', but How's prose style was less elegant and his person more dangerous to the social hierarchy, expressing a subversive strand in English life and thought which stretched back to Lollardy.[20]

His arguments were to be repeated, with individual idiosyncracies, by most of the radical pamphleteers. These do not require repetition here, except in certain respects relevant to this argument. The dominant emphasis of How's book was on the teaching of the Holy Spirit; it did not adopt a philosophical or scholastic method, which is not surprising, but relied on examples from the Bible — not the ambiguous Old Testament, but the New, particularly the writings of St Paul, who became something of an intellectual figurehead for many radicals. At the heart of the New Testament examples was the fact that Christ and the Apostles were unlearned in any worldly sense.[21]

The main point at issue was the 'gift of tongues', when the Apostles received the power of speech in many languages.[22] Defenders of universities used this as an illustration of the need for clergymen to have knowledge of different tongues, which by implication meant a need for traditional university education. To this straightforward, standard interpretation How presented an equally standard retort: the gift of tongues came directly from God, and history was full of examples of worldly learning which had conveyed no spiritual benefits.[23]

This question was at the heart of the debate on university education, but the different polemicists did not explore it in depth. How's approach cited here is typical: he never came to grips with the rôle of language in scriptural exposition, resting his case on the stark contrast between human and spiritual teaching. He was an iconoclast, but had no plans for reform. The dogged refusal to explore such vital questions, and the over-simplification of issues in order to present them in black-and-white terms is characteristic of the debate. The argument did not develop and pamphlets repeated the same themes incessantly: the Quakers, for example, were certainly regarded as radicals by contemporaries, but echoed traditional prejudices about the pride and sinfulness of man, the 'inordinate desire for knowledge', and the need to abolish the clergy.[24]

Such developments as there were tended to be inspired by political changes nationally. John Dury's *Motion Tending to the Publick Good*, published in 1642, was moderate, and sought only to add improvements to the existing educational system; this was in keeping with the irenic spirit which directed his work and writing. However, by 1645 his sermon *Israel's Call to March Out of Babylon*, which was influenced by the experience of the civil war, was speaking in directly apocalyptic terms of purging the universities of the 'gibberidge of Scholastical Divinity . . . the language of corrupt humane reason'.[25] Dury gave no details of what he envisaged, but the change in tone was significant: the carefully reasoned and elaborate plan of 1642 had given way to a harangue. This was an expression of despair:

strong language had to be used to whip up enthusiasm where logic had failed. With the advent of the Commonwealth, Dury felt more confident and he drew up detailed schemes for the future in his *Reformed School*.[26]

The belief that the Revolution might be ushering in the Millenium could encourage optimism and more explicit writing, in contrast to the old-fashioned underground literature of such as How. There were some who wanted genuinely radical change: Hugh Peters proposed 'That Academies may be set up for Nobility and Gentry, where they may know piety and righteousnesse, as wel as gallantry and Courtship . . . and that shorter ways to learning may be advanced, and that godlinesse in youth give them place in Colledges before letters and importunitie of men'.[27]

This egalitarian notion was extended to the entire social order by the communist Gerrard Winstanley, whose *Law of Freedom* viewed learning in starkly utilitarian terms. Winstanley thought constructively about the rôle of the universities in society: he saw the existing institutions as economically useless and socially divisive. In his ideal society, learning was to be an adjunct to trade, so that 'after children have been brought up at schools to ripen their wits, they shall then be set to such trades, arts and sciences as their bodies are capable of'.[28] Because he did not view education in isolation from the entire social order, Winstanley may be seen as the most 'modern' idealist from this period, but he was an isolated thinker.

The contrast between old-fashioned slogan-mongering and the more advanced ideals of such as Winstanley is particularly apparent in the work of William Dell, one of the most famous radical critics of the universities.[29] Dell's language, particularly his identification of human learning with Antichrist, was extreme, but he regarded himself as a traditionalist, heir to a line of critics of the universities which included Wycliff, Hus and Luther. He followed Barrow in seeing popish remnants in the universities' customs and teaching and followed standard radical practice in claiming that the clergy used their education as an excuse to exalt themselves unjustly over the people.[30]

Dell's self-evident desire to be seen as the harbinger of the new reformation resulted in a spate of works on the subject of university education in the years 1653-4, most of which were vigorous, straightforward polemics.[31] There was one crucial exception to this: in 1654 he published a short pamphlet entitled *The Right Reformation of Learning*, which was out of character in that it put forward constructive plans for a new educational system. The work showed strong sympathy with Winstanleyan ideals, especially concerning the practical utility of education, but Dell had no plans to change the social order, merely to increase the number of schools, which was neither new nor specifically radical.[32] Dell's other works were almost exclusively religious in aims and argument, whereas *The Right Reformation* concentrated on the practical aspects of education, as if Dell were trying to step beyond the confines of radical polemic; religion appeared only indirectly in the book. Dell's educational system was designed to free young men from 'that ease and idleness, which fills the hearts of University-Students with many corruptions, and noisome lusts, whilst they fill their heads only with empty knowledge and foolish notions; whereby neither can God be glorified, nor their neighbour profited'.[33]

It was not clear how God was to be glorified: under the scheme which Dell propounded, learned clergy would be made redundant, and their places be taken by part-time lay preachers, but these preachers would also have to be learned. It is clear that the learning which Dell envisaged was not old-fashioned scholasticism and Graeco-Roman philosophy, and he did believe that even the highest education should be socially relevant, but his failure to define the kind of learning which would benefit a lay preacher apart from the study of Scripture, which was open to any literate man, rendered his position ambiguous. Dell knew what he disliked, but was confused as to what should take its place.

The concluding section of the work recognised this pitfall, and Dell repeated that human learning could have a place only among purely earthly matters, but he maintained the existing ambiguity by reaffirming the value of an improved faculty of reason and sober learning to the extent of saying that, even if all men could not be Christians, they should at least be taught to live like men.[34] This is quite out of tune with his other writings. Hill notes that Dell was far from antagonistic towards learning in *The Right Reformation*, but does not stress sufficiently its unique place among his output.[35]

The idea that Dell may have been depressed, defeatist, or was attempting some sort of tactical compromise is unlikely from what is known of his character. But when his career is examined in detail, a possible answer emerges: in his messianic zeal — his utterance of the old slogans — Dell yielded to nobody, but he was less enthusiastic about some of the implications of more advanced thought, especially where reorganisation of the entire social order was suggested. Dell had been among those sectaries whom Hill describes as 'Masterless Men', who would not accept authority, but by the time he wrote *The Right Reformation*, he was no longer *déclassé*, as in his days as an outspoken chaplain in the New Model Army: he had acquired a comfortable parish living in Bedfordshire, where he settled down with his wife and children, and, incredibly, was also master of Caius College Cambridge; he had too much to gain from the existing social order.[36]

More moderate and practical thinkers were arguably more likely — in theory — to create intellectual preconditions for *viable* reform; however, many men of intellect and perception would go no further than admitting that something was wrong with the universities. Robert Greville attacked 'Criticall, Cabalisticall, Scepticall, Scholasticall Learning: which fils the head with empty, aeriall, notions, but gives no sound food to the Reasonable part of man', but he used this merely as an argument against episcopacy.[37] Richard Baxter also commented on the limited value of human learning: 'When I have studied hard to understand some abstruse admired book . . . I have but attained the knowledge of human imperfection, and to see that the author is but a man as well as I'.[38] But he would say no more on the subject.

A particularly interesting group of commentators on university questions were those Presbyterian divines who received masterships at Cambridge after the parliamentary purge of 1644-5. At first sight, it appears that their new position moderated their attitudes towards the universities, but closer examination reveals that they were not hypocrites like Dell, but had never held any constructive ideas about university reform; their previous utterances had been empty rhetoric. The most consistent speaker of this group was Thomas Hill, who became master of Trinity in 1645. His interest in university matters predated his appointment by some years and is shown in the fast sermons he delivered to the Long Parliament. In 1642 he noted that religion and learning were mutually dependant and drew attention to the continued use of Laudian ceremonies at Oxford and Cambridge; a year later he called for their 'purging and pruning'.[39] In another sermon he described the land's three main failings as: the lack of valid ordination, the insufficiency of maintenance for the clergy, and the decay of schools and universities. A close watch should be kept on the three 'chiefe springs' of the nation: the universities, the Inns of Court, and the families of the nobility; England could 'never expect pure streams, whilst the Fountains continue full of mud'.[40] However, whilst affirming the importance of godliness, he also defended traditional learning, on the grounds that 'Religion is the greatest Mysterie in the world. In any ordinary trade, before a man can bee acquainted with the secrets of it, you bind him Apprentice for six or seven years; truly, there are so many mysteries in Religion, that require the service of divers Apprentishipps to bee well acquainted with them'.[41] He did not therefore seek changes in the university structure, but merely the abolition of a few bad habits and a change in personnel; once this was accomplished, normal life and godliness would resume. Only once was he more detailed: in April 1644, preaching before the Corporation of London, he called on citizens to improve the quality of their schools, and to provide more scholarships and exhibitions for the most gifted pupils to go on to university; this too was well within the existing system.[42]

Herbert Palmer, intruded master of Queens' Cambridge in 1644, also recognised that the universities had an important role to play in national regeneration. In 1646 he observed that a constant supply of 'Ministers and Builders' from Oxford and Cambridge was essential for the nation's well-being; it would 'make way for all the rest, and make all other things prosper'. He had made a similar plea to the House of Commons in 1643 to 'Secure youth in the Universities, and Schools, with the utmost care; and even in Parents houses, what you can, specially the poorer sort. The young ones are the hopes or the bane of the Church and State in the next 20, or 10, or 7 years'. But both in 1643 and 1646 Palmer called solely for abolition of old and unnecessary statutes and oaths; like Hill, he saw reform in terms of the removal of the most cumbersome features of the old superstructure, rather than major institutional change.[43]

Anthony Tuckney, later to be master of Emmanuel and St John's colleges respectively, compared the universities to diseased bodies which needed medicine, and saw reform as a mixture of better 'Nurserie' for the patients (in other words, financial help for the universities) and 'Chirurgerie', by which he meant a purge of unsound members.[44] John Arrowsmith, intruded master of St John's, spoke in his fast sermon of 12 March 1645 of the violent changes recently effected and the need to return to normality, 'lest Cambridge become as a cottage in a vineyeard, as a lodge in a garden of cucumbers', and two years later he called on the House of Commons to 'give incouragement to learning, and continue nursing fathers to the nurseries of it', again thinking in terms of support for the recently purged university, not of reform.[45] Richard Vines, the new master of Pembroke Hall, took a consistently sympathetic and traditional stance: in November 1642 he urged parliament never to let the universities suffer, and in March 1645, with the benefit of first-hand experience, merely translated this into more specific terms by asking that financial burdens on the University of Cambridge be lifted, 'that learning may not be starved'.[46]

All these men expressed normality at least implicitly in terms of a *status quo ante* with different personnel, which was what the purges of Oxford and Cambridge were designed to achieve. Herbert Palmer felt that more could be done and called for further reforms to prevent inertia setting in, for spiritual regeneration, and for the provision of more preaching ministers, but he was vague about what should be done in practice. His absence at the Westminster Assembly and death in 1647 may have prevented him from demonstrating his ideas in his own college.[47] Ralph Cudworth, the new master of Clare, was the only intruded head to give much thought to the quality of learning in abstract terms. His fast sermon in March 1647 invited the House of Commons to 'promote ingenious learning, and cast a favourable influence upon it'. By this he meant not only the learning which 'furnisheth the pulpit', of which they were already well aware, but also 'that which is more remote from such popular use, in the several kinds of it, which yet are all of them, both very subservient to religion, and useful to the commonwealth'. He wanted men to have a greater understanding of nature as well as of languages and philology, so that they would learn more both of the workings and the Word of God. Knowledge was prized highly, but was not an end in itself; one of the nation's main failings was that 'we naturally prize truth more than goodnesse, knowledge more than holinesse', and Cudworth was particularly contemptuous of 'bookish Christians, that have all their religion in writings and papers, think they are compleatly furnished with all kinds of knowledge concerning Christ . . . as if religion were nothing but a little book-craft, a mere paper-skill'.[48] Yet Cudworth did not introduce reforms.

Even a sophisticated intellectual critic like John Milton had little to offer that was constructive and realistic. Milton echoed Hartlib, to whom his book *Of Education* (1644) was dedicated, by calling educational reform one of the 'greatest and noblest designs that can be thought on, and for the want whereof this nation perishes'.[49] But the vehemence of his language and the candid expression of his hatreds masked a basic traditionalism in his outlook, drawn from Renaissance humanism.

He adopted the standard view of the universities' opponents that the knowledge of languages was not an end in itself, but his main complaint of existing university methods was that languages were not taught well enough, and the curriculum of the ideal academy that he devised included a substantial amount of language teaching.[50] Although Hill has argued that Milton was closely connected with the contemporary radical underground, in this work he distanced himself from much of contemporary radicalism by his obvious intellectual snobbery.[51] Whereas How had been concerned that education failed to serve the needs of the people, Milton's complaint was that it was no longer adequate for the intellectual élite. Milton had long been obsessed with the need to defend intellectual freedom against all enemies, and he was afraid of the clergy slipping back into 'the sacerdotal ignorance of a former age'.[52]

Milton's academy was closely modelled on classical forms, aiming to fit men 'to perform justly, skillfully and magnanimously all the offices, both private and public, of peace and war', and, like the Romans, Milton was seeking to educate a patrician order.[53] His curriculum would have been too much for any but the exceptionally gifted, and Milton was out of touch with the realities of education, and of English society; his academy was as other-worldly as that of Plato, by which it was influenced, and provides a good example of the naive optimism of the Hartlib school at that time.

Two of the most able critics of the universities were John Hall and John Webster. Hall had failed to get a fellowship at St John's College, Cambridge, and turned to political journalism in the late 1640s, but when he wrote on the university question in 1649, he showed himself superior in argument to the usual bigoted pamphleteer. Like so many contemporary commentators, he was at his best when describing the inadequacies of the existing system, but his analysis was penetrating. He criticised the parliamentary purge of Cambridge in 1644-5 for having 'reached no further then Politicall aimes, it removed many persons of a more thriving and consistent growth in learning, then it either left there, or planted in their steads; it medled not at all with a view of reformation of those fundamental constitutions, on whose happy or weak designations, the interest and prosperity, the decay and ruin of such litterary Republicks principally depends'.[54]

He also wrote of the need for financial reform, for fewer fellowships (in order to encourage academic competition), for honours and rewards to the most innovative and creative minds, for copyright libraries in the universities, and for the more serious encouragement of individual skills, efforts and specialisations.[55] It is clear that Hall recognised that the universities had become less useful to society, by being élitist, isolated and introspective, and failing to utilise the real talents of their students.[56] He described the inadequate social animals produced by the existing system as 'detestable quacking Empricks, lewd, and contentious, Gownmen, or ignorant mercenary Divines'.[57] But Hall did not press home these tentative ideas of greater social integration; he was above all a patriot, concerned that the universities should help to re-establish national prestige, and learning was still designed to lift selected individuals from out of the masses, not to raise the general level of education.[58]

There is a strong sense of realism in John Webster's *Academiarum Examen* of 1653, a detailed, comprehensive critique of university studies and practices. Webster did not indulge in grandiose visions; his book was dedicated to John Lambert, the favoured recipient of several of the Revolution's more practical schemes. Webster was anxious to dissociate himself from the essentially negative attitude of many of the radical critics: 'he that would raise himself by the ruins of others, or warm himself by the burning of Schools, I wish him no greater plague than his own ignorance'.[59] His aims were avowedly limited: he did not wish 'to traduce nor calumniate the Academies themselves, but only the corruptions that time and negligence hath introduced there, but simply to attempt . . . some reformation, not eradication of their customes and learning'.[60] In some respects, this view was close to that of the intruded Presbyterian masters; it was a conservative mode of thought. Webster recognised the dangers of university élitism: 'those that teach in the Academies are but as others, and *homo* is a common name to all men', and that the universities had become isolated, creating a false impression of uniform quality among their graduates and maintaining that a university education qualified its recipient automatically for higher things.[61]

Webster's proposed reforms went no further than improving the existing curriculum, despite hoping that every graduate would have 'his honour according to his industry and proficiency'.[62] The need for more meaningful integration of the universities into society at large was only implicit in his work, and the strength of his attack came not from any adventurous new schemes of reform, but from his detailed and informed criticism of existing methods and the fluency and clarity of his arguments, which stood out in sharp relief from the repetitive bombast of so many of the pamphleteers.

The strength of the reformers' ideas can also be tested by examining some of the prominent defences of the existing order. To a critical, intellectual observer, these seem unimpressive: most of the defenders stuck rigidly, even thoughtlessly, to the best-tried arguments; yet it has already been shown that they were not unique in this, and because their opponents usually posed old questions, they had little need of new answers.

Their commonest device was that of mud-slinging. Thomas Hall said that 'to seek the destruction of humane learning is the badge and practice of wicked men I never read in History, Sacred or Divine, of any but wicked men that did ever oppose it'. Seth Ward described Dell as 'an angry fanatick man, who wanting himselfe such Academicall Learning as would become his relation, would needs persuade others against it', and he bracketed Webster with the Levellers.[63]

The defenders treated attacks on the universities as attacks on the whole body of the church.[64] This was quite consistent with the accepted view of the universities' role as being 'to fit men thence for the work of the Ministry'.[65] Such an approach meant that there could be no major compromises, but there were some who admitted minor failings. Robert Boreman admitted that 'in these tumultuous, disordered times, some dirt has gotten into our Fountaines, and mingled it selfe with our pure streams; but, what was ever in all Ages, we hope will not with aggravations be charged upon us, as the onely fault of ours'.[66] Joseph Sedgwick argued that justifiable criticisms could be countered if university authorities would 'maintain strictnesse of discipline, profitablenesse of study and reality of learning'.[67] Both Boreman and Sedgwick demonstrate the 'personalised' approach to university problems which was shared with so many thinkers of various types. Seth Ward, who disliked the ingrained attitudes of students and the gentry towards education, had only limited sympathy for traditional methods, but suppressed this feeling because he feared that even moderate and reasonable suggestions were a smokescreen for the destructive radical fringe.[68] On the main issues the defenders were intransigent, and sometimes evasive. Sedgwick, for example, pushed the questions of the Spirit's teaching and the value of languages into the background, and emphasised the need for national peace and unity; his claim that university degrees were a public witness to known and approved learning was ostentatiously blind to the reformers' complaints.[69] Edward Waterhouse's *Humble Apology* of 1653, a bigoted and élitist tract, reduced learning to the role of a guardian of social status, and simplified the debate to a choice between education and anarchy.[70] Yet in the context of contemporary beliefs, there was little more that could have been required of him; he and the other defenders were true to the most widely accepted attitudes towards the universities.

This study has not sought from these few selected examples to establish a new orthodoxy concerning the university debate during the Revolution, but merely to present one facet of the debate which has not been stressed. Although the Revolution ushered in a wave of new visions, many of the ideas expressed were traditional, but with a new opportunity for expression. Attitudes towards the universities were not yet ready to progress further; we should not blame revolutionary governments for doing 'so little'; they were consistent with the ideas of their age. Some of the reformers may have been correct in asserting that the universities were not doing enough for society as a whole, but they were doing all that was required of them within the traditional concepts of the social hierarchy. The reformers failed to produce clear and widely acceptable concepts of the university-in-society to challenge these orthodoxies, and until they did so there could be no accepted need for reform. Seventeenth century governments left the universities alone because they saw no need for social change; the universities guarded their independence to avoid being caught up in change of any sort. Their relative isolation from society prompted criticism, but also helped to shield them from its full effects.

Queens' College
Cambridge CB3 9ET

REFERENCES

1.   John Dury, *The Reformed School* (London, 1651), A3-4.

2.   M. R. James, *Social Problems and Policy during the Puritan Revolution, 1640-60* (London, 1930), chapter 7; C. Hill, *Change and Continuity in Seventeenth-Century England* (London, 1974), chapter 1; H. R. Trevor-Roper, *Religion, the Reformation and Social Change* (London, 1972), 237-293; T. C. Barnard, *Cromwellian Ireland* (Oxford, 1975), chapter 7; C.E. Whiting, *The University of Durham* (London, 1932), pp. 16-29; G. B. Tatham, *The Puritans in Power* (Cambridge, 1913), chapters 4 and 5; J. D. Twigg, 'The Parliamentary Visitation of the University of Cambridge, 1644-5', *English Historical Review* xcviii (1983), 513-528.

3.   M. H. Curtis, *Oxford and Cambridge in Transition* (Oxford, 1959), pp. 49-51.

4.   Margaret, Duchess of Newcastle, *The Life of the Duke of Newcastle* (London, 1915), p. 152.

5.   D. Cressy, *Education in Tudor and Stuart England* (London, 1975), p. 18; C. Wase, *Considerations concerning Free Schools as Settled in England* (Oxford, 1678), pp. 33-4.

6.   J. E. Stephens (ed), *Aubrey on Education* (London, 1972), p. 10; J. C. Davis, *Utopia and the Ideal Society* (Cambridge, 1981), p. 101.

7.   Cressy, 'Educational Opportunity in Tudor and Stuart England', *History of Education Quarterly* 16 (1976), pp. 303-6.

8.   C. Russell, *The Crisis of Parliaments* (Oxford, 1977) p. 269 and n.

9.   Edward Hyde, Earl of Clarendon, *Works* (London, 1751), pp. 313-333; T. Hobbes, *Works* (London, 1840), VI, pp.168, 192, 233, 236-7.

10.   *Life*, p. 153.

11.   Curtis, p. 172; there are countless examples in contemporary literature.

12.   C. H. Firth, *Cromwell's Army* (London, 1962), pp. 6-7.

13.   John Brinsley, *A Consolation for our Grammar Schools* (London, 1622), p. 8.

14.   I. Barrow, *Theological Works* (Oxford, 1818), III, pp. 69, 74; W. Fleetwood, *A Sermon Preached before the University of Cambridge in Kings-College Chapel* (Cambridge, 1689), pp. 20-2.

15.   Cambridge University Library, Guard Book CUR 11, 1.

16.   See footnote 2.

17.   James, pp. 321-2.

18.   C. Webster, *The Great Instauration* (London, 1975), p. 25; A. M. Quinton, *Francis Bacon* (Oxford, 1980), p. 74.

19.   H. Barrow, *Writings* (London, 1962), pp. 349-352; P. K. Christianson, *Reformers and Babylon* (Toronto, 1978), pp. 84-5.

20.   Webster, p. 19.

21.   S. How, *The Sufficiency of the Spirit's Teaching without Human Learning* (London, 1816), pp. 7, 12-14, 19-32; see Acts 17.15-34; 19.19; I Cor. 1.17; 2.10-14; 3.18-19; 8.1-2; Romans 1.22.

22.   Acts 2.1-4.

23.   How, pp. 38, 44, 45, 69.

24.   William Penn, *No Cross, No Crown* (London, 1930), pp. 96-8, 101-107; R. Schlatter, 'The Higher Learning in Puritan England', *Historical Magazine of the Protestant Episcopal Church*, 23 (1954), pp. 175-6.

25.   *A Motion Tending to the Publick Good* (London, 1642), *passim; Israel's Call to March out of Babylon* (London, 1646), p. 48.

26.   *The Reformed School* (London, 1651).

27.   H. Peters, *A Word for the Armie. And two words to the Kingdome* (London, 1647), p. 11.

28.   G. Winstanley, *The Law of Freedom and Other Writings* (London, 1973), pp. 361-5.

29.   His writings on the universities are best summarised in C. Webster, 'William Dell and the Idea of University', in M. Teich and R. Young, (eds.), *Changing Perspectives in the History of Science* (London, 1973), pp. 110-126.

30.   W. Dell, *A Plain and Necessary Confutation* (London, 1654), introduction, p. 24.

31.   *A Plain and Necessary Confutation; A Testimony from the Word against Divinity-Degrees in the University* (London, 1654); *The Testimony of Martin Luther upon the whole matter* (London, 1654).

32.   *The Right Reformation of Learning* (London, 1654), p. 29.

33.   *Ibid.*

34.   *Ibid*, pp. 29-30.

35.   C. Hill, 'The Radical Critics of Oxford and Cambridge in the 1650s', in J. W. Baldwin and R. A. Goldthwaite (eds), *Universities in Politics*, (London, 1972), p. 120.

36.   C. Hill, *The World Turned Upside Down* (London, 1975), pp. 41, 42, 59, 94; E. C. Walker, *William Dell, Master Puritan* (Cambridge, 1970), pp. 57-68, 104-6.

37.   W. Haller, *Tracts on Liberty in the Puritan Revolution* (Columbia, 1934), II, p. 53.

38.   R. Baxter, *The Autobiography of Richard Baxter* (London, 1974), p. 114.

39.   T. Hill, *The Trade of Truth Advanced* (London, 1642), pp. 42, 49-50; *The Militant Church Triumphant* (London, 1643), p. 23.

40.   *The Season for Englands Selfe-Reflection, and Advancing Templework* (London, 1644), p. 37; *The Right Separation Incouraged* (London, 1645), pp. 33-4.

41.   *The Good Old Way* (London, 1644), pp. 11, 36.

42.   *Ibid*, pp. 44-5.

43.   H. Palmer, *The Duty and Honour of Church-Restorers* (London, 1646), pp. 36-7, 44, 55; *The Necessity and Encouragement of utmost venturing for the Churches Help* (London, 1643), pp. 51-2, 54.

44.   A. Tuckney, *The Balme of Gilead* (London, 1643), p. 25.

45.   J. Arrowsmith, *Englands Eben-ezer* (London, 1643), dedication; *A Great Wonder in Heaven* (London, 1647), p. 40.

46.   R. Vines, *Caleb's Integrity* (London, 1643), p. 31; *The Happinesse of Israel* (London, 1645), p. 25.

47.   Palmer, *Duty*, pp. 13-14, 17, 37, 44-6, 55; he was one of the Assembly's assessors, see S.W. Carruthers, *The Everyday Work of the Westminster Assembly* (Philadelphia, 1943), p. 45.

48.   R. Cudworth, *A Sermon preached before the Honourable House of Commons* (Cambridge, 1879)), pp. 6, 7, 10.

49.   J. Milton, *Milton on Education*, ed. O. M. Ainsworth, (New Haven, 1928), p. 21.

50.   *Ibid*, pp. 53, 56-62.

51.   C. Hill, *Milton and the English Revolution* (London, 1977), pp. 93-115.

52.   Hill, p. 36; Ainsworth, p. 215.

53.   Ainsworth, pp. 55-8.
54.   J. Hall, *An Humble Motion to the Parliament of England* (Liverpool, 1953), p. 5.
55.   *Ibid*, pp. 29-31.
56.   *Ibid*, p. 17.
57.   *Ibid*, p. 27.
58.   *Ibid*, pp. 8, 14-16.
59.   J. Webster, *Academiarum Examen* (London, 1653), introduction.
60.   *Ibid*.
61.   *Ibid*, introduction, pp. 3, 91.
62.   *Ibid*, pp. 95-110, *passim*, 109.
63.   T. Hall, *Vindiciae Literarum* (London, 1654), p. 21; S. Ward, *Vindiciae Academiarum* (Oxford, 1654), pp. 6, 17.
64.   Ward, 3; R. Boreman, *The Triumph of Learning over Ignorance*, (London, 1653), p. 2.
65.   J. Sedgwick, *A Sermon preached at St Maries* (London, 1653), p. 12.
66.   Boreman, p. 13.
67.   Sedgwick, p. 15.
68.   Ward, p. 50.
69.   Sedgwick, pp. 2, 5, 7, 12, 25.
70.   E. Waterhouse, *An humble Apologie for Learning and Learned Men* (London, 1653), pp. 91, 188.

SCIENCE TEACHING AS A CAREER AT PADUA
IN THE EARLY EIGHTEENTH CENTURY:
THE CASE OF GIOVANNI POLENI

Brendan Dooley

Few members of eighteenth-century European university faculties had any illusions about the effectiveness of the instruction they imparted. In a report to the Venetian Republic's Riformatori of the University of Padua one law professor noted that the best aims of educational theory were too often perverted in practice:

> To the damage suffered by paternal economies one must add the distraction of the students themselves. They come to the university with the certainty of having to remain for four years. With this in mind, they just barely get to know the professors enough by sight to greet them on the street, while they do anything except those things which are conducive to study; and having formed this habit in the first year, they continue fatally till the last year of their degree, in which, overwhelmed like the foolish virgins of the gospel, without oil in their lamps, they run desperately to the professors with the inopportune, 'date nobis de olio vestro'.[1]

With such unenthusiastic students, it was not always the professors' fault if, at Padua, they were suspected of awarding degrees occasionally even to the local livestock ('si dottorono i bo').[2] Yet stipends at Padua and elsewhere were notoriously too low to recommend an academic career as a way to accumulate lands or country houses. Fortunately for the history of science and philosophy, there were other compensations for an unrewarding academic year. As another professor wrote, 'I've waited patiently to be relieved of the immense weight of my public lessons without enjoying myself by researching the most curious and most recondite operations of nature . . . now I return to look again at my old studies, ever widening their compass according to Nature's greatness and marvellousness'.[3] In mid-July the reopening of the University seemed far off indeed, and likewise the prospect of returning to rehash familiar arguments for students who, for the most part, wanted merely to obtain the social and economic advantages of a professional degree as painlessly as possible.

The professors who taught in European universities before the mid-eighteenth century are often forgotten in recent studies of the social function of universities. They do not seem to have played much part in determining significant changes in the patterns of student attendance at Oxford or in the universities of Castille.[4] They apparently had little to do with the developing strategies of recruitment in the French universities.[5] And they probably did little to enhance or to discourage the expectations of students in their choices of careers after their degrees at Oxford, Cambridge or Turin.[6] They may have had some role in questions regarding the addition of new subjects to the curriculum; but it was no doubt less important than that of the Italian bourgeois scholars who began to consider such subjects as suitable ornaments to a gentlemanly education or the English gentleman-scholars who began to consider them as suitable ornaments to their life in the country.[7] Even when they were directly affected by events within the university, as they were in Turin in 1720 when stricter competition was established for academic jobs, and again in Pisa in 1670, when their controversial scientific and philosophical positions were defended at the official level, their interests were soon forgotten as political issues arose which did not concern them.[8] Thus, professors seem to have had little or no concern for the university as an institution — or if they did, they expressed it in ways that have yet to be discovered.[9]

This neglect may be due at least in part to a lack of knowledge about what professors were doing in this period. Until recently, they have been studied only insofar as they published important work or made important discoveries while they happened to belong to university faculties. Thus, very little concerning the profession of teaching is to be found in the vast literature surrounding figures like Galileo, Vincenzo Viviani, Giovanni Alfonso Borelli, Marcello Malpighi, Giambattista Morgagni, and so forth. Those of them who published less important work or none at all, like Francesco Maria Grimaldi and Fabrizio Bartoletti at Bologna, innumerable professors before the arrival of Spallanzani at Pavia, and Francesco Garro at Turin, have been studied because their discipline, on the whole, seemed to have maintained a high standard of performance over a long period of time and because they are considered to have provided some sort of link between their more illustrious predecessors and successors within a particular university 'tradition'.[10] Relatively rarely, and almost never in Italy, they have been studied as bearers of particular strands of, for example, Newtonian thought, whose development cannot be studied in detail by recourse to the printed sources.[11] More often, they have been studied merely because they happened to form part of, say, the Universities of Parma, Pisa or

Turin, in a given epoch.[12] The most detailed treatment many professors from the Collegio Romano and the Universities of Jena, Modena, Rome, Bologna, Ferrara, Uppsala, and Mainz have got has been in the appropriate chapter of a 'university history'.[13]

Yet this view of the role of the professors does not fully do justice to the role they envisaged for themselves. The most recent research on Transalpine universities indicates that many professors took their teaching role so seriously that they attempted to convey to their students a body of knowledge that was constantly growing and changing. In the French *collèges* and universities and in the Academy of Geneva, they let Descartes' philosophy influence liberal arts instruction.[14] At the University of Paris, they adopted new analytical methods in mathematics, and at Basel, new experimental methods.[15] At Cambridge, they encouraged the selection of Newtonian topics for student disputations.[16] At Leiden and Halle, they introduced Newton's ideas into scientific instruction.[17] The situation in Italy may have been similar. At Pisa, professors let Galileo's physics creep into philosophical instruction in the early seventeenth century.[18] At Bologna, they are thought to have spoken, albeit 'modestly', about their own findings in medical instruction in the late seventeenth century.[19] At Padua, they taught the mechanical philosophy with such conviction that one of them was examined in 1689 by the local Inquisition.[20] At Turin, they introduced the Cartesian system into the teaching of physics in the early eighteenth century.[21]

The professors' conception of their role differed considerably from the role prescribed for them in the university statutes. In Italy, the statutes obliged them to convey a clearly defined and unchanging body of knowledge by infusing their students with a standard group of classical texts with the conventional commentaries.[22] Most of the statutes dated from the sixteenth century or before, but the same notion appeared in the most recent compilations. For instance, according to Nicolo Comneno Papadopoli's *Historia Gymnasii Patavini*, published in 1726, the list of 'interpretationes praescriptae' included practically the same texts that had been authoritative here and elsewhere at least a hundred years previously.[23] Judging by the more detailed information published yearly in the Paduan official rolls in the early eighteenth century, professors in the 'university of law' were still supposed to teach Gratian's *Decretum* and various selections from Justinian's *Corpus juris civilis*.[24] Professors in the 'university of arts' — the other half of the Italian two-faculty arrangement — were assigned similarly precise duties. Professors of medical theory taught a three-year course comprising Hippocrates' *Aphorisms*, Galen's *Methodus medendi*, and various treatises from

Avicenna's *Canon*. The four philosophy professors taught a three-year course combining elements from Aristotle's *De Anima* I, II, and III, *Physics* I, II, and 8, *On Generation and Corruption*, and *De Caelo*. The logic professors were enjoined to stick to Aristotle's *Posterior Analytics*. The astronomy professor taught Aristotle's *Meteorology*, I-III — a three-year course. The mathematics professor was supposed to teach Euclid's *Elements*. And the humanities professor was supposed to teach Aristotle's *Poetics* and a selection of Roman historians, poets and satirists. All professors were obliged to read — or recite from memory — four or five hour-long lessons per week for five months and to follow these with formal 'private' lessons in which they explained or elaborated upon the more difficult points raised.[25] Twice yearly they were supposed to give public disputations to show students how the material presented in class could be manipulated according to a set of rules. If they could find no one else to do so, they had to provide their own counter arguments or else pay a fine. All through May they were expected to sit exams designed to test students' mastery of passages chosen at random from the standard texts and of the standard formulae for explaining them. Professors of medicine, in particular, were required to demonstrate how the sum of knowledge they transmitted could be used practically by curing sick students (if not plague-infected) and to participate 'ad honorandum funus' if they failed.

Developments within the traditional disciplines did little to influence professors' changing conceptions of their role. The traditional texts in which the Italian universities guaranteed mastery were still, in the eighteenth century, considered essential for success in certain fields. In the Veneto, for example, Roman law held its ground in spite of the tradition of vernacular legal practice and the preference of many patrician administrators for the less comprehensive *ius venetum*.[26] Its authority here and elsewhere was nowhere better demonstrated than in the lively opposition to Lodovico Antonio Muratori's call for codification to restructure the old relationship between statute and common law (*Difetti della giurisprudenza*, Venice: 1742).[27] All over Italy, Galen and Hippocrates remained authoritative in medicine mainly because no one could agree on anything else as a legitimate basis for the examination and licensing of physicians. The possible alternatives, from Paracelsus to Van Helmont to Giorgio Baglivi, were impugned by many on theoretical as well as metaphysical grounds. Indeed, the universities themselves were the battlefields upon which vitalists, mechanists, and those belonging to the various intermediate hues fought for control of education.[28] The story told by Malpighi about the solemn burning of his house by those who disagreed with the conclusions he drew from his microbiological observations may have been his own invention. But Morgagni's move to the University of Padua to escape his 'Galenist' adversaries in Bologna was no myth.[29] So sharp was the disagreement that Giovanni Maria Bicetti, the proponent of immunisation, observed in 1765, 'all the harmful prejudices that society has regarding health are nothing but the products of the opinions of the doctors'.[30] The professors themselves occasionally resorted to miracle drugs in spite of statutory fulminations against these practices — as in the case of Alessandro Knips Maccope at Padua, who earned such a reputation by his use of mercury in the early eighteenth century that patients came to his studio from all over Europe 'as to the altar of Æsculapius'.[31] Since the best way to cure disease was often better arrived at by forgetting the theory for a moment and using pure good sense and intuition, most professors — 'ancient' and 'modern' alike — agreed that Galen and Hippocrates were at least not a useless foundation upon which to build solid medical knowledge.

The push for teaching innovation did not come from the students, since they had plenty of enticements for entering one of the fields in which the old teaching was still appropriate. Law students, who consistently made up 65% of the total registered at Padua, could count on the ever-increasing litigiosity by which, according to Gaetano Cozzi, the Venetian population seemed to express itself most characteristically in the seventeenth and eighteenth centuries.[32] Medical students, who consistently made up the other 35%, could count on the imminent danger of smallpox and other contagious diseases and — at least according to Giovanni Battista Davini, one of Vallisnieri's correspondents — the widespread decrepitude among the noble inmates of the Republic's crowded nunneries to keep them busy medicating.[33] They would thus contribute to what Morgagni termed 'the enormous crowd of surgeons that you see in every corner of this state'.[34] So overwhelming, indeed, was the percentage of students who prepared for the most lucrative lay professions that laureates in theology and philosophy are virtually untraceable in the documents. Theology students could count on the prospects of abundant easy jobs in the Church before the late eighteenth century waves of expropriations and the Josephine ecclesiastical reforms began a new period in its history.[35] But they were wasting their time if they attended the university since the best jobs required important family connections and most of the rest required no degree. Philosophy students could hope for one of the few possible university positions, but this was rarely considered to be a reasonable expectation. 'In so many hundreds of students, that I have had', lamented Antonio Vallisnieri, eighteenth century naturalist at Padua, after thirty years of teaching, 'I have not yet been able to train a single disciple that loved natural history or desired to write correct Italian prose . . . '. Instead, 'they all hanker after base profit'.[36]

Indeed, students were so uninterested in university teaching that they often allowed personal and practical concerns to govern the way in which they obtained their professional preparation. They tried to reduce studying to a minimum in order to save time for more earnings. As Gozzi observed, 'They would all start medicating or enter the forum with no other study except a few years of awkward practice, exalted by them above any doctrine, if the Most Excellent Senate had not decreed that noone who had not graduated from Padua could exercise these trades'.[37] And they tried to reduce their residence in Padua to a minimum in order to save money spent on room, board, and clothing for the changing seasons. After registration, many of them immediately went home to brush up, with the help of private tutors, on the texts that everyone knew would be covered on the exam. Sometimes the only listeners at the lessons were, as Cancelliere Bortolo Sellari reported in 1723, 'a few Greeks, [and] the others are nothing but the friends of the Public Professors'.[38] All the Senate could do in these circumstances was to publish decree after decree threatening ruinous penalties for any subject who dared to exercise his profession without the statutory preparation at the University of Padua.[39]

Far more important than student demand in changing the conception of official academic roles was government policy. Formed initially during the sixteenth century, the official attitude of Italian governments to universities was based on a conviction that education could serve useful political purposes if only it would begin to reflect some of the most recent conquests of humanistic thought.[40] But after the first chairs of botany, humanities, and anatomy were set up and the first gardens of simples were established, very little else was done to make sure university teaching would develop and change with the changing knowledge of the professors who imparted it. Finally in the late-seventeenth and early-eighteenth century, governments renewed their interest in university reform in order to produce functionaries for ever-growing state administrations in Tuscany, Lombardy, and the Papal States;[41] for excluding ecclesiastics from non-Church professions in Sicily;[42] for rationalising disorganised educational systems in the Este territories;[43] and for undermining the control of the urban guilds and corporations in Naples and Bologna.[44] The addition of new chairs like the chair of Algebra at the University of Bologna (1708) for the teaching of Cartesian and Leibnizian methods and the chair of Experimental Philosophy at the University of Turin

(1720) for the teaching of the new science began the slow process of once again making the statutes reflect changing views of the academic profession.

Even before they began to overhaul the statutes, Italian governments influenced the definition of academic roles by their hiring policies. Instead of selecting candidates on the basis of some expectation regarding possible contributions to the teaching of the traditional disciplines, they allowed other criteria to dominate. True, in some of the less important universities, candidates were selected according to the same social criteria used in German universities — for example, in Siena, where most professors belonged to the local aristocracy that dominated the city council.[45] But most of the time, candidates' scientific interests were the first things taken into account. In medicine, professors interested primarily in auxiliary fields such as zoology, microbiology, embriology, and the like could aspire to the two highest-prestige posts in the university: the first chairs of practical and theoretical medicine. The Riformatori sometimes had to ask their representatives if the candidate under consideration — in one instance, Johann Jacob Scheuchzer, naturalist at Basel — had ever had any interest in healing at all.[46] Likewise candidates with real interests in medical fields were often hired for chairs that were not medical, but which could be stepping-stones to the higher chairs — like Morgagni, who was almost resigned to accepting a chair in philosophy several months before his appointment to one in anatomy.[47] In fields such as mathematics, astronomy, botany, chemistry, and others that had worked their way in to the university curriculum generally by way of medicine and that, over time, had acquired a prestige all of their own, the divergence between the recognised capacities of the professors and the interests of the students was likely to be even greater. Galileo's curiosity about astrology, a study physicians could not afford to neglect because of the important effect the planets had on bodily humours, had less to do with his selection for a chair in mathematics at Pisa in 1589 than his important lectures at the Florentine Academy.[48] And when astronomy was finally separated from mathematics at Padua with the appointment of Geminiano Montanari in 1678, this was more in consideration of developments within these two disciplines than of the possible medical uses of one or the other.[49] Later, Giovanni Poleni was appointed to teach astronomy at Padua on the basis of a book containing his descriptions of experiments with the barometer and of his new calculating machine — nothing to do with medicine.[50] The work of Borelli and Lorenzo Bellini establishing the usefulness of mathematics in the study of physiology did nothing to influence the criteria by which mathematics professors were chosen.

At Padua, they continued to be hired in part because of the technical needs of the Venetian Republic. Thus, Jacob Hermann, in recommending Nicolas Bernoulli of the famous Basle mathematical family, was careful to emphasise the candidate's 'ability in hydraulic architecture, which he learned in Holland, so that he will be able to serve the public usefully in this important faculty'.[51] And the most important criterion for choices in all fields remained the candidate's participation in European discussions about their specialty and their contribution of significant work to its literature. Therefore, the Venetian Resident in London, informed about the vacant chair of Botany at Padua in 1718, 'spoke about the matter with Signor Cavaliere Newton'.[52] It took Newton's insistence, on the basis of his conversations with Dr. Hans Sloane, that 'this subject is particularly studied in Italy' for the choice to fall eventually on an Italian.

Likewise, government criteria for promotion within the university hierarchy had little to do with professors' success in teaching the traditional materials. At worst, promotions were awarded on the basis of favouritism, as in the case of Nicolo Calliachi, the well-paid professor of Belle Lettere at Padua who had privately tutored a senator; or else they were awarded on the basis of seniority, as in the case of Michelangelo Molinetto, Professor of Anatomy at Padua, who wrote practically nothing and was so unpopular that he sometimes had only one student a year.[53] At best, promotions were awarded on the basis of the same kinds of criteria that contributed to professors having been hired in the first place. Morgagni finished his career with a stipend of over 2000 ducats a year because of the productiveness of the relationship he had established with Albrecht von Haller, Athanasius Kircher and other important Transalpine scholars, because of the fame of his *Adversaria anatomia* (Bologna, 1706 - Padua, 1719), a treatise revising Vesalius and Fabricius ab Aquapendente, and because of the usefulness of his *De sedibus* (Venice, 1761), the first systematic work on pathology written in the eighteenth century.

The development of standards for measuring professional prestige may also have contributed to the changing views of academic teaching. More important than traditional official duties in determining status among professional colleagues was the professors' membership in learned societies. Thus, when there were no such societies in town, they got busy erecting them on the model of the Royal Society, formed by professors from Gresham College and Oxford. Professors from the University of Naples formed the Accademia delle Scienze, and professors from the University of Padua formed the Academia Patavina.[54] When the professors already belonged to these, they tried to become members of all the others. They even lumped literary societies in with learned ones to make their credentials look more impressive. Morgagni, for example, could claim membership in no less than eleven if he included the Royal Society of London, the Academie Royale des Sciences of Paris, the Academia Naturae Curiosorum of Schweinfurt, the Academia Scientiarum of St. Petersburg, the Ricovrati of Padua, the Inquieti of Bologna, the Arcadi of Rome, the Filergiti and the Icneurici of Forlì, the Fisiocritici of Siena, and the Filomati of Cesena.[55] Prestige was also determined by their ability to keep abreast of the debates carried on and the discoveries made outside their own countries. As Morgagni observed to Vallisnieri, 'You have to find out, before writing, whether the things were said before, mainly by reading the most famous journals — which, if I had not done it, oh! how many more things I would have put in the first part of my *Adversaria* as having been discovered by me!'[56] In Italy, their task was not often easy. Journals arrived late and got tied up for months in customs. Good bibliographical information was so hard to get and so highly prized that Antonio Magliabechi neglected everything else including his personal hygiene in an earnest effort to provide it to his numerous academic correspondents at the end of the seventeenth century; Giovanni Cinelli Calvoli became so thoughtless that he landed in jail while trying to provide it to the subscribers to his *Scanzie* (1677-1706).[57] Most of all, the professors' status in their disciplines was determined by their ability to ensure that their own contributions were conspicuous enough to be noticed. Sometimes the best way to do this when there was no good journal within easy reach was to start one up. Thus, Giovanni Ciampini of the Collegio Romano and Francesco Nazari of the 'Sapienza' of Rome began the *Giornale dei letterati* (1668-83), and Vallisnieri and colleagues at Padua helped the printer Girolamo Albrizzi compile the *Galleria di Minerva* (1696-1717).[58] When they could no longer trust these journals to publish regularly and to distribute widely, they started new and better-organised ones like the *Giornale de' letterati d'Italia* (1710) of Vallisnieri, Poleni, Morgagni, and their coordinator, Apostolo Zeno.[59]

Indeed, official duties seemed to interfere with all the pursuits that many professors considered to be stimulating and essential. Such duties took time away from the difficult work of preparing a few good disciples so that, like Montanari and Sebastiano Melli, they could surround themselves with a private academy of dedicated specialists.[60] They also impeded them from impressing their own views on the scientific and philosophical content of the university so that, like Lorenzo Bellini, medical professor at Pisa, they could, 'see the university each year more filled with my dependents, without my even saying anything, and now the principal chairs of practical and theoretical medicine are filled, with universal approval, by my scholars; likewise also the chairs of Simples, Logic, and Philosophy'.[61] They diverted their attention away from attainment of such a level of philosophical beatitude that they 'could not find [themselves] in any kind of circumstances, however strange, in which [they] should not find a huge wealth of things that could keep [them] always supplied with new, unusual, extraordinary, and immense knowledge, of uncountable value'. But worst of all, they got in the way of their obtaining a social position in which 'no one can detract from our well-being, our fame, and our noble satisfactions'. This was just as important in provincial centres like Padua, Pisa, and Bologna, where local politics had been reduced to pointless bickering, as it was in Rome, where family interest outweighed most other considerations in the constitution of the state bureaucracy.[62] When self-expression through political channels was a reasonable aspiration only for small traditional groups, the universities provided an institutional framework in which to realise alternative ones.[63]

To integrate official duties with other professional activities was no easy matter. Therefore, sometimes professors made no serious attempt to do so. Galileo, it is supposed, did not bother to stray too far from the texts assigned him in mathematics while he gazed at the heavens in his spare time; and Malpighi taught generations of young physicians about the mysteries of the human body while he stole every possible minute to look at chicken eggs.[64] Yet, when they attempted to go beyond the traditional texts, the necessity to reduce complex materials to a few essential points for the benefit of listeners with other interests sometimes rendered the difference with their own research as dramatic as it would have been if they had taught undiluted Galen and Hippocrates. Thus, Vallisnieri, explaining to medical students the most advanced seventeenth century preformationism in the generation of animals, began by warning them not to be fooled by the tiny dimensions of human genitalia: 'we are large with respect to eggs, or dogs, larger with respect to pigeons . . . while we are small with respect to elephants and whales . . . '.[65] The spheres of professional activity that took place inside and outside the classroom seemed to have little in common. Many professors resolved the contradiction in favour of their research. For them, the four-to-five month summer vacation suspending official duties that seldom varied from year to year and presenting the opportunity for enjoying what they considered to be the real pleasures of the academic profession must have seemed indeed a respite.

Some professors made serious attempts to resolve the contradiction between contemporary science and traditional teaching. One way was to bring personal research into the classroom. This did not always meet with the approval of the students. Geminiano Montanari was so uncompromising in his delivery that, of the 20 students who began the course, 'there are no more than two who pass the second book of Aristotle's *Meteorology* without leaving me'.[66] A better way was to inspire the respect of the students by assiduous performance. Morgagni risked his life by doing far more dissections for his students than the availability of disease-free cadavers should have permitted.[67] The best way of all was to use every available methodological variation in order to inculcate successfully in the students a love of science that would lead to formulation of independent conclusions about the most important questions. The professors' motivations in adopting this time-consuming approach probably ranged from the vain-glorious desire to impress whichever visiting experts might wander by the classroom to the patriotic desire to offer technical preparation to their state at the very highest level or even the altruistic desire to remove every obstacle from their students' fruitful exploitation of a few brief years of study. Usually these teaching drudges were easily recognisable by the few works they published and the enthusiastic reports they nevertheless left behind them — like Giuseppe Roma of the University of Turin, who so astounded his listeners by the effectiveness of his teaching of physics that an informer to the Roman Inquisition exclaimed in a report, 'He doesn't want to recognise the dangerous things he impresses upon the minds of the young'.[68] A few of them managed to combine education — both of the public at large and of a few advanced students — with voluminous scientific publication in an effort to expand the traditional limits upon the definition of their profession.

Giovanni Poleni, who taught at Padua from 1709 to his death in 1762, belongs to this last category. He is now almost exclusively remembered for his contributions to mechanics and its applications; he had a key role in the development of hydrostatics, kinetics, the stress principles of structural design and the editing of scientific texts.[69] In his own century he was also remembered as a great teacher, whose most brilliant student, Vitalino Donati, attained 'international importance' in a professorship at Turin.[70] During his own lifetime he was regarded by the Venetian government's Savi alle Acque as their precious consultant on all engineering questions dealing with the lagoon. By association with them he acquired their habit of saving every scrap of paper that had anything to do with official duties. Since he conceived of his profession of university professor as constituting an official duty resembling his others, he became a far more careful archivist of his personal papers than many contemporaries surer than he of having made an immortal contribution to learning. Among the things he kept, which also included thirty-odd volumes of personal correspondence and several unpublished treatises on subjects ranging from optics to moral philosophy, were several fascicles of his daily university lessons.[71] Annotated, apparently, up until the last moment before delivery, full of bibliographical indications and illustrated by sketches for visual aids, this documentation chronicles a long career dedicated to communicating an important message to undergraduates.

Poleni did not begin his career at Padua with much personal experience of what university teaching should be like. Yet he was fortunate to have received some of the best alternative education available to Venetian citizens in his period — at the Collegio alla Salute maintained by the Clerks Regular of Somaschi under the auspices of the Riformatori dello Studio.[72] And he was still more fortunate to have had as his tutor — with the close personal relationship characteristic of Somaschi pedagogy — one of the most learned members of the order in Venice: Francesco Caro, author of a five-volume compendium of lessons entitled *Philosophia amphisica ex Aristotelis Democratique mente illustrata* (Venice, 1695).[73] Since Caro's ambition was to ensure 'that my students should come regularly to school',[74] by promising them lessons in which their attention was to be rewarded by exciting discoveries, Poleni did not just copy down an exposition of the adulterated Aristotelianism that this work's curious title seemed to announce. He did not even really learn the unusual mixture of modern authors to whose doctrines Caro, later on in the text, claimed chiefly to adhere ('in logic, Bacon; in physics, Gassendi; Tycho in Astronomy; Galileo on motion; Boyle in experiments; Kircher in mechanics, Cabeo on meteors'[75]). Instead, he learned a complex syncretism. The structure of matter was explained atomistically. Indeed, his teacher was so determined to put across Gassendi's message that even the examples for types of syllogism were drawn from chemistry: 'every mixed body is made of atoms; every flower is a mixed body; therefore, every flower is made of atoms'.[76] Boyle's experiments with pumps and bell jars were apparently performed to prove the existence of some kind of vacuum. Yet the argument against occult qualities drew unexpected support from Descartes' *Dioptrique*. 'I will follow whatever reason, experiment, and truth suggest', proclaimed Caro.[77] Poleni's oft-repeated admonitions to his students against accepting untested hypothesis and his unwillingness to adhere faithfully to any one system may have been inspired by this education. During the course of his studies at the Somaschi college, Poleni changed his mind about going into law or theology. Since these were the only fields of practice besides medicine for which the government required a degree at Padua he was thus freed from the obligation of university attendance. And instead of seeking instruction in physics and other scientific subjects from the important professors in Padua around 1703 — Domenico Guglielmini, Michelangelo Fardella, Antonio Vallisnieri and others — the twenty-year-old college graduate turned to the science instruction available among the various religious orders in Venice. This choice did not promise to slip him into his life profession in the usual way, but it did promise to give him an opportunity to demonstrate his virtuosity within the intimate patrician circles that could prove useful to him later. And most of all, it promised him the only kind of solid training in experimental philosophy available locally.

Accordingly, he attended the 'school' of Tommaso Pio Maffei, a Neapolitan Dominican friar resident at SS. Giovanni e Paolo in Venice.[78] Maffei, after having been considered for a post in theology at Padua and dropped as a candidate because of his advanced opinions, had been invited finally to Venice by his Order in the 1690's on the recommendation of certain of the more inquisitive members of the patriciate. Since the Senate looked askance at extrauniversity cultural organisations, he was never encouraged to form a formal scientific academy on the model of the Cimento of Florence, the Investiganti of Naples, or the Inquieti of Bologna.[79] Instead, he held his demonstrations and gave his discourses in the noble household of the Duodo family and in his convent. With 'students' like Bernardino Zendrini, later Senate engineer, Bernardo Trevisan, noble virtuoso, and Antonio Conti, future acquaintance of Newton and Voltaire, his meetings may have produced much useful collaboration. According to Conti's recollection, he repeated many of Giovanni Battista Riccioli's experiments for measuring the speed and force of falling bodies and even invented a simple didactic device involving a pole marked off in degrees from which various weights could be dropped at different heights.[80] His convictions about the importance of demonstrations in science pedagogy were so profound that he never cared to divulge his voluminous systematic treatises on philosophy and physics. Only two small works Conti published for him posthumously remain (*De usu mathesos in theologicis et diversa circa principium universale staticum Galilei et Cartesii sententia dissertationes duae*[81]) for testing Giannantonio Moschini's assertion that he 'dispelled the gloom of the cloister' by his teaching.[82] To Poleni's education he may have contributed something about the methods for quantifying experimental results.

When Poleni left the protected environment of this private, individual instruction to teach in the University in 1709, he was by no means confident about his ability to dazzle a public accustomed to spectacular shows of oratorical prowess. He must have found some consolation when he heard the blunders of the worst professors during the forty-day circuit of all law and arts classrooms that the Riformatori required of him as a new member of the university community.[83] But his overall impression probably confirmed Morgagni's observation that 'Padua is an extremely difficult city'.[84] In his first audience he no doubt saw some of the six professors who would examine him within the usual two years to determine his worthiness of a real academic title. He knew that he might actually have to attend some lessons more than once — unlike colleagues educated in universities — in order to perform in a fashion commensurate with his stature by seizing all the possible nuances in his interpretation of the philosophy question from Aristotle's *De anima* and the medical question from Hippocrates' *Aphorisms* foreseeable in cases of a double degree.[85] He therefore admitted to his listeners, before proceeding to the subject of his prolusion, that 'there is so much reason to be afraid that my internal turmoil will appear not only in my face but also in my voice'.[86]

He made sure, as he proceeded in this first lesson, that whatever unfavourable impression his faltering delivery might have made was amply counterbalanced by his novel exposition. He did not even mention the first book of the *Meteorology* that the *rotulo* stated should be the basis of his lessons. And he left no doubt that 'superlunary' and 'sublunary' phenomena would be treated as observable data from which the properties of matter and the forces in nature could be deduced rather than as effects of eternal celestial motion that the interaction of the four elements could explain. He praised the wisdom of the Riformatori who had united the fields of astronomy and meteorology under a single professor because of the probability that the study of terrestrial meteorological phenomena could aid in speculations about the atmospheres on the many other possible worlds in the universe — 'according to observations, the supposition that every star is surrounded by an atmosphere no different from our earth is shown to be the most reasonable'[87] — and not because of any supposed communication between the spheres. Finally, he showed how the most recent geometrical analysis would be used in his course by assuring his audience that his discussion of comets would follow Newton, 'who by the admirable eloquence of his sublime genius so diligently emptied the material of the celestial spaces',[88] and not the popular Cartesian hypothesis. He did not promise a scandal, which was what many members of his audience always hoped for from the astronomy professor. But he assured them that he would explain the heavens at least as well as his cautious predecessors — from Andrea Argoli to Stefano Degli Angeli to Montanari[89] — by making the usual political allusion to the condemnation of Galileo and then positing a moving earth ('Let us pretend the earth moves . . . ').

By 1714-15, his last year in the lectureship of Astronomy and Meteorology, the cycle of lessons had passed through the next two books of Aristotle's *Meteorology* and through a two-year course called 'astronomiae rudimenta' and had come around again to the first book. After an opening oration composed for the occasion and containing the usual comparison of ancient and modern ideas, he merely threw together everything he had on hand from the previous four years and taught from his notes.[90] He divided the course in the customary way, basing himself loosely on the Aristotelian text but taking into account Aristotle's error in considering comets to be meteorological effects rather than heavenly bodies. He therefore did not worry about repeating some of the material he had already covered in the course on the rudiments of astronomy any more than he did about anticipating some of the material he would cover the following year when, as second-chair Professor of Philosophy, he would be asked to explicate the *De caelo*. His topics and the way in which he taught them were dictated more by his own preferences, the university's facilities, and his students' limited capacities than by the structure of the traditional programme.

He found himself somewhat inhibited in teaching the section on astronomy. This was not because he was no expert. With one of the world's great telescopes easily accessible at Palazzo Correr in Padua — constructed under Montanari's guidance well before John Flamsteed conceived the Royal Observatory at Greenwich[91] — Poleni had had little trouble in continuing the university's long tradition of original astronomical observations. He became so polished, in fact, that he even communicated them from time to time to Daniel Bernoulli, an undisputed expert in mathematical matters.[92] But his research was not easily reducible to a form well adapted to eighteenth-century university conditions, where most of his students possessed no more than the rudiments of geometry, where the program was so constructed that he had to make allowances for a large percentage of first-year students every year, and where his only visual aids were a blackboard ('pietra nera', as he called it)[93] and some chalk. Therefore, he was probably not surprised to find that the Riformatori regarded excellence in practical astronomy as a useful addition to a scientific career but were so uncertain of its place among official activities that they waited until 1767 to build a university observatory. And when he taught astronomy he did not furnish his lessons with a sophisticated set of personal observations.

Instead of overburdening his students with an unfamiliar technical apparatus, he preferred to introduce them to the study of astronomy by way of those aspects of it for which the usual texts in ethics, rhetoric, and geography were still sufficient preparation.[94] Explaining the objects of the discipline as celestial events that occurred through time in a way analogous to the political changes observable in civil history, he showed his students how to become intelligent amateurs in the science of chronology. In his lessons on comets he implied that some heavenly bodies seemed indeed to have a determinable lifespan like men since their appearance and disappearance could be accounted for. In the lessons on astrology he showed how many changes went on in the heavens while mankind recorded a single year. He knew that the search for points of contact between terrestrial and celestial events had led to bitter controversies about the age and origins of the human race with theological implications that were probably better to avoid in the classroom. The debates between Georg Horn and Isaac Voss in the seventeenth century were being continued by Jacob Fay and John Toland in his own day: 'indeed, there is so much dissent between the most famous authors', he told his students, 'That it is impossible to choose between them'.[95] So instead of mentioning the birth date of Moses or bringing up the widely believed antiquity of the Chinese, he took Claude François Dechales' advice and pointed out that the Egyptian system of dating was so completely incompatible with the Christian one that it was impossible to find out when their empire began.[96] Then, beginning with a hypothetical first year of the reign of Nebuchadrezzar I, the Babylonian king who conquered Elam, he divided time roughly into the familiar categories of Egyptian, Greek, Roman, and modern history with appropriate references to Joseph Scaliger, Johannes Kepler, Johannes Hevelius, Stanislas Lubienski, and others who had used astronomical observations as one of the tools for chronological research.[97]

He insisted that the parallel between cosmological history and human history went beyond the mere contemporaneous unfolding of separate stories. Unusual celestial events seemed to occur in relation to historical ones, like the comets that coincided with the birth of Alexander the Great, with the Roman conquest of Egypt, and with the death of Pope Innocent VIII.[98] The story of man and the story of the heavens seemed inseparably intertwined. Therefore it was of vital importance to all that an accurate description of the cosmos should be obtained. He showed how this had been made possible by the discovery of a method of basing oneself, on the one hand, on the theorems of geometry and arithmetic and, on the other, of those of optics.[99] He showed the part played by improvements in scientific instruments, using Galileo's remarks on the phases and apparent changes in size of Venus and Mars in *Dialogo* III. In his only visual demonstration in this section, he covered the blackboard with diagrams drawn from André Tacquet's elementary astronomy manual to show how the exact positions of the heavenly bodies could be determined by parallax.[100] After mentioning discoveries made in his own day, including Borelli's and Cassini's explanations for the behaviour of comets, he proceeded to the causes for the forces in nature. Dividing his argument into the scholastic quadruple scheme he considered appropriate to metaphysical discourse, he explained that the formal and material (secondary) causes for the generation of the celestial bodies were light, heat, and stellar matter. The efficient and final (primary) causes reposed in God, who 'by his infinite wisdom so organised this machine of nature that the secondary causes proceed from the primary causes', and who demonstrated his will to man by the unpredictable celestial events attested by the Psalmist in Psalm 115.[101]

Since the section on meteorology lent itself to an entirely different methodology, he virtually threw himself into teaching it. The philosophical content was difficult and complicated, involving the structure of matter, the doctrine of the elements, and the properties of water and air. But the material he wished to teach was based on observations that did not always require equipment that was too bulky to bring into class or time period that were too long for the class schedule. He had plenty of glass apparatus and pumps on hand, and what he did not have he was in the habit of borrowing from his friend Christian Martinelli, the new keeper of the observatory in Palazzo Correr. He had used them in experiments conducted at home with Morgagni while building his early reputation at Padua and in work he published in his *Miscellanea* (1709), in the *Giornale de' letterati d'Italia* (vol. 5, 1711), and in the two major treatises on hydrostatics that he was preparing for publication within the next three years (*De motu aquae mixtae*, 1717, and *De castellis*, 1718).[102] Whether or not he actually showed students some of his equipment and, as seems probable, performed some simple experiments in class, his expressions of the effectiveness of a good demonstration as a didactic tool were enthusiastic and frequent. For example, in regard to one series of experiments he exclaimed, 'without any other aid, they suffice to establish certain laws about the nature of the air'.[103] The descriptions he gave were so detailed and so well illustrated by diagrams both on the blackboard and in his handouts that students must have felt as though they had been in a real laboratory even when they had never left the lecture hall.[104]

He chose experiments that demonstrated some of the most important scientific discoveries of the seventeenth century, concentrating particularly on pneumatics. He explained the Torricelli experiment and showed how it could be used to prove the error in Galileo's conception of the air as a substance with little weight and no pressure.[105] He showed how it could be varied by using different lengths of tube to prove that the suspension of the liquid was caused not by a sucking power from within but by external conditions.[106] He suggested other variation to demonstrate the error of Pascal and Borelli, who thought humid air to be heavier than dry air. He showed how experiments with capillary tubes done by the Accademia del Cimento and by Robert Boyle could be repeated. He suggested variations to prove that the rise of water in these tubes was due to viscosity and not to the supposed difference, alleged by Honoré Fabri, between the quantity of air pressing upon the cistern and the quantity of air that could squeeze in a the tube's upper opening. He recounted Otto von Guericke's invention of the air pump and the improvements made upon it by Boyle and Hooke.[107] He drew a diagram of a cross section showing how the simplest models functioned. He suggested various experiments for demonstrating the elasticity of air and eliminating the Aristotelian idea of the *horror vacui* — at least in the absolute sense no longer tenable in contemporary physics. He showed the air thermoscope explored by Galileo and Santorio Santorio, encouraging students to discover for themselves why *experientia repugnat* any other hypothesis for explaining the fall or rise of the liquid than the communication of heat or cold in the surrounding atmosphere to the air in the bulb.[108] Even students with no interest whatsoever in becoming great scientists must have found both enjoyment and instruction in seeing this popularised experimental philosophy at work.

His purpose in these demonstrations was not, however, to insist upon a set of dull, unadventurous and possibly commonplace conclusions. He knew that by the second decade of the eighteenth century many basic ideas about the air could already be considered as unassailable conquests of experimental physics and the glass industry. As the editors of the *Journal de Trévoux* had remarked in 1710 in regard to Christian Wolff's *Aerometria* (1709), 'if anyone still doubts that the air is heavy, can be compressed, and expands, and what effects proceed from this weight and these properties, it is his own fault'. When contemporary research, such as that of Francis Hauksbee and Philippe de La Hire and contemporary attempts at synthesis such as that of Newton (*Opticks*, Query 31) reached back to these experiments, it was not to reinforce the conclusions of Torricelli, Boyle and Mariotte. Rather, it was to find in them some hint or sign that could lead to the discovery of the laws of hydrostatics and the kinetic properties of gasses that seemed to elude even the most careful investigation.[109] In a basic physics course, where there was no reason to assume that students had already acquired the intellectual matrix into which an intense program uf up-to-date demonstrations could be situated, this kind of analysis was not easy to communicate. Therefore, Poleni did not risk confusing the issues by making observations about the important refinements that were being made on the old instruments — from Guillaume Amonton's closed barometer to Hauksbee's tube-strewn tables — to permit their use under more rigorous experimental conditions.[110] Instead of broadening the technical or practical foundations of his course, he tried to show his class demonstrations contributed to a broad understanding of natural philosophy. He accompanied his lectures with synopses of various theories, indicating which ones he preferred and offering his own when he couldn't find one that suited him. He did not merely dictate to them a collection of selections from books they could easily consult in the university library. He gave them a careful synthesis.

In many cases he stayed very close to Descartes. His explanation of the structure of matter, for example, was drawn straight from the *Principia* and the *Météorologie*. He showed how the three elements were produced — how the vortical motion of the globular particles of the second element drove the subtle matter of the first element inward to form the sun and how the coarsest particles of the third element, intermixed with the first and the second, joined to form the earth. He defended Descartes' purely mechanistic physics from Gassendi's attempt to solve many of the problems associated with the concept of motion by infusing the mechanical world with a general hylozoic sensitivity. To Gassendi's use of a biological metaphor for explaining the circulation of vapours in the earth, he responded, 'I don't believe those philosophers, who ineptly and impiously supposed the Earth to be a kind of giant animal, can have found any analogy between the bodies of animals and that of the earth, except that the interior parts of both animals and the earth are perpetually heated'.[111] And when Descartes seemed uncertain or unclear, he used commentaries of such steadfast Cartesians as Pierre Silvan Régis, the sworn enemy of Daniel Huet and Nicolas Malebranche.[112] He believed, for example, that the sun induced a whirling motion in the elongated particles of water issuing from the earth and went to the blackboard with the *Metéorologie* diagram of two strings flying outward from a spinning pole to show how it happened. Yet he did not believe that this effect was sufficient to explain why vapour rose. So he adopted Régis' gloss, saying that if the particles issuing bore an outer layer of the first element, the increasing diameter of the sphere they described by their heat-induced spinning would reduce their density with respect to this outer layer, allowing it to carry them up to the rarer parts of the atmosphere. 'This adherence of the subtle matter is considered to be very apt for explaining both the elevation and the suspension of the vapours', he told his students.[113] Furthermore, he agreed with one of the Leibnizian objections to Newton: that the void, and Newton's concept of space as *sensorium divinitatis*, seemed an unnecessary — and probably dangerous — metaphysical notion. As he remarked in class, 'That eminent man tries to expel all celestial material in his work which (allow me to say) seems to savour of something superhuman, yet that which his opinion about the vacuum suggests seems human [upon further examination]'.[114]

He was by no means afraid to stray far from the strict Cartesians when it suited his purpose. In hydrostatics, for example, he sometimes relied on Louis Carré, Malebranche's right-hand man in the Academie des Sciences, whose theory of attraction advanced in a report published in the *Histoire de L'Academie des Sciences (1705)*, seemed so timed, according to Poleni, that 'multum probabilitatis ammittit'.[115] Without directly asserting action at a distance, he noted that water's propensity to adhere to substances favoured its movement in one direction rather than in another under certain circumstances. This accorded with Carré's insistence that 'l'adherence n'est pas une force mouvant', but pointed the way clearly for the doctrine of attraction asserted by Hauksbee in connection with capillary action.[116]. And his solution to the problem of cohesion in matter followed another Malebranchiste, Jacob Bernoulli (now better known for the *Ars conjectandi* than for the mechanical works). Like Bernoulli and many other contemporaries, he was not entirely satisfied with Descartes' principle of relative quiet — the state implied in Descartes' law of inertia — as an explanation for why the particles of an object stuck together. He therefore welcomed the suggestion that the pressure of the ether, accompanied by that of the air itself, was sufficient to account for the rigidity of even the hardest metal.[117] At the same time, he by no means avoided Newtonians. For example, he enthusiastically endorsed Edmund Halley's 1692 memoir in the *Philosophical Transactions* (partly translated in the *Acta eruditorum* of the same year, where he probably read it) regarding the inner structure of the earth.[118] He occasionally went directly to Newton, as when he paraphrased *Principia* III Prop. 41 in connection with the habitability of the earth in relation to Mercury or Saturn because of the inverse square law that governed the Sun's heat emissions.[119] He had so much respect for Newton's work, indeed, that he breathed a nearly-audible sigh of relief in his section on the ether when he noted that as far as this particular subject was concerned, 'it suffices to note that the question of the weight of the ether has no place in the Newtonian hypothesis'.[120] With the publication of the second edition of the *Opticks* in 1717 he would have had to revise this statement and come to terms with Newton even in this difficult matter. For the moment, however, he, his students (who were probably confused enough already), and his philosophy were safe.

During this period from 1709 to 1715, when he continued to use the same pile of notes for his teaching, he was apparently satisfied with this mixture of recent theories and simple class demonstrations. One thing is clear: he never attempted to alter the traditional classroom set-up, with the rostrum or *cattedra* up front and the benches for the students before it. After all, he knew he could always lard his course with ever larger chunks of philosophical text when he had exhausted all the other practical possibilities of the current teaching methods. Yet the advantages of a style of teaching that might give greater emphasis to the experimental side of natural philosophy were too alluring to ignore. And he was no doubt encountering some of the inconveniences that he noted in his after-thoughts to a class on mechanics in which he had not been able actually to perform the appropriate experiment: 'The explanation of Mariotte's experiment that I gave in class was extremely difficult', he wrote; 'Therefore it is necessary to write down diligently and in detail the things pertaining to it as well as those pertaining to the explanation of the law'.[121] How much the Riformatori would be inclined to consider seriously Poleni's thoughts on this matter depended on their belief in the precarious self-supported University economy to which the old methods seemed perfectly adapted.

In 1719 Poleni suggested, in a long letter to the Riformatori, the establishment of a new laboratory for experimental philosophy. By operating alongside the traditional lecture series, it would have relieved the professors of science from the responsibility and expense of bringing in their own instruments. Like the recently opened laboratory of experimental philosophy at the Institute of Bologna, it would have provided a point of contact between the scientists' professional interests and the interests of the best students. In a frank appeal to the well-known parsimony of the Riformatori, he included practical suggestions down to the last detail and a list of expenses for the first year down to the last ducat. Without allowing his imagination to suggest to him everything that he would have liked on hand for his own work, he listed a few key instruments for experiments in hydrostatics, phonics, aerometry, optics, chemistry, and the science of, as he put it, 'the bodies that have the quality of attracting each other'.[122] He assured the Riformatori that they would get a good return on their investment, inasmuch as students would be profoundly edified by a new kind of instruction based on the in-class discovery of the properties of matter and the principles of natural philosophy: 'New discoveries', he pointed out, 'enlarge the minds of those who make them and are a great object of excitement for those who observe them'.[123] If realised, the new lab would have been a strong selling point for Padua among the greatly sought-after foreign students that wars, pestilence, and the convenience of local institutions had long discouraged from attending.

The Riformatori, however, had other plans. They did not welcome Poleni's project and immediately set about putting it into action. Instead, they brushed it aside just as their predecessors had done with the similar projects presented by Domenico Guglielmini and Pompeo Sacco at the end of the previous century and by Scipione Maffei in a report on university reform of 1715.[124] In 1724 they still had no intention of digging it up again. They accepted Poleni's second and much more modest proposal: the acquisition of a set of brass interlocking squares, circles, and triangles that he could use for mathematical demonstrations whenever he tired of the clouds of chalk dust he raised by trying to draw things freehand on the blackboard. They were so pleased with this new acquisition, indeed, that they insisted that his name be engraved upon them for display after his death[125] — where they are to this day — in one of the halls of the University.

When in 1738 the Riformatori finally granted official recognition to experimental philosophy at Padua by establishing a professorship and outfitting a laboratory, over fifty years had passed since similar arrangements had been made at the University of Leiden, and somewhat fewer at Utrecht, Cambridge, the Institute of Bologna, and the University of Turin. Finding a good foreign candidate did not promise to be easy, now that experimental philosophy had come into vogue all over Europe. As Poleni told the Riformatori, 'the men who cut the biggest figures in the Experimental Art these days, and they are very famous, would not without the greatest difficulty (besides the fact that they follow a different religion) be induced to leave their comfortable and lucrative positions'.[126] Not by chance, the choice fell on Poleni himself, whose blueprint was to constitute the new course's practical and theoretical foundation.

When he assumed his new responsibilities he never lost sight of the divulgative nature of the science he was supposed to teach. He continued the practice begun in his lessons on astronomy decades before, reducing the complicated mathematical content of his demonstrations to a minimum. He thus followed the popularised Newtonianism of writers like Pieter van Musschenbroeck and Willem Jacob 'sGravesande and others who, he claimed, 'have turned experiments into an art'.[127] Like them, he proposed experiments that were designed not to arrive at new conclusions, but to prove a didactic point. For example, during one of his Sunday afternoon lessons in 1724 he illustrated the physics of simple machines by attaching various weights to a block and tackle and hoisting them by a device that permitted the measurement of the work done. This experiment, drawn out of 'sGravesande's *Physices* was supposed to show students that in cases of two or more pulleys, 'the ratio of force to weight, when the movement is uniform, is composed of the proportion between the diameters of the last wheel pulling the weight and the first wheel whose circumference is subject to it on the one hand and, on the other, of the proportion between the revolution of the last wheel to that of the first wheel in the same time'.[128] The experiment thus constituted a simplified scheme for translating the mathematical notion into visual terms. The exact form it took depended upon Poleni's directions to the firm that furnished the university with its machines. From the point of view of Newtonian science, this was bound to lead students into a number of serious misconceptions. The whole idea of demonstrating, through the use of mathematical reasoning, that the universe was an integrated and harmonious whole was turned inside out.[129] Instead of being centred upon the broader inferences that could be drawn from the interplay of simple mechanical laws, discussions were centred upon the chaotic world of observable mechanical phenomena from which everything — and nothing — could be deduced in the absence of a proper mathematical foundation. At the same time, students were warned to shun unfounded hypotheses and encouraged to test meticulously every mathematical conclusion. From a technical point of view, the most Poleni could hope from this kind of teaching was that his students should learn to respect the usefulness of higher mathematics and to regard it as something more than a recondite game for intellectual initiates.

This did not prevent him for hoping that his students would also obtain something new and original in spite of the limits to their abilities to appreciate experimental science. He proposed that careful research be conducted into previous results of even the simplest experiments. 'this is a *mare magnum*', he told the Riformatori, 'which depends upon a great quantity of books and upon long reading and application'.[130] Then he insisted that the results of every experiment be recorded on separate charts for his own future reference and that of his successors: 'I think that in this way a useful, clear, and scientific order would arise by itself, from which a completely and entirely regular course could be constructed according to an exact method'.[131] He constantly sought to bring as much as possible of his own laboratory experience into his teaching. At first the outcome did not satisfy him: 'After each lesson', he wrote to his fellow-scientist in Venice, Giovanni Francesco Pivati, 'I was disturbed by the unsurmountable inconvenience of the locale [lessons were held at first in the same place where simples were shown to medical students], by the crowd, by the heat, and by the difficult task of saying and performing at the same time while trying to make sure that both should come out pleasing and correct.'[132] He hoped that with continuous practice of 'saying the things in the lessons that will subsequently be done during the demonstrations for listeners who will also be the spectators in the experiments' he would eventually find 'the system most adapted to the purpose'.[133] In the end, he apparently found such a system. His teaching was so successful that he earned honourable mention along with Jean-Théophile Desaguliers, Daniel Bernoulli, Christian Wolff, and Musschenbroeck in the preface to the third edition of 'sGravesande's *Physices* (1742) even though he never published a major compendium of his experimental work.

When the new instruction was well under way at Padua, Jacopo Facciolati reported the inventory of the experimental philosophy laboratory in his *Fasti Gymnasii Patavini* (1758) from a handlist given to him by Poleni. The catalogue was impressive — over 250 machines of all kinds, many of them from German, Dutch and French shops. He described Musschenbroeck's famous pyrometer (first introduced in the *Tentamina* of 1731) consisting of a metal rod fastened down at one end and, at the other, fitted with gears and wheels to permit the measuring of its expansion when heated.[134] He described the heliostat, another specialty from the Musschenbroeck shop, which consisted of a mirror fixed to a clock that could be set so that the mirror followed the sun's passage in the sky permitting the operator to study the sun's rays without having to readjust the apparatus continuously.[135] He mentioned a machine whose 'construction and the motion of its parts are such that various bodies can be made to rotate in various ways for exploring the properties of centrifugal force'.[136] The Musschenbroeck models had a bell that rang when the weight on the spinning bar had slid out beyond a certain point. He described a crank-operated electrical machine with 'various cylinders and various globes of glass or crystal', probably activated by the friction of the operator's hand. It featured 'two plates with little chains and tubes, all of iron', apparently a variation of Georg Matthaias Bose's recently proposed apparatus for demonstrating the conductivity of metal.[137] He listed a set-up involving a 'large wooden pole for holding the scale-pan of a balance. Conjoined is another iron for holding the beam of the balance. Cylindrical scale-pans and balls of various weights'.[138] This was clearly to be used for experiments of the type mentioned by 'sGravesande, where weights were tied by a string and allowed to fall into the pan at one end of the balance in order to show how much liquid had to be poured into containers in the pan at the other end for equilibrium to be maintained in explanations of inertia and impact.[139] Then there were the usual air pumps and their attachments for such demonstrations as that old textbook favourite, the equal fall of a lead ball and a feather in an evacuated jar.[140] There were also the usual telescopes of various dimensions, including the *telescopium catoptricum dioptricum sive Newtonianum*, two feet long.[141] He even described some devices whose usefulness has long been forgotten, like the one for investigating 'the pores of bodies', which he claimed to be 'a recent invention'. It consisted of 'four closed-off metal capsules with a wooden instrument inserted along which they can slide'.[142] Clearly, few science professors could resist the temptation to spend much of their work time in this lab, whether or not they had to teach students in it.

The kind of curiosity that the new laboratory aroused was far too great for Poleni to continue much longer in his immunity to all the more theatrical aspects of scientific teaching. Indeed, the most widespread and successful version of experimental philosophy in Europe was not so much that preached by Desaguliers at Mr Brown's, Bookseller, in London or by Martinus Martens in various locales around Amsterdam.[143] Rather, it was the version preached by the professional wandering experimenters — from Bose in Wittenberg, with his 'wonderful displays' of electrical fluid, full of surprises for his awe-struck public, to John Banks in Manchester, with his half-crown lessons on such useful subjects as 'the application of water to Bucket Wheels', which imparted, according to one listener, 'a wonderful insight into the laws of nature'.[144] Not to mention the various performers who showed up at fairs and public houses to turn science into something like a mountebank show. Poleni, accordingly, recognised that even the simplest principles could engage the attention of the layman when accompanied by elaborate technology. Among the duties he assumed was that of entertaining the various visitors who came through Padua to admire

the wisdom of his employers in having outfitted the University so
handsomely. For example, upon the arrival of 'Il Signor Capitano
Venier and Dame Correr' in 1753 he showed 'the double cone that
ascends an inclined plane', 'the centre of gravity, with the litte statue',
'the friction machine of Signor [Jean-Antoine] Nollet', and, his own
invention, 'the machine for extinguishing fires'.[145] He even kept a
master list of 'experiments done' with notes on whether they were
'good' or not. One of his best, which not only demonstrated a
fundamental biological principle but also performed a useful service,
no doubt winning him the applause of the Venetian noblemen and
noblewomen for whom he performed it, was listed as 'with the air
pump, death of a pigeon'.

   Thus Poleni's noblest purposes were fulfilled in the teaching of
science at Padua. Not only did he manage to adapt his teaching
methodologies to the needs of his public by convincing the university
administration to make the necessary modifications, but he brought
to his lessons some of the scientific expertise that had won him two
prizes from the Academie des Sciences of Paris (1733 and 1737). He
knew that most of his students had no interest in broadening and
deepening the perspectives they had gained in their course with him.
He found consolation in his belief that the few students who showed
signs of sudden illumination during his public lessons and the few
students who came to his house after his ordinary hours to take extra
lessons in trigonometry and the calculus were enough to justify all the
trouble he went to. And a sufficient number of students considered his
profession to be attractive enough for them to abandon more
lucrative ones. They contributed to the complicated momentum that
Paduan science had continued to maintain, in spite of whatever
metaphysical problems it encountered, even in periods when it was
eclipsed by the appearance of greater genius — and, no doubt, more
abundant publishing opportunities — elsewhere.[146]

   The inability of universities to respond to the demands put upon
them by society was much discussed in the eighteenth century. More
often than not, the blame was placed on their ancient statutes. 'One
must consider that the universities were for the most part instituted in
a blind middle age between the preceding barbarism and the
successive civilisation', Maffei declaimed in 1715.[147] It was thought
that the best way to make them function in a useful way would be to
make them resolve whatever were considered to be the most
important problems of the time. Maffei suggested new professorships
and institutes to make them more attractive to the ruling noble classes
that he believed would show more interest in governing ably the states
of Italy if they would only study the arts and sciences. When many of
the organizational reforms Maffei called for had been made, Carlo

Antonio Pilati insisted in 1768 that these were not enough. He suggested that other reforms be enacted so that students would receive an education in the defects of the Italian legal system and in the injustices perpetrated by the Church.[148] Only one group was interested in the social function that the universities served best of all — that of providing a workplace for science. And the professors were rarely the best advocates of their own cause.

Department of History
University of Chicago
1126 E 59th St.
Chicago, IL 60637, U.S.A.

REFERENCES

* Adriano Carugo, Piero Del Negro, and Eric Cochrane provided valuable suggestions when they read an earlier draft of this paper. My thanks for the comments of Charles Schmitt and two anonymous referees on the final version.

1. Venice, Archivio di Stato, *Riformatori dello Studio di Padova* (hereafter, *Riformatori*), filza 409, Antonio Bombardini, 8 December 1717: 'Al pregiudizio dell'economia paterna, s'aggiunge la distrazione dello scolare. Viene questo allo Studio con la certezza di dovere tornare per quattr'anni. Questo riflesso fà che il primo anno appena appena imparano a conoscere i professori di vista per salutarli per strada, applicando a tutto ciò che meno conviene allo studio, e questo habito fatto nel primo anno continua fatalmente fino all'ultimo anno del dottorato, in cui abbattutisi come le vergini pazze del Vangelo senza olio nel lume, corrono freneticamente dai Professori con l'inopportuno: date nobis de olio vestro'.

2. *Riformatori*, filza 89, 2 March 1731/2.

3. Florence, Biblioteca Nazionale Centrale, Magl. cl. VIII, cod. 1089, c.7^r (10), Antonio Vallisnieri to Antonio Magliabechi, 17 July 1700: 'Ho fatto assai ad attendere al grave peso delle pubbliche lezioni, senza divertirmi a ricercare le operazioni più curiose e più astruse della natura. Non potevo scrivere, che cantilene da farsi sopra le cattedre, e gloriosi inganni dell'Arte nostra. Ora torno a dare un occhiata a vecchi studi, dilatandoli a quanto di grande e di rimarcabile sà operare la Natura'.

4. L. Stone, 'The Size and Composition of the Oxford Student Body, 1580-1910', in L. Stone (ed.), *The University in Society*, 2 vols (Princeton, 1974), I, 3-110; R.L. Kagan, 'Universities in Castille, 1500-1810', in *ibid.*, I, 335-405.

5. R. Chartier and J. Revel, 'Université et société dans l'Europe moderne', *Revue d'histoire moderne et contemporaine*, 25 (1978), p. 369.

6. M. A. Curtis, *Oxford and Cambridge in Transition, 1558-1642: An Essay on Changing Relationships between the English Universities and English Society* (Oxford, 1959), pp. 83ff; C. Hill, *Change and Continuity in Seventeenth-Century England* (Cambridge, Mass., 1975), pp. 128-35; J.K. McConica, 'The Social Relations of Tudor Oxford', *Transactions of the Royal Historical Society*, ser. 5, vol. 27 (1977), 115-34; D. Balani, 'Studi giuridici e professioni nel Piemonte del '700', *Bollettino storico-bibliografico subalpino*, 76 (1978), 175-278.

142   *History of Universities*

7.   E. Garin, *L'educazione in Europa*, 1400-1600 (Bari, 1976), pp. 109-113; V. Morgan, 'Cambridge University and the Country', in Stone (ed), *The University in Society*, I, p. 184.

8.   G. Ricuperati, 'L'Università di Torino nel Settecento', *Quaderni storici*, 23 (1973), 575-602; P. Galluzzi, 'Libertà scientifica, educazione, e ragion di stato in una polemica universitaria pisana del 1670', *Atti del XXIV Congresso Nazionale di Filosofia* (Florence, 1973), II (2), 404-12.

9.   As J. B. Morrell suggests in review of Stone (ed.), *The University in Society*, *History of Science*, 15 (1977), 145-52.

10.   V. Busacchi, 'Il nuovo spirito di ricerca e lo sperimentalismo nell'opera poco nota di medici e non medici nel Seicento a Bologna', in *Studi e memorie per la storia dell'Università di Bologna*, 2 vols (Bologna, 1957), I, 417-33; C. Jucci, 'Contributo dell'Università di Pavia al progresso della biologia naturalistica', in *Discipline e maestri dell'Ateneo pavese* (Pavia-Milan, 1961), pp. 111-35; S. Ramazzotti and L. Briatore, 'Appunti di storia della fisica: didattica e ricerca fisica nell'Ateneo torinese nel diciottesimo secolo', *Giornale di fisica*, 16 (1975), 141-52.

11.   For example, W.G. Hiscock, *David Gregory, Isaac Newton, and Their Circle* (Oxford, 1937), *passim*; L. M. J. Coleby, 'John Francis Vigani, First Professor of Chemistry in the University of Cambridge', *Annals of Science*, 8 (1952), 46-60; idem, 'John Mickleburgh, Professor of Chemistry in the University of Cambridge, 1718-56', *Annals of Science*, 8 (1952), 165-74; F.W. Gibbs and W.A. Smeaton, 'Thomas Beddoes at Oxford', *Ambix*, 9 (1961), 47-9.

12.   G. Berti, *Lo Studio universitario parmense alla fine del Seicento* (Parma, 1967), *passim*; M.A. Dellacorna, 'I lettori dell Università di Torino dal 1630 al 1659', in *L'Università di Torino nei secoli 17 e 18*, Memorie dell'Istituto Giuridico dell'Università di Torino, ser. 2, no. 145 (Turin, 1972), 221-346.

13.   See, for example, R.G. Villoslada, *Storia del Collegio Romano* (Rome, 1954), chaps. entitled, 'I teologi del Seicento e del Settecento', pp. 214-32, and 'La filosofia, il diritto canonico, la storia, la liturgia', pp. 233-58; *Geschichte der Universität Jena, 1548-1958*, 2 vols (Jena, 1958), I, ch. 4: 'Die Universität Jena im Zeichen vom Pietismus und Aufklärung vom Beginn des 18 Jahr. bis zur Reorganisation der Universität unter Anna Amalia', pp. 167-216; C. G. Mor and P. Di Pietro, *Storia dell'Università di Modena*, 2 vols (Florence, 1973), ch. 3: 'Lo Studio Pubblico di S. Carlo, 1682-1772', pp. 49-90; and similar chapters in such works as N. Spanio, *L'Università di Roma* (Rome, 1935); L. Simeoni, *Storia dell'Università di Bologna, II: L'Età moderna* (Bologna, 1940); A. Visconti, *La storia del'Università di Ferrara* (Bologna, 1950); S. Lindroth, *A History of Uppsala University, 1477-1977* (Stockholm, 1977); H. Mathy, *Die Universität Mainz, 1477-1977* (Mainz, 1977). On the English contributions, see M. Feingold, 'Oxford and Cambridge College Histories: An Outdated Genre?' *History of Universities*, I (1981), 207-13.

14.   L. W. B. Brockliss, 'Medical Teaching at the University of Paris, 1600-1720', *Annals of Science*, 35 (1978), 221-151; idem, 'Philosophy Teaching in France, 1600-1740', *History of Universities*, I (1981), 131-68; idem, 'Aristotle, Descartes and the New Science: Natural Philosophy at the University of Paris, 1600-1740', *Annals of Science*, 38 (1981); T. McClaughlin, 'Censorship and Defenders of the Cartesian Faith in Mid-Seventeenth Century France', *Journal of the History of Ideas*, 40 (1979), 563-81; M. Heyd, *Between Orthodoxy and the Enlightenment: Jean-Robert Chouet and the Introduction of Cartesian Science in the Academy of Geneva* (The Hague, 1982), pp. 116-44.

15.   M. Lacoarnet and Mme. Ter-Maissian, 'Les universités', in R. Taton (ed.), *Enseignement et diffusion des sciences en France au XVIIIe siècle* (Paris, 1964), pp. 125-68; W. Rother, 'Zur Geschichte der Basler Universitäts-philosophie im 17. Jahrhundert', *History of Universities*, 2 (1982), 170-1.

Science Teaching as a Career in Padua 143

16. R. G. Frank, Jr., 'Science, Medicine and the Universities of Early Modern England: Background and Sources', *History of Science*, II (1973), 194-216 and 239-69.

17. E. G. Ruestow, *Physics at Seventeenth and Eighteenth-Century Leiden: Philosophy and the New Science in the University* (The Hague, 1973), pp. 61-72; L. C. Palm, 'Snellius and his Newtonian Teaching in Halle', *Janus*, 64 (1977), 15-24.

18. M. Bellucci, 'La filosofia naturale di Claudio Berigardo', *Rivista critica di storia della filosofia*, 26 (1971), 363-411.

19. H. B. Adelmann, *Marcello Malpighi and the Evolution of Embryology*, 5 vols (Ithaca, N.Y., 1966), I, 157n.

20. A. De Stefano, 'Un processo dell'Inquisizione veneziana contro Michelangelo Fardella', *Siculorum Gymnasium*, 1 (1941), 135-46.

21. G. Ricuperati, 'L'Università di Torino e le polemiche contro i professori in una relazione di parte curialista del 1731', *Bollettino storico-bibliografico subalpino*, 64 (1966), 341-74.

22. This role of the standard curriculum in the Italian universities is sustained in B. Lesnodorski, 'Les universités au Siècle des Lumières', in *Les universités européens du XVIème au XVIIIème siècle* (Geneva, 1967), pp. 143-60; 'Das juristische Vorlesungsprogramm der Universität Padua im 17. und 18. Jahrh.', in *Studi in onore di Edoardo Volterra*, 6 vols (Milan, 1971), IV, 179-95; S. De Bernardin, 'La politica culturale della Repubblica di Venezia e l'Università di Padova nel secolo diciassettesimo', *Studi veneziani*, 16 (1974), 443-502; E. Mango Tomei, *Gli studenti dell'Università di Pisa sotto il regime Granducale*, (Pisa, 1976), pp. 61-64; M. R. Di Simone, *La 'Sapienza' romana nel Settecento* (Rome, 1980), pp. 19-28; G. Ricuperati, 'Università e scuola in Italia', in *La letteratura italiana, I: Il letterato e le istituzioni* (Turin, 1982), pp. 983-1007.

23. Information about the earlier dispensation can be obtained from *Statuta et privilegia almae universitatis dd. philosophorum, medicorum, ac theologorum Archgymnasii Patavini* (Padua, 1648), pp. 80, 161. For the late sixteenth and early seventeenth century curriculum in other Italian universities, C.B. Schmitt, 'Science in the Italian Universities in the Sixteenth and Early Seventeenth Centuries', in M. P. Crosland (ed.), *The Emergence of Science in Western Europe* (New York, 1976), pp. 35-56.

24. Here and below, Padua, Archivio Antico del Bò, busta 242.

25. Here and below, *Statuta et privilegia . . .* , pp. 82, 98, 102.

26. G. Cozzi, *Repubblica di Venezia e stati italiani: politica e giustizia dal secolo XVI al secolo XVIII* (Turin, 1982), pp. 314-15.

27. G. D'Amelio, 'Sui rapporti fra Illuminismo e scienza del diritto in Italia', *Annali di storia del diritto*, 7 (1963), 832-114; F. Venturi, *Settecento riformatore, I: Da Muratori a Beccaria*, (Turin, 1963), pp. 161-77; G. Tarello, 'Ideologie settecentesche della codificazione e struttura dei codici', *Filosofia*, 29 (1978), 17-34.

28. J. Roger, *Les sciences de la vie dans la pensée française du XVIIIème siècle* (Paris, 1963), pp. 25-6; 69-70; and, as far as the situation in Italy in particular is concerned, S. Moravia, 'Filosofia e "Sciences de la vie" nel Secolo diciottesimo', *Giornale critico della filosofia italiana*, 45 (1966), 64-109; M. Caporaso, 'Vitalismo e meccanicismo nel dibattito sulla generazione spontanea', *Medicina nei secoli*, 17 (1980), 85-110; M. T. Marcialis, 'Meccanicismo e unità dell'essere nella cultura italiana settecentesca', *Rivista critica di storia della filosofia* 37 (1982), 3-38.

29. Adelmann, *Malpighi*, I, 542-3; G. B. Morgagni, *Opera postuma, I: le autobiografie*, ed. A. Pazzini (Florence, 1964), pp. 18-19.

30. Cited in B. Fadda, 'L'innesto del vaiolo: un tema di storia della medicina e di storia della cultura nel Settecento', *Società e storia*, 4 (1981), 867.

31.   D. Giordano, 'Alessandro Knips Maccope', *Rivista di storia delle scienze mediche e naturali*, 27 (1936), 127.

32.   On the characteristics of the student community, see M. Saibante, C. Vivarini, and G. Voghera, 'Gli studenti all'Università di Padova dalla fine del '500 ai nostri giorni (studio statistico)', *Metron*, 4 (1924-5), 163-223. On the legal profession in Venice, G. Cozzi, *Repubblica di Venezia e stati italiani: politica e giustizia dal secolo XVIII* (Turin, 1982), pp. 314-15.

33.   Rovigo, Accademia dei Concordi, mss. *Concordi* (hereafter, *Concordi*), 370-4, Davini, n.d.

34.   *Riformatori*, filza 409, Morgagni, 8 December 1717.

35.   This statistic was compiled from *Anagrafi di tutto lo stato della Serenissima Repubblica di Venezia*, 5 vols (Venice, 1768). On clerical education and religious demand, E. Brambilla, 'Società ecclesiastica e società civile: aspetti della formazione del clero dal Cinquecento alla Restaurazione', *Società e storia*, 4 (1981), 299-366. Registration in the theology faculty at the University of Turin was under 1.5%. See D. Balani, D. Carpenetto, and F. Turletti, 'La popolazione studentesca all'Università di Torino nel Settecento', *Bollettino storico-bibliografico subalpino*, 76 (1978), 65.

36.   *Concordi*, 323-64, Vallisnieri, 16 July 1723: 'Gran miseria in Italia, e segnatamente in questa città, mentre in tante centinaia di Scolari, che ho avuto, non ho ancora potuto fare un'allievo, che si diletti di Naturale Storia, né di scrivere in Italiano con qualche pulitezza, attendendo tutti al vile guadagno'.

37.   *Relazione ai Riformatori dello Studio di Padova di Gasparo Gozzi* (Venice, 1845), p. 3. (This text, dated 6 August 1771, has been republished in *Opere di G. G.*, Turin, 1960, pp. 753-68.)

38.   *Riformatori*, filza 197, Sellari, 7 November, 1723: 'È più costante che mai l'opinione che lo Studio si veda in un'estrema miseria in quest'anno. Si legge, ma alla riserva di pochi greci, gli altri non sono che gli amici dei Pubblici Professori'.

39.   Accounted for at length in De Bernardin, 'La politica culturale della Repubblica di Venezia', (cited, note 22), *passim*.

40.   On the sixteenth-century reform of universities, see P. O. Kristeller, 'The University of Bologna and the Renaissance', in *Studi e memorie per la storia dell'Università di Bologna*, 2 vols., (Bologna, 1956), I, 313-23; Schmitt, 'Science in the Italian Universities', pp. 47-50; and E. Cochrane, *The Harvest of the Italian Renaissance* (forthcoming), ch. 3: 'The New Political Order'.

41.   B. Peroni, 'La riforma dell'Università di Pavia nel Settecento', in *Contributi alla storia dell'Università di Pavia* (Pavia, 1925), pp. 117-74; A. Marongiu, 'I professori dell'Università di Pisa sotto il regime granducale', in *Studi in memoria di Lorenzo Mossa*, 3 vols (Padua, 1961), II, 591-602; M. R. Di Simone, *La 'Sapienza' romana nel Settecento* (Rome, 1980), pp. 123-138.

42.   E. Baeri, 'Il dibattito sulla riforma dell'Università di Catania, 1778-88', *Archivio storico per la Sicilia orientale*, ser. 4, vol. 32 (1979), 297-337; L. Villari, 'L'Università degli Studi di Piazza Armerina', *Studi meridionali*, 12 (1980), 91-110.

43.   G. P. Brizzi, 'Riforme scolastiche e domanda di istruzione', *Contributi, Biblioteca Municipale A. Panizzi*, 11-12 (1982), 53-98.

44.   M. Schipa, 'Il secolo diciottesimo', in *Storia dell'Università di Napoli* (Naples, 1924), pp. 433ff; U. Marcelli, 'Insegnamento e pratica delle dottrine economiche nel secolo diciottesimo: Giacomo Pistorini, Lettore allo Studio e consultore del Senato', in *Studi e memorie per la storia dell'Università di Bologna*, 2 vols (Bologna, 1957), I, 487-503; P. Zambelli, 'Una lettera inedita di Celestino Galiani', *Bollettino del Centro di Studi Vichiani*, 7 (1977), 118ff; M. Cavazza, 'Riforma dell'Università e nuove accademie nella politica culturale dell'Arcidiacono Marsili', in L. Boehm (ed.),

Università, accademie e società scientifiche in Italia e in Germania dal '500 al '700,
Annali dell'Istituto Storico Italo-Germanico, Quaderno 9 (Bologna, 1980), pp. 245-82.
45. D. Marrara, *Risieduti e nobiltà: Profile storico-istituzionale di un'oligarchia* (Pisa, 1976), p. 131. Compare R.S. Turner, 'University Reformers and Professional Scholarship in Germany, 1760-1806', in Stone, ed., *The University in Society*, pp. 495-532.
46. *Riformatori*, filza 81, 5 January, 1714.
47. *Riformatori*, filza 191, 29 August, 1711.
48. S. Drake, *Galileo at Work: His Scientific Biography* (Chicago, 1978), p. 16.
49. M. Soppelsa, *Genesi del metodo galileiano e tramonto dell'aristotelismo nella scuola di Padova* (Padua, 1974), p. 117.
50. P. Cossali, *Elogio di Giovanni Poleni* (Venice, 1813), p. 16.
51. *Riformatori*, filza 192, 14 December 1712: 'Il a aussi beaucoup d'habilité dans l'Architecture des Eaux, qu'il a apprise en Hollande de sorte qu'il pouvroit servir utilement le Publique dans cette partie si importante'.
52. *Riformatori*, filza 195, 3 June 1718: 'Non ho lasciato però nel frattempo di tener linguaggio del proposito col Sig. Cavaliere Newton, soggetto di molto accreditata virtù e presidente di questa Società Reale, il quale in primo luogo mi disse esservi in Londra scarsezza di persone intelligenti nelle Bottaniche, e che non me ne potrebbe contare che due o tre, cioè un medico assai erudito di famiglia Sloone [sic, for Sloane] e due speciali. Mi aggiunse poi, bene sapere essere in Italia particolarmente coltivato, e professato tale studio . . . '.
53. M. Fardella, *Lettere ad Antonio Magliabechi*, ed. S. Femiano (Cassino, 1978), p. 101.
54. V. Ferrone, *Scienza, natura, religione: mondo newtoniano e cultura italiana nel primo Settecento* (Naples, 1982), pp. 502-5; M. Cavazza, 'Accademie scientifiche a Bologna dal 'Coro Anatomico' agli Inquieti (1650-1714)', *Quaderni storici*, 48 (1981), 884-921; P. Del Negro, 'Giacomo Nani e L'Università di Padova nel 1781. Per una storia delle relazioni culturali tra il patriziato veneziano e i professori dello Studio durante il diciottesimo secolo', *Quaderni per la storia dell'Università di Padova*, 13 (1980), 90. In general, concerning the essential aspects of a profession seen from a sociological point of view, E. Greenwood, 'The Attributes of a Profession', *Social Work*, 2 (1957), 44-55; and the remarks of G. P. Prandstraller in his Introduction to *Sociologia delle professioni* (Rome, 1980), pp. 7-100.
55. Morgagni, *Autobiografie*, p. 94.
56. Venice, Biblioteca Nazionale Marciana (hereafter, Bibl. Marc.), cod. ital. cl. X: 148 (= 6685), c. 12, 1 December 1710.
57. Magliabechi's personal habits were discussed at length in a contemporary pamphlet: *Joannis Cinelli et Antonii Magliabechi vitae* (Fori Vibonum [= Florence], 1684), attributed to N. Bertolini. More recently, S. Mastellone, 'Antonio Magliabechi: un libertino fiorentino?', *Il pensiero politico*, 8 (1975), 36-51. On Cinelli, see the entry by G. Benzoni in *Dizionario biografico degli italiani*, XXV (Rome, 1981), 583-9.
58. On which, see L. Felici, 'Giornali romani dal '700 al '800, III: Il *Giornale dei letterati*', *Palatina*, ns. vol. 5 (1961), 64-66; D. E. Rhodes, 'Libri inglesi recensiti a Roma, 1668-81', *Studi Seicenteschi*, 5 (1964), 151-60; W. E. K. Middleton, 'Science in Rome, 1675-1700, and the Accademia Fisicomatematica of G. G. Ciampini', *British Journal for the History of Science*, 8 (1975), 138-54. On Italian journalism in general, with bibliography: G. Ricuperati, 'Giornali e società nell'Italia del Ancien Régime, 1668-1789', in N. Tranfaglia and V. Castronovo (eds.), *La Stampa italiana dal Cinquecento al Ottocento* (Bari, 1976), pp. 67-372. See now the recently published J. - M. Gardair, *Le 'Giornale de' letterati' de Rome (1668-1681)* (Florence, 1984). On Albrizzi, see the entry by G. E. Ferrari, *Diz. Biog. ital.*, II (Rome, 1960), pp. 58-9.

59.   See B. Dooley, 'The *Giornale de' letterati d'Italia* (1710-40): 'Journalism and "Modern" Culture in the Early Eighteenth Century Veneto', *Studi veneziani*, n.s. vol. 6 (1982), 229-270.

60.   S. Rotta, 'Scienza e "publica felicità" in Geminiano Montanari', in *Miscellanea Seicento*, Università di Genova, Istituto di Filosofia della Facoltà di Lettere e Filosofia (Genoa, 1971), p.95; M. Maylender, *Storia delle accademie d'Italia*, 5 vols (Bologna, 1925-9), IV, 34.

61.   This and the following are from Bellini's letter, 17 November 1689, in H. B. Adelmann (ed.), *The Correspondence of Marcello Malpighi*, 5 vols (Ithaca, N.Y., 1975), V, 1553.

62.   On Padua, see M. Berengo, *La società veneta alla fine del Settecento* (Florence, 1956), p. 25. On Pisa, Pietro Leopoldo, *Relazione sul governo della Toscana*, ed. A. Silvestrini, 3 vols (Pisa, 1970), II, 63-4; and, in general, R. Burr-Litchfield, 'Ufficiali ed uffici a Firenze sotto il Granducato Mediceo', in E. Fasano Guarini (ed.), *Potere e società negli stati regionali italiani del '500 e '600* (Bologna, 1978), p. 147. On Bologna, A. Giacomelli, 'La dinamica della nobiltà bolognese nel diciottesimo secolo', in *Famiglie senatorie ed istituzioni cittadine a Bologna nel Settecento, I: Colloquio* (Bologna, 1980), pp. 85-6. On Rome, V. E. Giuntella, *Rome nel Settecento* (Bologna, 1971), pp. 1-54.

63.   Here I differ in my interpretation from J. Ben David, *The Scientist's Role in Society* (Englewood Cliffs, N.J., 1971), ch. IV.

64.   C.B. Schmitt, 'The Faculty of Arts at Pisa at the time of Galileo', *Physis*, 14 (1972), 263. With particular regard to the Paduan period, compare A. Favaro, *Galileo e lo Studio di Padova*, 2 vols (Padua, 1883), I, 168; L. Geymonat, *Galileo Galilei* (Turin, 1969⁵), p. 34. For my information on Malpighi I used Adelmann, *Malpighi*, I, 157.

65.   Bibl. Marc. cod. ital. X:148 (= 6685), n.8: 'Nos sumus magni respectu ovis, aut canis, maiores respectu aquilae, galli, polli, maiores etiam respectu columbae; e contra nos sumus parvi respectu elephantis aut balenae, minimi respectu terrae, etiam magis minimi respectu spatii quod est inter nos et Stellas fixas'.

66.   S. Rotta, 'Scienza e "pubblica felicità"', p. 98.

67.   G. B. Morgagni, *Autobiografie*, p. 53.

68.   G. Ricuperati, 'L'Università di Torino e le polemiche contro i professori in una relazione di parte curialista del 1731', *Bollettino storico-bibliografico subalpino*, 64 (1966), 366.

69.   Biographical details are drawn from the anonymous life in Bibl. Marc. cod. ital. cl. XI: 220 (= 6940) datable to just after Poleni's death in 1761. Also, Cossali, *Elogio*; G. Gennari, *Elogio di G. P.* (Padua, 1839). On his scientific contribution, summarised in the entry by B. A. Boley in *D. S. B.*, XI (1975), 65-66, see the articles in the collection, *G. Poleni (1683-1761) nel bicentennario della morte*. (Atti e memorie dell'Accademia Patavina di Scienze, Lettere ed Arti, 74, Padua, 1961-2, special number); and, in addition, P. Verrua, 'La macchina calcolatrice di G. Poleni', *Bollettino dell'Accademia Italiana di stenografia*, 7 (1931), lxix-lxxvi; F. Vivian, 'Joseph Smith, G. Poleni and Antonio Visentini in the Light of New Information Derived from the Poleni Papers in the Marciana Library', *Italian Studies*, 18 (1963), 54-66; L. Guadagnino Lenci, 'Per G. Poleni: note ed appunti per una revisione critica', *Atti dell'Istituto Veneto di scienze, lettere, ed arti*, 134 (1975-6), 543-67; A. Cavallari-Murat, 'Collaborazione Poleni-Vanvitelli per la cupola vaticana, 1743-8', in *Atti del congresso di studio Luigi Vanvitelli ed il Settecento europeo* (Napoli, 1978), pp. 171-210; Idem, 'Le *Exercitationes Vitruvianae*: approdo neoclassico di Simone Stratico (1733-1824)', *Filosofia*, n.s. vol 29 (1978), 445-76; S. Bergia and P. Fantazzini, 'Dalla regolamentazione delle acque alle leggi dell'urto centrale elastico: una rivalutazione del ruolo di G. Poleni', *Giornale di fisica*, 21 (1980), 46-60; D. Nardo, 'Scienza e filologia nel primo Settecento padovano:

gli studi classici di Giovanni Battista Morgagni, Giovanni Poleni, Giulio Pontedera e Leone Targa', *Quaderni per la storia dell'Università di Padova*, 14 (1981), 1-40.

70.   U. Baldini, 'L'attività scientifica nel primo Settecento', in *Storia d'Italia, Annali III: Scienza e tecnica* (Turin, 1980), p. 509 with bibliography.

71.   In Bibl. Marc. Precise indications will be given in due course.

72.   On the Collegio alla Salute, see G. A. Moschini, *La Chiesa ed il Seminario di S. M. della Salute in Venezia* (Venice, 1842), pp. 53-147; S. Tramontin, 'Gli inizi dei due Seminari di Venezia', *Studi veneziani*, 7 (1965), 313-77; G. Gullino, *La politica scolastica veneziana nell'Età delle Riforme* (Venice, 1973), pp. 76; 107.

73.   There is no study of Caro. On the Somaschi programme, M. Tentorio, 'I Somaschi', in *Ordini e congregazioni religiose*, ed. M. Escobar (Turin, 1951), p. 626; F. De Vivo, 'Indirizzi pedagogici ed istituzioni religiosi nei secoli 16 e 17', *Rassegna di pedagogia*, 16 (1958), 1-23.

74.   F. Caro, *Philosophia amphysica*, 5 vols (Venice, 1695), III, 6.

75.   *Ibid*, p. 47. Nicolas Cabeo is remembered rather for his experiments on electrical repulsion.

76.   *Ibid*, I, 155.

77.   *Ibid*, III, 6.

78.   On Maffei, see *Giornale de' letterati d'Italia*, 28 (1717), 387; *Scriptores Ordinis Predicatorum*, III (1910), 258.

79.   On the Venetian government's cultural policy, see B. Dooley, 'Giornalismo, accademie e organizzazione della scienza: tentativi di formare un'accademia scientifica veneta all'inizio del Settecento', *Archivio veneto*, Ser. 5, vol. 120 (1983), 5-39.

80.   See Conti's letter to Poleni, Bibl. Marc., cod. lat. cl. VIII:136 (=2147), 9 July 1728.

81.   *Raccolta d'opuscoli scientifici e letterari*, 2 (1729), 355ff and 468ff.

82.   G. A. Moschini, *Della letteratura veneziana*, 3 vols. (Venice, 1806), III, 167.

83.   For an account of these practices at Padua, see Morgagni, *Autobiografie*, p. xxxvii.

84.   *Ibid*, p. xxxviii.

85.   Poleni's diploma and the minutes of the exam sitting are in Bibl. Marc. cod. lat. cl. VIII: 157 (=2734), n.p.

86.   Bibl. Marc. cod. lat. cl. VIII: 147 (=2724), n.p.: 'Etsi obsequium erga illos, qui hanc mihi provinciam demandarunt, eam timoris partem, quae ex mei ipsius cognitione exoritur dissimulare doceat; attamen alteram timoris partem, quae ex iudicio vestro subeundo enascitur, neque dissimulare vellem, si possem, cum sit meae venerationis erga vos argumentum, neque possem, si vellem, cum tanta sit timendi causa, ut iam interna commotio non tantum in oris verum etiam in vocis perturbatione compareat'.

87.   Bibl. Marc. cod. lat. cl. VIII: 147 (=2724), n.p.: 'Ex observationibus rationi maxime consentaneum extitit supponere quodcumque sidus peculiari atmosphaera non secus ac tellurem nostram circumdari'.

88.   Bibl. Marc. cod. lat. cl. VIII: (=2724), n.p.: 'Ipse celeberrimus Newtonus, qui admirabili sublimis ingenii pompa caelestium spatiorum materiam tam sedulo exinanuit, censit tamen, quod cometae cauda nihil aliud sit, quam vapor longe tenuissimus, quem caput, seu Nucleus cometae per calorem amittit.'

89.   On Andrea Argoli, see entry by M. Gliozzi in *Dizionario biografico degli italiani* IV (Rome, 1962), 132-4; and Soppelsa, *Il metodo galileiano*, pp. 70-9. On Degli Angeli, see L. Tenca, 'Stefano Degli Angeli', *Atti Acc. Sci. dell'Ist. di Bologna*, ser. II, vol. 5 (1958), 194-207.

148   *History of Universities*

90.   Opening prolusion for 1714-15 is in Bibl. Marc. cod. lat. cl. VIII: 147 (=2724), n.p.

91.   S. Rotta, 'Sulla costruzione e diffusione in Italia dei telescopi a riflessione', *Le macchine*, I (1968), 97-8.

92.   See Bernoulli's letter in Bibl. Marc. cod. ital. cl. IV: 642 (=5503), 26 April 1726.

93.   *Riformatori*, filza 83, 30 January 1720-1.

94.   The lessons on astronomy for the academic year 1714-15 are in Bibl. Marc. cod. lat. cl. VIII: 157 (=2734), (hereafter Lessons, 1714-15, I), numbered consecutively. Lessons will be indicated in the notes by these numbers.

95.   *Lessons, 1714-15*, I, n. 36: 'Tanta etenim inter celebriores auctores dissensio est ut cuinam standus sit distingui non patitur'. These debates are discussed in P. Rossi, *I segni del tempo: storia delle nazioni e storia della terra da Hooke a Vico* (Milan, 1979), pp. 179-80; 184-5.

96.   *Lessons, 1714-15*, I, n. 36: 'Nobis liquide non innotescat quot annus primum separatae salutis antecesserit annis primus Nabonassari'. Dechales' advice was in his *Cursus seu mundus mathematicus*, 4 vols (Leiden, 1690[2]), IV, 722. Indeed, it was not particularly helpful advice, as most accurate observations made in antiquity were dated from Nabonassar.

97.   On the seventeenth-century chronologists, A. D. Momigliano, 'Roman "Bestioni" and Roman "Eroi" in Vico's *Scienza nuova*', in A. D. Momigliano, *Terzo contributo alla storia degli studi classici e del mondo antico*, 2 vols (Rome, 1966), I, 153-77; A. Grafton, 'Joseph Scaliger and Historical Chronology: the Rise and Fall of a Discipline', *History and Theory*, 14 (1975), 156-85.

98.   *Lessons, 1714-15*, I, n. 37. Compare Hevelius, *Cometographia* (Gdańsk, 1668), an obvious source.

99.   *Lessons, 1714-15*, I, n. 38: 'Caelestium rerum periti duplici usi sunt methodo pro tali determinatione assequendo qua geometricis et arithmeticis, qua opticis theorematibus insistendo'.

100.   *Lessons, 1714-15*, I, n. 44. See A. Tacquet, *Opera, I: Astronomia* (Antwerp, 1669), Bk. 8, Ch. 2. On Tacquet's 'annoyingly erudite eclecticism', see the entry by P. Stromholm, *D. S. B.*, XIII (1976), 235-6.

101.   *Lessons, 1714-15*, I, n. 47: '[Deus] infinita sapientia sua hanc naturae machinam ita cohordinasse ut causae secundae previa causae primae ordinatione agant'.

102.   His experiments with Morgagni are discussed in Bibl. Marc. cod. ital. cl. XI: 220 (=6940), n.p.

103.   Bibl. Marc. cod. ital. cl. IV: 592 (=5555) (Hereafter, *Lessons, 1714-15*, II), c. 70. These lessons will be indicated by page number.

104.   Some of his figures are in *Lessons, 1714-15*, II, cc. 119-22. They are in multiple copies on squares of paper identical in size, probably made up for distribution to students.

105.   *Lessons, 1714-15*, II, c. 75. To place these pneumatic experiments into the context of the history of technology I used W. E. K. Middleton, *History of the Thermometer* (Baltimore, 1966), Chaps. 1-21; Idem, *The Invention of the Meteorological Instruments* (Baltimore, 1969), pp. 1-29; 43-63; 70-1.

106.   *Lessons, 1714-15*, II, cc. 103-4.

107.   *Lessons, 1714-15*, II, cc. 105-6.

108.   *Lessons, 1714-15*, II, c. 128.

109.   See M. Kerker, 'Hermann Boerhaave and the Development of Pneumatic Chemistry', *Isis*, 46 (1955), 36-49; W. E. K. Middleton, 'Jacob Hermann and the

Kinetic Theory', *British Journal for the History of Science*, 2 (1965), 247-50; R. Zouckermann, 'Poids de l'air et pression atmosphérique', *Physis*, 24 (1982), 133-56; F. Sebastiani, 'Le teorie microscopico-caloristiche dei gas di Laplace, Ampère, Poisson, e Prévost', *Physis*, 24 (1982), 197-236.

110. W. E. K. Middleton, *History of the Barometer* (Baltimore, 1964), pp. 94-8.

111. *Lessons, 1714-15*, II, c. 86: 'Philosophi illi, qui inepte, atque impie Tellurem magnum quoddam animal esse finxerunt nullam crediderim inter animalis et Telluris corpora analogiam invenire potuisse, nisi hanc, quod et animalis et telluris interiores partes calore iugi foveantur'. Gassendi's simile is in *Opera*, 6 vols (Lyon, 1658-75), I, 556-7. On this and other aspects of Gassendi's thought I have followed K. Lasswitz, *Geschichte der Atomistik vom Mittelalter bis Newton*, 2 vols (Hamburg-Leipzig, 1890), II, 140-67; T. Gregory, *Scetticismo ed empirismo. Studio su Gassendi* (Milan, 1961), pp. 179-250; O. R. Bloch, *La philosophie de Gassendi: Nominalisme, matérialisme et métaphysique* (The Hague, 1971), pp. 155-284.

112. Poleni cites Régis' *Système de philosophie*, 5 vols (Lyon, 1691), III, 235ff. On Régis, I used R. A. Watson, *The Downfall of Cartesianism 1673-1712* (The Hague, 1966), pp. 75-81.

113. *Lessons, 1714-15*, II, c. 97: 'Haec vero materiae subtilis adhaesio tamquam aptissima ad explicandas vaporum, et elevationes, et suspensiones predicatur, tum quia revera, hypothesi admissa, res apte exprimitur, tum quia semel admissa vaporum suspensionem propter talem causam, ipsorum etiam descensus quam faciliter explicatur'.

114. *Lessons, 1714-15*, II, c. 123: 'Vir ille eximius coelestem omnem materiam exinanire contendit in opere illo, quod (liceat ita loqui) redolet quid plus quam humanum, at quod spectat hoc de coelesti vacuo placitum videtur humanum'. On the position of Leibniz and his followers, A. Koyré, *From the Closed World to the Infinite Universe* (Baltimore, 1957), Ch. II; A. Koyré and I. B. Cohen, 'The Case of the Missing *Tamquam*: Leibniz, Newton, and Clarke', *Isis*, 52 (1961), 555-66.

115. *Lessons, 1714-15*, II, c. 75. On Carré, see *Oeuvres de Malebranche, XX: Documents biographiques et bibliographiques*, ed. A. Robinet (Paris, 1967), pp. 147-53.

116. Compare Hauksbee's conclusions in *Physico-Mechanical Experiments on Various Subjects* (London, 1719), Sec. V, Exp. 8. On early eighteenth-century transformations in Cartesianism, T. L. Hankins, 'The Influence of Malebranche on the Science of Mechanics During the Eighteenth Century', *Journal of the History of Ideas*, 28 (1967), 193-210; R. Hahn, *The Anatomy of a Scientific Institution: the Paris Academie des Sciences 1666-1803* (Berkeley, 1971), pp. 31-44; C. Iltis, 'The Decline of Cartesianism in the Leibniz-Cartesian Debates', *Isis*, 64 (1973); H. Guerlac, 'Some Areas for Further Newtonian Studies', *History of Science*, 17 (1979), 75-101; As far as Italy is concerned, the most trustworthy studies are now R. Ajello, 'Cartesianismo e cultura oltremontana al tempo dell'*Istoria civile*', in *Pietro Giannone e il suo Tempo. Atti del Convegno di Studi nel Tricentenario della nascita*, 2 vols (Naples, 1980), I, 1-182; and V. Ferrone, *Scienza, natura, religione: mondo newtoniano e cultura italiana nel primo Settecento* (Naples, 1982), pp. 3-108.

117. *Lessons, 1714-15*, II, cc. 123-5. Compare Bernoulli, *Opera Omnia*, 2 vols (Geneva, 1744), II, 106. On the importance of Bernoulli's theory, besides Lasswitz, *Geschichte der Atomistik*, II, 430-5, see C. Truesdell, 'A Program Toward Rediscovering the Rational Mechanics of the Age of Reason, 1687-1788', *Archive for the History of the Exact Sciences*, I (1960), 14.

118. He refers to Haley's 'On the Circulation of the Water Vapors of the Sea and the Cause of the Springs', *Philosophical Transactions*, 17 (1692), 468ff.

119. *Lessons, 1714-15*, II, c. 93.

120. *Lessons, 1714-15*, II, c. 127: 'Sufficit indigitare quod quaestio de aetheris gravitate in Neutoniana hypothesi locum non habeat'.

121. Bibl. Marc. cod. lat. cl. VIII: 138 (= 2715), 'Sectiones Conicae et Mechanicae, 1723-4', n. 5: 'Explicatio experimenti Mariotti ex exedra dicta difficilis admodum fuit. Quare oportet cum diligentia minutimque scribere tam quod attinet ad modum experimenti, tam quod attinet ad explicationem legis'.

122. *Riformatori*, filza 195, 23 April 1719: 'I corpi, i quali hanno la virtù di attrarsi l'un l'altro non solo sono degni d'osservazione, ma vi è ai nostri giorni qualche sistema famoso di filosofia, il quale dalle attrazioni dei corpi tutto dipende'.

123. *Riformatori*, filza 195, 23 April 1719: 'Vorrei porre più in vista ciò che in quel tempo fosse o intorno alla medicina o intorno altre cose più dalla curiosità degli uomini ricercato. E andare poi investigando il modo d'inventare nuove esperienze, perchè le nuove scoperte accrescono l'anima a quelli che le fanno, e sono un grande eccitamento a quelli che prima li vedano'.

124. The projects of Guglielmini and Sacco were mentioned by Maffei in his *Parere* (1715), published by B. Brugi, 'Un parere di Scipione Maffei intorno allo Studio di Padova sui principi del Settecento', *Atti dell'Istituto Veneto di Scienze, Lettere, ed Arti*, 69 (1909-10), p. 582. On the general policies of the Riformatori, I follow Del Negro, 'Giacomo Nani', pp. 77-114.

125. *Riformatori*, filza 85, Poleni, 2 December 1723.

126. Bibl. Marc. cod. ital. cl. IV: 592 (= 5555), c. 191, to G. F. Morosini, n.d., but 1738: ' . . . gli uomini che fanno adesso nell'Arte Esperimentale la figura prima, e notissimi sono, troppo difficilmente (oltre che seguono una diversa religione) si indurrebbero a lasciare i loro commodi e lucrosi posti'.

127. Bibl. Marc. cod. ital. cl. IV: 592 (= 5555), c. 191: 'Sono essi i Signori Christian Wolff in Germania, Desaguliers in Inghilterra e in Ollanda, Musschenbroeck e 'sGravesande. Questi degli Esperimenti fanno un'arte, e li vanno eseguendo in serie, e con l'ordine ricercato dal sistema della Natura'. In my remarks on the Dutch tradition in experimental philosophy I follow C. A. Crommelin, 'Die holländische Physik im 18 Jahr. mit besonderer Berücksichtigung der Entwicklung der Feinmechanik', *Sudhoffs Archiv*, 28 (1935), 129-42; and G. Goril, *La fondazione dell'esperienza in 'sGravesande* (Florence, 1972), pp. 7-159.

128. Bibl. Marc. cod. lat. cl. VIII: 145 (= 2722), 'Lezioni, 1743-44', n. 18. Compare W. J. 'sGravesande, *Physices*, 2 vols (Leiden, 1742), I, Bk. 1, Ch. 15.

129. On Newton's methodology, A. Koyré, *Newtonian Studies* (Cambridge, Mass., 1965), Ch. 2; I. B. Cohen, 'Hypotheses in Newton's Philosophy', *Physis*, 8 (1966), 163-84. For my comments on the transformations of this methodology in the practice of popular experimental lecturers, I consulted A. Pala, 'Lo sperimentalismo francese dal 1650 al 1750', in G. Solinas (ed.), *Saggi sull'Illuminismo* (Cagliari, 1973), pp. 226ff.

130. Bibl. Marc. cod. ital. cl. IV: 592 (= 5555), c. 128: 'Bisogna sapere più che si possa l'Istoria di tutti gli Esperimenti che sono stati fatti, i modi, gli artefici, e le Macchine adoperate. Di più, il successo degli Esperimenti medesimi, e le consequenze, che ne sono state fatte per la filosofia naturale o per la matematica. Questo è un *mare magnum*, che dipende da gran quantità di libri e da lunga lettura ed applicazione'.

131. Bibl. Marc. cod. ital. cl. IV: 592 (= 5555), c. 129: 'Credo che in tal forma nascerebbe come da se stesso un ordine utile, chiaro, e scientifico, onde dappoi si potrebbe fare un corso in tutto e per tutto regolare, secondo un metodo esatto'.

132. Bibl. Marc. cod. ital. cl. IV: 592 (= 5555), c. 194, 21 April 1739: 'Sono rimasto male in assetto per l'incommodo, cui non si può reggere, del luogo, per la folla, per il caldo, e per la gran fatica di dire e fare, e procurare assieme che l'uno e l'altro aggradevole e pulito riesca'.

133. Bibl. Marc. cod. ital. cl. IV: 592 (= 5555), c. 185, to the same, 18 March 1738/9: 'L'Operare, il lavorare in presenza degli altri, il dichiarare le cose con le lezioni, che nel mostrare si farano agli uditori, i quali saranno nello stesso tempo spettatori dello sperimento, in una parola, la pratica mi aiutaranno a costituire quel sistema che mi sembri più adatto per ben servire'.

134. J. Facciolati, *Fasti Gymnasii Patavini* (Padua, 1758), p. 423. On the major contributions of the shop in Leiden of Samuel van Musschenbroeck and his heirs Jan and Pieter, see M. Daumas, *Les instruments scientifiques aux dix-septième et dix-huitième siècles* (Paris, 1953), pp. 325-7.

135. Facciolati, *Fasti*, p. 426.

136. *Ibid*, p. 418: 'Machina ex plurimis partibus constans, quarum aliae ligneae, aliae ferreae, aliae ex orichalco, aliae plumbeae. Compositione et motibus earum partium fit, ut varia corpora variis modis in varios gyros agantur; atque adeo proprietates vis centrifugae ita explorentur'.

137. *Ibid*, p. 425: 'Machina ex trabibus, cum magna rota axe munita, manubriis ferreis, et cheloniis aeneis. Laminae duae, catenulae et tubuli; haec omnia ferrea. Cochleae ligneae, cylindrus ferreus cum axe et tympanis . . . '. On electrical research in Italy in the first half of the eighteenth century, S. Ramazzotti and L. Briatore, 'Appunti di storia della fisica: dalle calze di seta di Symner all'alettroforo di Volta', *Gior. di fisica*, 15 (1974), 52-9; J. L. Heilbron, *Electricity in the Seventeenth and Eighteenth Centuries*, (Berkeley, 1979), pp. 362-72.

138. Facciolati, *Fasti*, p. 418: 'Stylobata ligneus grandis ad sustinendam unam bilancis lancem. Adjunctus est alter ferreus ad sustinendam bilancis jugum. Lances cylindracae et pilae ponderis varii. Et jugum, quod stylobatae illi bilancis adjungitur, cum aliis partibus'.

139. Compare 'sGravesande, *Physices*, II, Bk. II, ch. V.

140. Facciolati, *Fasti*, p. 414. Compare 'sGravesande, *Physices*, II, Bk. IV, ch. V; P. van Musschenbroeck, *Essai de physique . . . traduit du Hollandaise*, 2 vols (Leiden, 1739), I, Ch. VII.

141. Facciolati, *Fasti*, p. 426.

142. Facciolati, *Fasti*, p. 413: 'Instrumentum recens inventum: compositum est ex capsulis quatuor metallicis cancellatis, ligneo instrumento insertis, per quod discurrere queunt'.

143. M. Rowbottom, 'The Teaching of Experimental Philosophy in England, 1700-30', in *Actes du onzième congrès internationale d'histoire du science, Varsovie, 1965* (Warsaw, 1968), IV, 46-53; W. D. Hackmann, 'The Growth of Science in the Netherlands in the Seventeenth and Early Eighteenth Centuries', in M. P. Crosland (ed.), *The Emergence of Science in Western Europe* (New York, 1976), pp. 89-110.

144. On Bose, see the entry by J. L. Heilbron in *D. S. B.*, II (1979), 324-5. On Banks, see A. E. Musson and E. Robinson, 'Science and Industry in the Eighteenth Century', *Economic History Review* 13 (1960), 233-4.

145. Here and below, Bibl. Marc. cod. lat. cl. VIII: 153 (=2735), n.p.

146. For a discussion of this problem in general, U. Baldini, 'La scuola galileiana', in *Storia d'Italia, Annali III: Scienza e tecnica* (Turin, 1980), pp. 383-468.

147. Brugi, 'Un parere di Scipione Maffei', 578. On Maffei's political ideals, C. Donati, 'Scipione Maffei e *La scienza chiamata cavalleresca*. Saggio sull'ideologia nobiliare al principio del Settecento', *Rivista storica italiana*, 90 (1978), 30-71.

148. C. A. Pilati, *Di una riforma d'Italia*, 2 vols (Chur, 1779²), II, Ch. XV. On Pilati, see F. Venturi, *Settecento riformatore, II: La chiesa e la repubblica dentro i loro limiti*, (Turin, 1976), pp. 251-325.

Research Notes

THE KUTTENBERG DECREE AND THE WITHDRAWAL OF THE GERMAN STUDENTS FROM PRAGUE IN 1409: A DISCUSSION

František Šmahel

On the 18th of January, 1409 a decree was issued from the Royal Chancellery of Wenzel IV in Kuttenberg (Kutná Hora) which fundamentally altered the old constitution of Prague University, giving a voting majority to the representatives of the 'Bohemian nation' in all important decisions.[1] After four months of fruitless negotiation trying to find a compromise, the masters and students of the three non-Bohemian nations represented at the university withdrew to Germany to found a new university in Leipzig. So Prague University became a state university *sui generis* as well as in legislative terms. Of the many issues connected with this development I have chosen for discussion two which relate to the general methodology of research into medieval universities. The first concerns the absolute and relative strength, in terms of numbers, of the four nations represented at Prague University before the Kuttenberg Decree. The second verifies estimates of the extent of the secession in May, 1409.[2]

For decades Czech historians ignored the relation between the number of indigenous university students and teachers and their representation in the faculty and university organs which was only a quarter. The explanation is quite simple. In 1846 V. V. Tomek published a statistical study of the numbers of students at Prague University in the 14th century. This study, notable for its time, nipped in the bud any possible attempts to vindicate the Kuttenberg Decree by citing the rights of the Bohemian majority.[3] By simply adding up the number of the various students entered in the register of the Law Faculty, the author deduced that in the 1370s and 1380s only a sixth of these professed Bohemian nationality.

Although the Bohemian proportion rose to almost a fifth in the next two decades even this remained a surprisingly low minority representation. For that reason it was decided not to investigate too closely whether the picture might have been different in other faculties. It was only considered possible, and even then more or less on a basis of guesswork, that Czechs might have gained in numbers among the masters of the Arts Faculty.[4]

Only a hundred years after Tomek, in 1947, did there emerge the supposition only hinted at before, that there was a major redistribution at Prague University in favour of the Czech people at the turn of the 14th and 15th centuries.[5] It was only one further step to the next assumption that the decree of Wenzel IV was not only consistent with the normal aspirations of the indigenous people represented at the university, but also with their annually increased representation at the university. Furthermore the compromise proposals of the three protesting nations included one to divide uneven vote numbers by half to achieve a 50:50 situation. Thus this interpretation appeared to match not only true conditions at the university but also the otherwise undeniable upsurge of the Czech emancipation movement in Prague and elsewhere. Due to its superficial plausibility, the new interpretation gained currency to such an extent that no one attempted to check its unproven claims.[6] It was in any case no longer possible to list the composition of the university according to nationality, but only that of the students entered in the Dean's graduation roll (*liber decanorum*) of the Arts Faculty. The difficulty of such a task created a disincentive from the outset, because research had to be based on a reconstruction of the nationalities of almost a thousand graduates during the decade 1399-1409.

It was only by chance that I set out to verify what appeared to be an obvious set of facts. While working on the Prague Secession, I saw the possibilities which the application of electronic methods could offer to medievalists. Apart from the fascination of the speed of computers I was even more impressed by certain theoretical possibilities such as the effect of feedback and formulating reverse control questions, which was something new to a historian.[7] This new way of setting the same research task made work appear attractive which would otherwise not have been worth the effort. It could now be asked whether the proportion of Bohemian graduates had *really* risen continuously from a minority to a majority.

Not only was the answer itself a surprise, but so was its numerical expression.[8] During the period under review, from the winter semester of 1398 to the end of the winter semester of 1409, only a fifth of the candidates (19.81 per cent) for the bachelor's degree, and not quite a third (29.12 per cent) for the master's degree belonged to the Bohemian nation. But the surprises were not yet over. To prevent the results of an entire decade distorting a decisive period before the Kuttenberg decree was issued, the representation of indigenous candidates for five semesters between autumn 1406 and spring 1409 was also calculated. Instead of the expected increase, the results revealed a *drop* to 16.47 per cent among the bachelor group and 21.95

per cent in the masters' category of the Arts Faculty. Still more curious was the fact that this drop was only relative, since the number of Bohemian graduates from the university continued to increase in absolute figures. This trend was also confirmed by the results of an independent investigation into a group of university teachers known as the *magistri regentes*.[9] During the period 1381-1390 only 19.3 per cent of the College of Masters of the Arts Faculty were of the Bohemian nation. In the following decade they represented 26 per cent, and 29.3 per cent during the period 1401 to 1409. Seen from the perspective of the national problems of the time, it is noteworthy that the Bohemian minority did not even add up to a third of the Masters' College.

But let us now return to the surprising increase in the number of foreign students matriculating at Prague University. The increase in the three non-Bohemian nations represented at the university, in both relative and absolute terms, corresponds to the decline in attendance which can be discerned at all the central European universities about 1405. The increase in foreign students at Prague cannot be explained conclusively. There were specific reasons at the various universities, such as a students' war and the plague in Heidelberg and economic stagnation in Vienna. But probably another reason was increasing interest in the controversy over Wyclif's conception of universals.[10] Although the relative dip in the numbers of students of the Bohemian nation could not have any direct influence on an immediate reduction in the numbers of Czechs among the *magistri regentes*, the Wyclif faction undoubtedly saw a serious danger in the increase of foreign students. This trend meant, above all, more prestige and support for the group of conservative theologians, nominalists and moderate reformers who were aiming, with the help of the archbishop, to eradicate Wyclifism from the university as a heretical teaching. Secondly, a potential danger was growing that the number of masters among the three non-Bohemian nations would increase sooner or later among the teaching staff, whereas in the meantime the Bohemian representatives could point to their own numerical superiority to plead unfair distribution of votes. And finally a larger number of future foreign graduates meant a deterioration of the prospects for a livelihood of the local Bohemian students, which were doubtful enough as things stood.

No further details need be listed here.[11] It was not a marked increase in numbers which provided the impetus towards emancipation by the leaders of the Bohemian nation at the university: on the contrary, it was the relative decline in numbers. In the end it was the stand of Wenzel IV which decided matters, since he would obtain the necessary support of the University for his Council and arrived at from Prague (see Appendix II). Moreover there are some names which could not be confirmed as ever having been enrolled at Prague university.[19]

The next step is inevitable. In the case of four universities — Paris, Bologna, Cracow and Heidelberg — Dr. Schumann either adopted my data or confirmed it.[20] A difference of three in the number of students who moved from Prague to Cologne is of little importance.[21] What should be examined more closely is the secession via Vienna and Erfurt, for here Dr. Schumann arrived at a figure 55 to 60 less than my figure of 96 persons. A list of differences is found in Appendix III (although in fact *pars pro toto* only for Vienna University.).

Dr. Schumann studied the Prague students and masters on the basis of direct evidence in the matriculation lists and the frequently incomplete and inaccurate registers of names. My research was based on an examination of the university careers of the students, bachelors, licentiates, masters and doctors who could be shown to have studied or otherwise been active at Prague University between the years 1399 and 1419. In a word I used a prosopographical method.[22] The documentation I put together was too extensive to be published, but I retain the information for future use. Similar problems arise with Dr. Schumann's interpretation of Leipzig.[23] Here I shall limit myself to one example: she concludes that only two of the 12 bachelors described as being of the Meissen nation during the 1409 winter semester were proved also to have been in Prague. In fact, seven are proved with certainty to have come from Prague and the others probably also did so.[24]

Throughout my research I made a distinction between clear and debatable cases, including in the former category those who could be said with great probability to have studied in Prague. I included in this group, for example, those students who took their bachelor's examination just after arriving in Leipzig. The Leipzig statutes for the bachelor's examination stipulated at least 18 months' study, so that the candidates in the first two terms must therefore have previously studied elsewhere. Of the 33 candidates in the first two semesters 15 had previously studied in Prague according to my estimate, which I do not consider exaggerated.

If a critical historian is going to examine the sources directly he cannot ignore what these sources actually tell him. Even though the editor of the Leipzig matriculation roll had grasped that the term *pragensis* had to do with the claim to exemption from the matriculation fee, Dr. Schumann regards this adjective in the narrow sense merely as a description of one of the participants in the Prague

Secession and therefore confines herself to entries in the imperial policy by altering the ratio of votes at the university; but his decree of 18 January 1409 had further historical consequences. The king's intervention turned what was originally a *studium generale* into a state university where the Hussite reform party grew into the dominating force. On the other hand the secession of several hundred masters, bachelors and students prompted great excitement and animosity against the Czech heresy in neighbouring countries even before the Hussites could enter their revolutionary phase.

There is also a long history attached to the second question, viz. how many masters and students left Prague in the spring of 1409? In the second half of the 19th century estimates ran to several thousand[12]. Unswerving faith in the statistics of medieval chroniclers could not hold its own against the revised figures provided by newly edited registers of the medieval universities. First Friedrich Paulsen, then Heinrich Denifle refuted the old premises. Paulsen estimated the Prague Secession at 400 to 500 persons. By comparing the numbers of matriculations at European universities shortly before and after 1409, Denifle excluded the possibility of a uniquely large influx of former Prague masters and students.[13] The later analysis of the Cracow and Viennese registers only confirmed the lower estimates.[14] These lower estimates are the basis of the results of the complex research which I published in 1967.[15] The extent of the secession, established at 700 to 800 persons, would then agree with the assumed attendance of 1,000 to 1,200 students, as well as with the overall numbers of the Bohemian nation in relation to the other nations.

However, the issue was not simply set aside after that. In her 1975 dissertation 'The *Nationes* at the Universities of Prague, Leipzig and Vienna', Sabine Schumann concluded that my estimate was too high and suggested that the maximum which had withdrawn from Prague was 500.[16] Although her procedure was in fundamental agreement with mine, she was able to establish only 251 identifiable persons according to the university registers compared to my 513 proven participants in the Secession. The large gap, particularly noticeable by medieval standards, was seen as due to my 'decisive methodical error'.[17] Greater importance must be attached to the method of quantitative research, however, than to the actual figures themselves. I do not intend to increase the figure of 251, which serves as the starting point for this issue, but to reduce it. Dr. Schumann calculated each individual matriculation without taking into account whether the student concerned might have also enrolled at another of the universities in question.[18] *Peregrinatio academica* by the Prague students, bachelors and masters was frequent after May 1409, for not everyone was content to settle down at the first university town he matriculation roll up to the end of 1411.[25] In fact, in the next few years a further 94 undisputed and 14 possible cases from the Prague Alma Mater availed themselves of this exemption. The reason why they should have delayed their matriculation for so long (the last *pragensis* was enrolled as late as 1433) were doubtless varied, but do not alter the merits of the case.

As I have already indicated, students of medieval history cannot afford to take their sources too literally. They must apply as much care in establishing what is *not* stated in the sources, doing so by means of reverse checks and verification or the quantitative and qualitative aspects of the entire system to which the material under investigation belongs. This applies to the 109 bachelors and 15 licentiates from three foreign nations who took their examinations in Prague between the summer semester of 1407 and May 1409. I could not prove that any of these 124 graduates was at Prague or any other university after this date, so that in all probability, following their exodus from Prague they either became clergymen or teachers in the lower schools, or found work in municipal administration. This assumption is perfectly legitimate given that the members of the three foreign nations had committed themselves on oath to the obligation to leave Prague as long as the Kuttenberg Decree was not revoked or revised.[26]

So even after many years I do not feel obliged to alter anything essential in the results of my research. Perhaps I made a mistake in listing in my summary the precise figure of 513 positively identified participants in the Prague Secession, especially as a figure of 'about 500' would have sufficed in view of the approximate character of the numerical expression.[27] Since of these 500 or so not quite a third were students and the ratio between graduates and undergraduates at medieval universities was the opposite, there must have been at least twice as many students. That is why I have estimated the overall figure of participants in the Prague secession in the spring of 1409 at 700 to 800.

Na strži 39
Praha 4
Czechoslovakia

REFERENCES

1. As the original of the Kuttenberg Decree was not preserved, the basic text used is the copy in the notarial deed of 18 September 1414. The last critical edition in M. Jana Husi, *Korespondence a dokumenty* [Jan Hus, *Correspondence and Documents*], ed. Václav Novotný (Prague, 1920), n. 83, pp. 199-202.

2. Generally on this subject see Ferdinand Seibt, 'Johannes Hus und der Abzug der deutschen Studenten aus Prag 1409', *Archiv für Kulturgeschichte* 39 (1957), pp. 63-80; papers and contributions to the academic conference on the significance of the Kuttenberg Decree under the title *Dekret kutnohorský a jeho místo v dějinách* [*The Kuttenberg Decree and Its Place in History*] (Prague, 1959), [Acta Universitatis Carolinae—Philosophica et Historica, 2]; and Jiří Kejř, *Sporné otázky v bádání o Dekretu kutnohorském* [*Controversial Questions in the Research on the Kutna Hora Decree*] (Acta Universitatis Carolinae—Historica Universitatis Carolinae Pragensis), 3 — 1 (1962), pp. 83-95. This series is afterwards cited as: AUC-HUCP.

3. V. V. Tomek, 'O počtu študentů v učení Pražském ve 14.století' [On Student Numbers at Prague University], *Časopis Musea Království Českého* 20 (1846), pp. 212-230. Tomek's calculations were made more precise by a collective investigation by Professor Zatschek's historical seminar: Heinz Zatschek, 'Studien zur Geschichte der Prager Universität bis 1409',*Mitteilungen des Vereines für Geschichte der Deutschen in den Sudetenländer* 77 (1939), pp. 14-28.

4. Particular consideration was often given to the utterance by Jan Hus: 'magistri Bohemi sunt super Teutonicorum magistros multiplicati et in omni sciencia et facultate ultra extraneos elevati'. Cf. e.g. Václav Chaloupecký, *Karlova universita v Praze, 1348-1409* [*The Charles University, Prague, 1348-1409*] (Prague, 1948), pp. 92, 97, where there is also an approximate calculation of the number of professors of the Bohemian nation.

5. F. M. Bartoš, *Čechy v době Husově 1378-1415* [*Bohemia at the Time of Hus 1378-1415*] (Prague, 1947) (*Česke dějiny*, vol. 2—6), p. 256.

6. Cf. Zdeněk Fiala, 'O vzniku Dekretu kutnohorského' [On the Creation of the Kuttenberg Decree] in: *Dekret kutnohorský a jeho místo v dějinách*, pp. 29, 37 n. 53; *Stručné dějiny University Karlovy* [*Concise History of Charles University*] (Prague, 1964), p. 42; and *Handbuch der Geschichte der böhmischen Länder* I (Stuttgart, 1967), p. 490.

7. See, for example, Norbert Wiener, *The Human Use of Human Beings: Cybernetics and Society* (New York, 1954[2]).

8. I also summarise the results of the research which I published in the paper 'Pražské universitní studentstvo v předrevolučním období 1399-1419' [The Student Body at Prague University from the Hussite Revolution 1319-1419, a Statistical and Sociological Study] (Prague, 1967) *Rozpravy ČSAV* 77, SV series, vol. 3, pp. 24-27, 63-68. See the numerical data in table one. Also see the data for 1367-1398 of Hana Václavů 'Počet graduovaných a negraduovaných studentů na pražské artistické fakultě v letech 1367-1398 a jejich rozdělení podle universitních národů [The Numbers and Origins According to Nations of Students Represented in the Prague Arts Faculty, 1367-1398], AUC-HUCP 17, (1977) pp. 18-20.

9. František Kavka, 'Mistři-regenti na artistické fakultě pražské univerzity v letech 1367-1420' [*Magistri regentes* at the Arts Faculty of Prague University, 1367-1420) in: *Z českých dějin* (Prague, 1966), pp. 77-96.

160   *History of Universities*

10.   See František Šmahel, 'Wyclifs Fortune in Hussite Bohemia', *Bulletin of the Institute of Historical Research* 43 (May, 1970), pp. 16-34; *idem*, 'Leben und Werk des Magisters Hieronymus von Prag', *Historica* 13 (1966), pp. 92, 94 and 'Le mouvement des étudiants à Prague dans les années 1408-1412', *Historica* 14 (1967), pp. 33-75.

11.   More about the emancipation struggle of the Bohemian nationality at the university can be found in František Šmahel, 'The Idea of the "Nation" in Hussite Bohemia', *Historica* 16 (1969), pp. 163-180.

12.   Konstantin Hoefler, *Johannes Hus und der Abzug der deutschen Studenten aus Prag 1409* (Prague, 1864), p. 247. He estimated the maximum secession at 20,000 although even before him V. V. Tomek, *Geschichte der Prager Universität* (Prague, 1849), p. 125, had suggested a figure only a quarter of this. At the end of the last century Zikmund Winter was still insisting on a figure of a least 2,000: *Děje vysokých škol pražských od secesí cizích národů po dobu bitvy bělohorské, 1409-1622* [*History of Prague University since the Secession of Foreign Nations at the Time of the Battle of White Mountain, 1409-1622*] (Prague, 1897), p. 9.

13.   Cf. Friedrich Paulsen, 'Die Gründung der Universitäten im Mittelalter', *Historische Zeitschrift* 45 (1881), p. 251 and Heinrich Denifle, *Die Universitäten des Mittelalters* (Berlin, 1885) I, 600-601, esp. note 1554. Fr. Matthesius, 'Der Auszug der deutschen Studenten aus Prag 1409', *Mitteilungen des Vereins fur die Geschichte der Deutschen in Boehmen* 53 (1915), pp. 77-79 arrived at a figure of 800 to 1,000 students.

14.   Ivan Hlaváček, 'Matriky vídeňské a krakovské univerzity a Dekret kutnohorský [The Kuttenberg Decree and its Effect on the Numbers Enrolled at the Universities of Vienna and Cracow] in: *Dekret kutnohorský a jeho místo v dějinách*, pp. 75-81.

15.   F. Šmahel, 'Pražské universitní studentstvo', pp. 61-81.

16.   Sabine Schumann, *Die 'nationes' an den Universitäten Prag, Leipzig und Wien. Ein Beitrag zur älteren Universitätsgeschichte* (Dissertation, Free University, West Berlin, 1975).

17.   *Ibid.*, pp. 183-184, 204.

18.   This is applicable, for example, to all Prague students appearing in the *Acta Nationis Germanicae Universitatis Bononiensis*. See F. Šmahel, 'Pražské universitní studentstvo', p. 74. Furthermore the four Erfurt students whom Schumann provides as evidence (*Die 'nationes'*, p. 193) left very soon for Leipzig: Johannes Hammo de Lubeke, Johannes Trunczemann and Ludolfus Lankaw in the winter semester 1409, and Cristianus Cultelificis de Briczen in the summer semester 1412. See *Die Matrikel der Universität Leipzig*, ed. Georg Erler (Leipzig, 1895) I, 26, 27, 39.

19.   With regard to the Viennese group this is applicable to Wenczislaus de Brunnan, Conradus Eberhardi de Hallis and Petrus de Spinis, (Kom. Bihar, Hungary). The last enrolled in Vienna, but was still in Prague in January of the same year. This indicates that, belonging as he did to the Bohemian nation, he did not take part in the Prague Secession of May, 1409.

20.   See F. Šmahel, 'Pražske universitní studentstvo', p. 74 and S. Schumann, *Die 'nationes'*, p. 184.

21.   With the exception of one Johannes de Helden who appears in the Cologne register as a *magister artium Pragensis* (see *Die Matrikel der Universität Köln*, ed. Hermann Keussen (Bonn, 1928) I, pp. 83-84), Schumann includes them all, but treats three of them as indisputable cases. Bernardus de Monasterio, who continued his studies in Cologne after Prague, must be distinguished from another Bernardus Vorschove de Monasterio, who became a doctor of medicine at Bologna. For more information see Šmahel, 'Mistři a studenti pražské lékařské fakulty do roku 1419' [Masters and Students of the Prague Medical Faculty up to 1419], AUC-HUCP 20-2 (1980), p. 51. It is true that two masters, Johannes de Monte and Johannes de Helden,

could not be proved definitively, but this is no surprise in view of the frequent written variations of names. The two masters would not have been allowed to matriculate in Heidelberg as *magistri Pragenses* without relevant certificates, so they can be considered participants in the secession.

22. See, *inter alia*, 'Personenforschung im Spätmittelalter', *Zeitschrift für historische Forschung* 2 (1975), pp. 1-93 and 'Prosopographie als Sozialgeschichte? Methoden personengeschichtlicher Erforschung des Mittelalters', in *Sektionsbeiträge zum 32. deutschen Historikertag, Hamburg 1978* (Munich, 1978).

23. Cf. esp. Siegfried Hoyer, 'Die Gründung der Leipziger Universität und Probleme ihrer Frühgeschichte' in: *Karl-Marx-Universität Leipzig, 1409-1959* (Leipzig, 1959) I, 8f., and F. Šmahel, 'Pražské universitní studentstvo', p. 69f.

24. See Schumann, *Die 'nationes'*, p. 190. In the interests of brevity I will cite only the entries in the *Liber decanorum* in *Monumenta historica Universitatis Carolo-Ferdinandeae Pragensis* Tomus 1, Pars 1 (Prague, 1832) [Hereafter MUPR] and in the Leipzig matriculation list [hereafter, Leipzig]: (1) Jodocus de Karlowicz MUPR I-1, 329; Leipzig, 26; (2) Augustinus Buernchin de Kemnicz MUPR I-1, 389; Leipzig, 26; (3) Paulus de Worczin MUPR I-1, 377, Leipzig, 26; (4) Wenczeslaus Strenczlonis de Kempnicz MUPR I-1, 394; Leipzig, 26; (5) Simon Bernbecker de Lypczig MUPR I-1, 373; Leipzig, 26; (6) Franciscus Eylemburk MUPR I-1, 399, Leipzig, 26; (7) Johannes Tufel de Kemnycz MUPR I-1, 390, Leipzig, 26.

25. Cf. G. Erler, *Die Matrikel*, I, Introduction p. XLVIIIf. and LXXXlf.

26. On the oath of the foreign nations see Z. Fiala *O vzniku Dekretu*, pp. 26, 36 note 39 and J. Kejř, *Sporné otázky*, p. 102.

27. I established 319 participants as beyond doubt. Dr. Schumann also includes persons in the overall figure whom she could not identify with certainty.

Appendix I:
Matriculations and bachelors' examinations at Prague University 1399-1418

Prague	*Group*	*Period* *	*Nationes*											
			Bohem.		*Bavar.*		*Polon.*		*Sax.*		*??*		*Total*	
			no.	%	*no.*	%	*no.*	%	*no.*	%	*no.*	%	*no.*	%
Universitas iuristarum	*studentes*	WS 1399—WS 1408	112	20.9	45	8.4	176	32.8	203	37.9	-	-	536	100
		SS 1409—SS 1419	71	66.4	4	3.7	19	17.8	13	12.1	-	-	107	100
Facultas artium	*baccalarii*	WS 1399—WS 1408	170	19.8	138	16.1	253	29.5	220	25.6	77	9.0	858	100
		SS 1409—SS 1419	144	84.2	3	1.8	23	13.4	1	0.6	-	-	171	100
		WS 1406—WS 1408	44	16.5	46	17.2	71	26.6	82	30.7	24	9.0	267	100
	licentiati	WS 1399—WS 1408	53	29.1	27	14.8	60	33.0	38	20.9	4	2.2	182	100
		SS 1409—SS 1419	48	96.0	-	-	2	4.0	-	-	-	-	50	100
		WS 1406—WS 1408	9	21.9	8	19.6	13	31.7	9	21.9	2	4.9	41	100

* WS = Winter Semester SS = Summer Semester

Appendix II:
The secession of foreign students from Prague

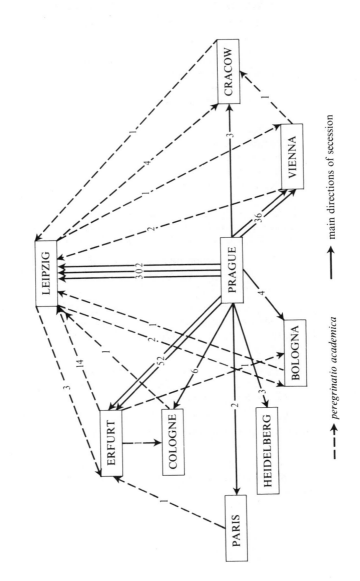

ʃ   **Appendix III:**
Additional register of the participants
in the Prague Secession via Vienna

In this list I confine myself only to the most important essentials, mainly entries in the university registers and other official documents. I do not include those masters, bachelors and students whom Dr. Schumann identifies in *Die nationes*, pp. 196-200).

WS   Winter semester
SS   Summer semester
M   Matriculation
BE   Bachelor's examination
LE   Licentiate examination

MUPR I-1   — *Monumenta Historica Universitatis Carolo-Ferdinandeae Pragensis* Tom. I., Pars I. *Liber decanorum Facultatis Philosophicae Universitatis Pragensis* (Pragae, 1830).

MUPR II   — *Monumenta Historica Universitatis Carolo-Ferdinandeae Pragensis* Tom. II. *Album seu Matricula Facultatis Juridicae Universitatis Pragensis* (Pragae, 1834).

GALL   — *Die Matrikel der Universität Wien*, ed. Franz Gall, Publikationen des Instituts fur Österreichische Geschichtsforschung, VI series, Quellen zur Geschichte der Universität Wien, sect. 1, vol I, 1377-1450 (Vienna, 1956).

KLICMAN   — *Processus iudiciarius contra Jeronimum de Praga habitus Viennae a. 1410-1412*, ed. Ladislav Klicman (Praha, 1898) [Historický archiv, I. třída, č. 12].

PERLBACH   — M. Perlbach, *Prussia scholatica: Die Ost- und Westpreussen auf den mittelalterlichen Universitäten* (Braunsberg, 1895).

UIBLEIN   — *Acta Facultatis artium Universitatis Vindobonensis, 1385-1416*. Based on original handwritten MS, ed. Paul Uiblein, Publikationen des Instituts fur Österreichische Geschichtsforschung, sixth series, sect.2 (Graz-Vienna-Cologne, 1968).

ERLER   — *Matrikel der Universität Leipzig*, ed. Georg Erler vol. I: *Immatrikulationen, 1409-1559* (Leipzig, 1895) [Codex diplomaticus Saxoniae Regiae, 2 Hauptteil, vol. 16].

1. *Achacius Cheuczel de Salzburga*: Prague, comp. KLICMAN, p. 26; Vienna WS 1409, GALL Renenses 43.

2. *Andrea Fafendorff*: Prague BE WS 1405, MUPR I-1, p. 389: Vienna SS 1417, GALL Saxones 2, comp. PERLBACH, p. 160.

3. *Bernardus Nebraw do Torn*: Prague BE WS 1407, MUPR I-1 p. 397; Leipzig WS 1409, ERLER, 27, Pragenses 9; Vienna SS 1414, GALL Saxones 22 comp. PERLBACH p. 160.

4. *Betholdus de Monaco*: Prague BE WS 1408, MUPR I-1, p. 402; Vienna comp. KLICMAN, pp. 31-32.

5. *Caspar Weinstein de Ingolstadt*: Prague comp. KLICMAN p. 27f.; Vienna SS 1410 GALL Renenses 18.

6. *Conradus Domini de Nornberka*: Prague BE WS 1405, MUPR I-1, p. 389, LE WS 1407, MUPR I-1 p. 397; Vienna WS 1414 GALL Renenses 19.

7. *Daniel Hohenkircher*: Prague comp. KLICMAN p. 11 note 1; Vienna WS 1409, GALL Renenses 26.

8. *Hainricus Biberg de Awra*: Prague comp. KLICMAN p. 32; Vienna SS 1409, GALL Renenses 60.

9. *Johannes Kro de Kothebus*: Prague BE SS 1404, MUPR I-1, p. 382, LE WS 1407, MUPR I-1 p. 397; Vienna SS 1413, GALL Hungari 5.

10. *Johannes Kroll de Besskow*: Prague M 1408, MUPR II, p. 157; Vienna SS 1409, GALL Saxones 9.

11. *Johannes Münich dictus Tesser de Mergetheim*: Prague comp. KLICMAN p. 24f.; Vienna SS 1409, GALL Renenses 59.

12. *Johannes Pauli de Karintia de Müsburg*: Prague comp. KLICMAN p. 31; Vienna SS 1409, GALL Australes 12.

13. *Johannes Swab de Buczbach*: Prague BE WS 1405, MUPR I-1, p. 389, IM 1406, MUPR 11, p. 83; Vienna comp. KLICMAN p. 15 and UIBLEIN p. 538.

14. *Johannes Stuckler de Patavia*: Prague BE SS 1408, MUPR I-1 p. 399; Vienna WS 1409, GALL Renenses 15. Comp. KLICMAN pp. 29-30.

15. *Laurencius Meysner de Oschatz*: Prague BE WS 1406, MUPR I-1 p. 392; Vienna SS 1411, GALL Saxones 8. Comp. UIBLEIN, p. 544; Leipzig WS 1414, ERLER p. 46.

16. *Leonardus Purkardi de Monaco*: Prague BE WS 1406, MUPR I-1 p. 392; Vienna, comp. KLICMAN p. 20, UIBLEIN p. 544.

17. *Nicolaus Zungl de Gmunden*: Prague, comp. KLICMAN p. 22f.; Vienna SS 1409, GALL Australes 39.

18. *Peregrinus de Czegenbach*: Prague BE WS 1405, MUPR I-1 p. 389, LE WS 1407, MUPR I-1 pp. 396-7; Leipzig WS 1409, ERLER p. 26; Vienna SS 1413, GALL Saxones 10. Comp. PERLBACH p. 255.

19. *Theodoricus de Brunswick*: Prague BE WS 1404, MUPR I-1 p. 383 (see also MUPR I-1 p. 402-3); Leipzig WS 1409, ERLER p. 26; Vienna SS 1411, GALL Saxones 2. Comp. UIBLEIN p. 564.

CARDINAL FRANCESCO SODERINI'S PROPOSAL FOR AN ITALIAN COLLEGE AT PARIS IN 1524*

K. J. P. Lowe

Francesco Soderini (1453-1524) was a member of a famous Florentine family who were perhaps the leading opponents of the Medici in the late fifteenth and early sixteenth centuries. His brother Piero was *gonfaloniere* for life of the Florentine republic from 1502 to 1512. Soderini attended the Universities of Bologna and Pisa in the 1470s and taught law for a time at Pisa. His ecclesiastical career began in 1478 when he was made bishop of Volterra and in 1503 he became a cardinal.[1] This note is concerned with a bequest of Soderini's designed to found a college at the University of Paris, and it attempts to place this projected foundation in the overall political context of Soderini's opposition to the Medici.

The fourth and final will[2] of Cardinal Francesco Soderini is dated 22 February 1524, three months before his death on 17 May. The supplier of this information, Staglia de Actis, a clerk from Todi, one of Francesco Soderini's *familiares*, stated that Soderini had made several wills[3], one a long time ago, one while he was living in Fondi (i.e. between 1517 and 1521), another while he was in prison in Castel Sant'Angelo during Adrian VI's pontificate (i.e. between February and May 1524). The one written in Castel Sant'Angelo was reputed to have been written in Soderini's own hand. Only the first of the other three wills[4], dated 10 February 1511, is known to survive; it was drawn up in Bologna after Soderini had followed Julius II there with the papal court. Unfortunately it is therefore impossible to know the point at which Soderini first thought of founding a college in Paris but it was conceivably as early as 1512 in response to the return of the Medici to Florence. This will of 1511 and that of 1524 are completely different in emphasis, stemming from the need to take into account the changes in the position and structure of the Soderini family, as well as the position of Soderini himself. One of the ways in which this manifests itself is in the novel appearance in the 1524 will of a bequest to found a college in Paris for Italian students of canon law and theology.

Bequests by ecclesiastics, especially by bishops and cardinals, to found new colleges or bursaries at existing ones, were commonplace. For example in Paris (leaving aside other universities), Cardinal Jean Cholet founded the Collège des Cholets or de Beauvais in 1295,[5] Cardinal Jean Le Moine composed the statutes for the college which bore his name on 1 May 1302,[6] Cardinal Pierre Bertrand founded the Collège du Cardinal Bertrand or d'Autun in 1337[7] and Cardinal Jean de Dormans, bishop of Beauvais, founded the Collège de Dormans or de Beauvais on 8 May 1370.[8] Cardinal Pierre de Montaigu left money on 7 November 1388 to endow bursaries at the college set up on 13 December 1314 by Giles Aicelin, archbishop of Rouen and later of Narbonne.[9] What was unusual was the idea of a foundation in Paris by a foreigner and, more particularly, by an Italian. Italians were renowned for their *campanilismo* and generally left their money, if they had an educational bent, to their home universities or, at worst, to the universities of their place of adopted residence. Soderini would therefore have normally been expected to endow the Universities of either Pisa or Rome. He chose to do neither. The only precedent was the foundation of the Collège des Lombards[10] on 25 February 1334 by four Italians: Andrea Ghini, a Florentine, who was bishop of Arras; Francesco Ospedale, a Modenese citizen who was a captain of artillery to the king of France; Raniero di Giovanni, a citizen of Pistoia and an apothecary in Paris; and Emmanuele Rolandi from Piacenza who was a canon of Saint-Marcel near Paris.[11] They were an unlikely quartet to found a college. Their two points of contact were that they were all Italian and that they all had French interests; indeed they all lived in France, with the possible exception of Ghini.

Soderini had longstanding and diverse French connections. He had first encountered the French king, Charles VIII, on 16 November 1494 as a preliminary to accompanying, in a diplomatic capacity, the victorious monarch on his takeover of the kingdom of Naples. He was subsequently Florentine ambassador to France on three occasions: from December 1495 to September 1497, from September 1501 to May 1502 and from November 1502 to June 1503.[12] He was in Lyons when, on 5 June 1503, news reached him of his elevation to the cardinalate and it was reported that Louis XII reacted just as enthusiastically as if he had been French.[13] He was given a French bishopric, that of Saintes in the diocese of Bordeaux, sometime after the death of Cardinal Bertrand Perauld on 5 September 1505.[14] As a preliminary to this, for the latter part of 1504 and the early part of 1505 he had been consistently acting as Cardinal Proposer in consistory for French bishoprics and benefices. For example, on 8 November 1504 he related Cardinal Francesco della Rovere for

Mende, a suffragan bishopric of Bourges and on 31 March 1505 he related Antonio de Foro for Nevers, a suffragan bishopric of Sens.[15] This could have been because he was acting as Cardinal Protector, but there were French cardinals who could have fulfilled this function.[16] His intellectual ties are harder to reconstruct but as the addressee of a letter from Mario Equicola[17] in Paris praising Jacques Lefèvre d'Étaples' commentaries on Aristotle,[18] the world of Parisian cultural and university life must have been at least indirectly familiar to him and his Florentine humanist background could have given him an entrée to literary gatherings in the capital during his stay there.[19]

Francesco was not the only francophile in the family. One of his elder brothers, Piero, had equally strong political links with France, and enormous French approval greeted the news that he had been made *gonfaloniere a vita* in September 1502; one of the reasons given for this was his great experience of both Italian and French affairs.[20] Once in power Piero's implementation of pro-French policy and persistent reliance on French support may be seen as a cause of his downfall in 1512. Medici use of Spanish and imperial aid would in any case have forced the Soderini into the arms of the French. This bond between the city of Florence and France was criticised not only by Piero's adversaries, but questioned also by one of his supporters, Machiavelli, who wrote rather bitterly in the *Decennale Primo*:

E per esser di Francia buon figliuoli
Non vi curasti, in seguitar sua stella
Sostener mille affanni e mille duoli. (106-108),

and

Voi vi posavi qui col becco aperto
Per attender di Francia un che venisse
A portarvi la manna nel deserto. (122-144)[21]

But although the French monarchy may have failed materially to support the Soderini, especially during their hours of greatest need, their protestations of support never wavered and the backing of the most Christian Kings was not to be despised; France was still the most powerful country in Europe and had been a successful invader of the peninsula in the recent past. François I gave his backing to Soderini at certain strategic points in his career; for example, in 1517 when he took the entire Soderini family under his protection after the alleged conspiracy by Cardinals Riario, Sauli, Petrucci, Castellesi and Soderini against Leo X, and in no uncertain terms warned of the dire consequences for any who should attempt to molest his 'chers et bien amez . . . Sodorins . . . que sont esté tousiours bons et loyaulx serviteurs de la couronne de France'.[22] Soderini maintained contact with the French king whenever he could during his exile at Fondi from 1517 to 1521. He reputedly sent Giovanni Girolami to Vicenza in November 1517 with instructions to recommend his and Piero's affairs to the king, an act which was viewed with the utmost suspicion by the Medici.[23] François came to the rescue once again in July 1522 after Soderini's involvement in the conspiracy against Cardinal Giulio de'Medici, giving the goods and persons of the Soderini family, Zanobi Buondelmonti, Luigi Alamanni, Bernardo da Verrazzano and Battista della Palla a safe conduct and personal guarantee.[24] The letter patent for this states in the preamble that the Soderini family had also served Charles VIII and Louis XII, thus stressing the continuous relationship between this Florentine house and the French monarchy.[25]

Just as the Soderini were allies of the French so they were enemies of the Medici. The potentially unsatisfactory nature of the French alliance appeared even more dubious when there was a Medici on the papal throne, although at these points the Soderini, and especially Francesco, had to rely still more heavily on their French connections. Conversely the Medici were most worried when the Soderini managed to obtain the ear of a non-Medici pope. In the complicated run up to the election of Adrian VI in December 1521, Francesco Soderini backed the Colonna who backed Adrian who also enjoyed the support of the emperor, thereby leaving the Medici out in the cold.[26] But at the time Soderini's emergence on the winning side had not been a foregone conclusion, because on his return from Fondi he had made a virulently anti-Medici speech, attacking the family in general and Leo in particular, which turned even the moderates against him.[27] One of the pasquinades written during the conclave advised him to ally his fortunes with those of the emperor and not those of the French, in case a Medici pope emerged.[28] But Soderini's preferences were so well known at the papal court that this suggestion amounted to little more than a joke, whilst François' friendship for him was taken seriously. After letters from Soderini to the French king inviting him to invade Sicily and help oust the Medici from Florence were discovered (through Medici sharp practice), Adrian VI asked the college of cardinals for its opinion on Soderini's behaviour and the correct response to it. One cardinal wrote that they ought to beware of fanning a great fire through their desire to extinguish a tiny spark,[29] that is that they ought to beware of offending the king of France by attacking his friend.

It was these two strands in Soderini's life — French patronage and a hatred of the Medici — which must have determined him to leave money to the University of Paris. The Medici were firmly back in control of Florence, which ruled out an endowment to the University of Pisa. There was a new Medici pope, Clement VII, which discouraged a bequest to the University of Rome. Conceivably as a grateful *alumnus* Soderini might have chosen to favour the University of Bologna where he had studied before September 1473 when he moved back to Pisa to study law,[30] but he had no other loyalties to or interests in the city. Therefore Paris, which was well away from the Medici sphere of influence, must have seemed the obvious choice to an anti-Medicean. The other possibility was the University of Rome. Soderini had been involved once in a transaction with that university but at a very menial level. Cardinal Domenico Capranica left a provision in his will of 14 August 1458 for a college of thirty-one scholars to study theology, arts and canon law. Very precise instructions were left for the presentation of these scholarships.[31] To provide the money for this foundation he bequeathed to the college five pieces of property — the Palazzo delle Due Torri, the casale di Boccamazzi, the casale di Monimento, the casa del Trullo (which he had been using as a stable) and his own palace in S. Maria in Aquiro — the revenues from which should have been sufficient to finance the project, and he decreed that the first three of these should never be sold.[32] On 22 January 1490 Soderini and Niccolò Capranica, a nephew of Domenico and a canon of St Peter's, presided over the exchange between the Collegio Capranica and Falco Sinibaldi, the Papal Treasurer, whereby the college gave Sinibaldi the casale di Boccamazzi in return for a house on Via Sacra in the Borgo.[33]

It would appear, then, that Soderini's bequest was more an expression of political discontent than of educational zeal. He had spent only a few weeks in Paris in 1502, between the beginning of February and the 9th or 10th of March.[34] As far as is known, he did not meet any one who might have encouraged him to endow the university — Erasmus, for example, had left Paris at the end of April or the beginning of May 1501 and was not to return until December 1504.[35] He may have encountered and (as indicated above) was certainly aware of the teaching of Lefèvre d'Étaples. As he was not only a former student of law but an ex-teacher of it (for he had taught, probably the *Institutes*, at the University of Pisa during the academic year 1477-1478), he would have been aware of the University of Paris' excellence in the fields of theology and canon law. Equally as a churchman he could have been expected to found a college for students of these subjects rather than for students of civil law.

The form of Soderini's bequest was extremely conventional and only departed even slightly from the familiar in one respect, that the Soderini were to have first refusal in the matter of places, and only after that were the doors to be opened to anyone from Florence, and then to anyone from Italy. Nearly all the bequests to the University of Paris had restrictions on the acceptability of would-be scholars, but they were usually, as in the case of the Collège des Lombards, restrictions of locality; Francesco Ospedale's candidates had to originate ideally from the city of Modena or, if not, from the diocese of Modena or, if not, from the province of Lombardy, and if still no one suitable were available, from any part of Italy.[37] As many of the foundations were set up by bishops or archbishops, the qualification was often that of belonging to a certain diocese. Only one other of these foundations gave preference to members of the founder's family, that of Cardinal Jean de Dormans of 1370.[38] Of the two colleges founded at Paris within ten years of Soderini's bequest, one, the Collège de Merci, set up in 1515, was for regulars,[39] and the other, the Collège du Mans, founded on 9 June 1526 by Cardinal Philip of Luxemburg, was for students of the arts.[40] Soderini was quite correct to leave to François I and the rector of the University who in February 1524 was Jean Lothon,[41] the mechanics of the foundation, as this was one of the rector's duties.[42] It was also usual practice to stress the erection of a chapel with a bell tower and a bell.[43] It is unfortunate that there is a *lacuna* in the text where the expected number of students ought to be, but it may well be blank in the original too. As the precise sums of money owed to him are not mentioned, it is probable that he did not know exactly what these were, nor could he have known how much of a residue would be left for bursaries after the building of the new college.

This uncertainty was at least partially responsible for the failure of Soderini's project. For there is no evidence that any initiatives were ever made to further the foundation. It is notoriously difficult to recoup debts, especially those relating to church revenues. Cardinal Jean de Lorraine was a new, young friend, who was even more adept a pluralist than Soderini, and who had already made use of Soderini in several minor ecclesiastical matters.[44] It is to be expected that neither he nor Antonio Verze, the archbishop of Besançon, redeemed their pledges, nor did the various unnamed person in France whose repayments might have allowed the building and endowment of the college to take place. Another and more sinister reason for the failure of the plan is that less than two years later there was a court case to assert the falsity of the will. The verdict of the judge is not known, but several of Francesco Soderini's old retainers who had witnessed the will then claimed that they had not been present. The clue to the reason for this case may lie in one of the examiner's questions, 'Has the witness ever heard that Soderini had not made a will during his last illness but that it had been done by his brothers and next of kin in an attempt to salvage his goods and heredity from the clutches of the

Pope and the Apostolic See?"[45] However, Clement VII's papal brief
giving Soderini permission to make a will is not a forgery and there is
no reason to suppose that his will was not in order. In fact it is much
more likely that the case was, in some fashion, prompted by a
Medici/papal desire to keep the Soderini possessions under their
control. Soderini's attempt to provide an alternative base in Paris for
disenchanted or outlawed members of his family and possibly other
anti-Mediceans by founding a college at the university, could well
have been thwarted at a preliminary stage by direct or indirect
interference from Clement VII, a Medici pope. The utterly orthodox
text of the bequest belies the political struggle which prompted it.

The Warburg Institute
Woburn Square
London WC1H 0AB

REFERENCES

*   I would like to thank Conte Luciano Soderini for his kind permission to work in
his private archives, John Ormerod for his help in taking photographs of material in
these archives and David Chambers for reading and commenting on a first draft of this
note. I shall use the following abbreviations:

ASod	Rome, Archivio Soderini
AV	Archivio Segreto Vaticano
AS	Archivio di Stato
ASF	Florence, Archivio di Stato
BNF	Florence, Biblioteca Nazionale
BV	Biblioteca Apostolica Vaticana
ACap	Rome, Archivio Capitolino

1.   There is no detailed account of Soderini's career. The most recent articles on him
are by F. Apolloni Ghetti, 'Il cardinale Francesco Soderini restauratore nel 1519 di un
monumento classico' in *Strenna dei Romanisti* (21 April 1976), pp. 258-270, 'Nuovi
appunti su Francesco Soderini Cardinale Volterrano' in *L'Urbe* XXXIX (May-August
1976), pp. 1-14, and 'Nuovi appunti su Francesco Soderini Cardinale Volterrano
(continuazione e fine)' in *L'Urbe* XXXIX (September-October 1976), pp. 1-17. These
contain satisfactory bibliographies of the secondary literature.

2.   ASod, III, 185^r-190^r.

3.   ASod, III, 242^v and 243^r. The document is a copy of part of a case dating from
February 1526 to ascertain whether or not this final will was false. He had obtained
leave to make this last will on the very day that it was drawn up, AV, Armadio 29, 72,
243^r-244^r.

4.   The first will is in AS Bologna, Archivio Notarile, Tommaso Grengoli, busta 18,
filza 13, under date. There are serious problems involved in tracing the second and
third wills. The second would be difficult to find as it was presumably *rogato* either by
one of the notaries in his household (and none of their records survive in any

profusion) or by a local notary (in which case the registered copy would have remained in Fondi and later been sent to Naples). The third is even more difficult to locate as few of his personal papers have survived and, since no notary was involved, it would not have been registered.

5.   M. Félibien, *Histoire de la ville de Paris* (Paris, 1725), III, p. 301, and M.-E. Rabut, 'Les Cholets. Étude historique et topographique d'un collège parisien' in *Positions des thèses élèves de l'École des Chartes* (1971), pp. 149-155. H. Rashdall, *The Universities of Europe in the Middle Ages* ed. F. M. Powicke and A. B. Emden (Oxford, 1936) has a list of colleges at the University of Paris before 1500, II, pp. 536-539.

6.   Félibien, op. cit. , I, pp. 504-505 and V, p. 607, and C. Jourdain, 'Le Collège du Cardinal Lemoine' in *Mémoires de la Société de l'Histoire de Paris et de L'Île-de-France* III (1876), pp. 45-47. Jean Lemoine was French and set up the college during a sojourn in Paris as legate of Boniface VIII.

7.   Félibien, op. cit. , I, p. 592.

8.   Ibid. , I, p. 668, and M. -D. Chapotin, *Le Collège de Dormans-Beauvais* (Paris, 1870), p. 59.

9.   Ibid. , I, pp. 526-527, V, p. 623 and p. 676, and M. Godet, *La Congrégation de Montaigu (1490-1580)* (Paris, 1912), p. 1.

10.   It must have been this college which Vespasiano referred to in his life of Cosimo de' Medici. He wrote that there was a college in Paris which was called *di Fiorentini* after a Florentine cardinal who built it, which stood beside the house of Bernardetto de' Medici, which was almost in ruins and which Cosimo repaired (Vespasiano da Bisticci, *Le Vite* ed. A. Greco (Florence, 197), II, p. 181). No Florentine cardinal had ever built a college and Vespasiano must have been thinking of the Collège des Lombards, founded by a Florentine bishop.

11.   Félibien, op. cit., I, p. 588 and III, p. 427.

12.   The dates of the first mission can be found in ASF, Signori, Carteggi, Legazioni e Commissarie, Elezioni e Istruzioni, 21, 149ᵛ and Signori, Carteggi, Missive Prima Cancelleria, 51, 33ᵛ, and those of the second and third in ASF, Signori e Collegi, Deliberazioni . . . di speciale autorità, 40, 34ᵛ and 45ʳ.

13.   ASF, Dieci di Balìa, Carteggi, Responsive, 72, 248ᵛ, letter from Alessandro Nasi, Soderini's fellow ambassador, from Lyons, 5 June 1503: 'Sua Maestà ne mostrò essere benissimo contenta et satisfacta non altrimenti che se fussi electo uno cardinale franzese', and also in the register of letters, BNF, Ginori Conti, 21, 28ʳ.

14.   C. Eubel, *Hierarchia Catholica Medii Aevi* (Munster, 1910), III, p. 359, and P. B. Gams, *Series Episcoporum Ecclesiae Catholicae* (Regensburg, 1873-1886), p. 624. Eubel, following Gams, gives the date of 27 January 1507 for his appointment as administrator, but it is obvious from letters to the chapter of Saintes of 16 June 1506, to the king of France of 17 August and a similar one to the Cardinal of Rouen (AV, Armadio 39, 24, 248ʳ-249ʳ and 379ʳ & ᵛ, and Armadio 39, 29, 184ᵛ) that his appointment took place before this.

15.   AV, Fondo Concistoriale, Acta Miscellanea, 6, 111ʳ-135ᵛ, 8 November 1504 to 22 May 1505. This is the only prolonged batch of propositions that exists for him; rather surprisingly, in all eleven of them he was relating someone to a French benefice whose locations ranged from Besançon to Rheims to Virdun to Clermont. He continued to agitate on behalf of those desirous of French patronage, as is shown by a letter he wrote to Louis XII of 13 March 1513 on behalf of the bishop of Nice, Paris, Bibliothèque Nationale, Collection Depuy 262, 14.

16.   See D. S. Chambers, *Cardinal Bainbridge in the Court of Rome 1509-1514* (Oxford, 1965), p. 73 where he discusses Cardinal Francesco Alidosi acting as Cardinal Protector for the English when Bainbridge had already been given a red hat. Bertrand Perauld, Guillaume Briçonnet, Georges d'Amboise and François Guillaume de Clermont for example were all cardinals at this period.

17. For information on Equicola's life see S. D. Kolsky, *Mario Equicola: A Biographical Reappraisal* (Ph. D. London, 1981).

18. Aristotle, *Totius philosophiae naturalis paraphrases a Francisco Vatablo recognitae* (Paris, 1528), 356ᵛ and 357ʳ, 11 December 1504. A discussion and English translation of this is found in E. F. Rice, 'Humanist Aristotelianism in France: Jacques Lefèvre d'Étaples and his Circle' in *Humanism in France* ed. A. H. T. Levi (Manchester, 1970), p. 132.

19. E. F. Rice, 'The Patrons of French Humanism 1490-1520' in *Renaissance Studies in Honor of H. Baron* ed. A. Molho and J. A. Tedeschi (Florence, 1971), p. 691, mentions Lefèvre's presence at Germain de Ganay's *litterata convivia*.

20. A. Gherardi, 'Come si accogliesse in Corte di Francia la nuova dell'elezione del Gonfaloniere Soderini' in *Archivio storico italiano* series V, i (1888), p. 133. Louis XII wrote of this creation: 'dont avons este et sommes très ioyeux, pur la bonne et grande congnoissance que avons de luy et de ses sens, vertuz, droicture, et grande experience tant des affaires d'Ytalie que des nostres deca les monts'.

21. N. Machiavelli, 'Decennale primo' in *Il teatro e gli scritti letterari* ed. F. Gaeta (Milan, 1965), p. 240. For a very interesting analysis of other Florentine attitudes towards France during this period, see C. Bec, 'Les florentins et la France ou la rupture d'un mythe (1494-1540)' in *Il pensiero politico* XIV, 3 (1981), especially pp. 382-386.

22. This letter from François I to the *gonfaloniere* and commune of 4 July 1517 is in ASF, Diplomatico, Riformagioni, Atti Pubblici, and is published by G. Canestrini and A. Desjardins, *Négociations diplomatiques de la France avec la Toscane* (Paris, 1859-1886), II, pp. 778-779.

23. ASF, Copialettere di Goro Gheri, IV, 86ʳ, Goro Gheri to Baldassare da Pescia, where one of Soderini's circle Piero Contugi, brother of Zachario, bishop of Assisi, was tortured in order to extract information about Soderini and 'dice ancora che quando Govani Girolami dua mesi fa andò a Vicentia che hebbe commissione andare dipoi in Francia per raccomandare le cose sua et di suo fratello al re'.

24. ASF, Signori, Carteggi, Responsive 37, 251.

25. ASF, Capitani di Parte Guelfa, Numeri Rossi, 75, 75ᵛ: 'Notum sit et manifestum dum nobiles viri de domo et familia Soderinorum cives florentini fuerunt iampridem in servitio bone memorie Caroli Octavi et Ludovici XII predecessorum nostrorum . . . '.

26. G. Molini, *Documenti di storia italiana copiati su gli originali autentici e per lo più autografi esistenti in Parigi* (Paris, 1836), pp. 156-157, postscript to a letter from de Abbatis to Florimond Robertet, the chancellor of France, of 7 February 1522: 'Donda al presente Medicis se trova più disperato che may fu ala vita soa, et non sa sel hè in celo o in terra perché don. Io. Manuel à scripto alo imperador che per il Cardenal Colona hè stato electo papa Maistro Adriano . . . et dicto Medicis sta suspeso, per esser unito el Cardinal Sodorino de Fiorenza con casa Colonesa, che non labiano aiutar con favore de larmata che à al Sign. Prospero in retornarlo in Fiorenza, per esser li Soderini dela factione gebelina'.

27. M. Sanudo, *Diarii* (Venice, 1892), XXXII, 230: Soderini 'fece una elegantissima oration, ringratiando Idio che havia liberato la Chiesia di questa tyrannide di Leon pontifice, dicendo grandissimo mal di la caxa di Medici, exortando li cardinali a elezer bon pontifice e non come questo che teniva il mondo in guerra etc.' and ibid., XXXII, 280.

28. BV, Ottob. lat. 2817, 27r: 'Ad Cardinalem Soderinum
E'ti bisogna Soderin star forte,
Poi che tu hai fatto così bel sermone
In el collegio contra di Leone
Ch'à posto sottosopra questa corte;
Che se per caso o per tua mala sorte
Medici havessi questa electione,

Salvar non ti potria falce o falcione
Perché sol Dio te camparia da morte.
Donque non ti ritrar dal ghibellino,
L'aquila sequi e non guardar al giglio
Se voi dar scaccomatto al medicino,
Perché mutar al tempo el suo consiglio
Vien da prudente. Onde el mio Soderino
Opra il tuo ingegno con ogni tuo artiglio
Che mai cade im periglio
Il bon nocchiero con li soi sergenti
Che navigare sa secondo i venti'.

29. BV, Vat. lat. 3920, 140^r: 'nedum scintillam extinguere cupimus, incendium maximum excitemus'.

30. BNF, Magl. XXI, 155, 114^r and, more securely, ASF, Carte Strozziane, CXXXVIII, 47^r.

31. BV, Barb. lat. 1625, p. 1 and pp. 16-17. This is the book of statutes for the college drawn up by Domenico Capranica.

32. BV, Vat. lat. 7971, pp. 32-33. See also M. Morpurgo-Castelnuovo, 'Il Cardinale Domenico Capranica' in *Archivio della R. società romana di storia patria* LII (1929), especially pp. 89-94.

33. AV, Armadio 39, 21, 138^v-140^r.

34. ASF, Signori, Carteggi, Responsive 20, 97^v and 136^r.

35. *Erasme et Paris*, Institut Néerlandais, Paris, 1969-1970 (Paris, 1969), pp. 15-16.

36. In an autobiograpical account Marco Strozzi, a Florentine canon and rector of S. Miniato, who met Soderini in 1477 and was closely associated with him during the following years, wrote: 'Et anno 1477 circa septuagesimam cum ipso [Soderini] Florentiam accessi et in die cinerum pro quibusdam negociis remisit me Pisas precipue ut alius vices suas in legendo persolveret', ASF, Carte Strozziane, CXXXVIII, 47^r. Septuagesima in 1478 was 19 January and Ash Wednesday was 5 February. A. Verde *Lo Studio Fiorentino* (Florence, 1974), I, p. 303, does not give his name as a teacher but it is extremely likely that he was sharing the teaching of the *Institutes* with Filippo Decio as there were normally two people doing it.

37. Félibien, op. cit., III, p. 428.

38. Chapotin, op. cit., p. 60. But Noël Mesleau who left money to the Collège du Plessis on 27 October 1519 for the endowment of several bursaries also stipulated that members of his family should take precedence. See C. Brechillet Jourdain, *Index chronologicus chartarum pertinentium ad historiam Universitatis Parisiensis* (Paris, 1862), p. 326.

39. Félibien, op. cit., II, p. 934.

40. Ibid., III, p. 586.

41. C. Égasse Du Boulay, *Historia Universitatis Parisiensis* (Paris, 1673), VI, p. 156. Lothon was rector from 16 December 1523 to 18 March 1524 when he was succeeded by Robert Bouchigny.

42. C. Égasse Du Boulay, *Remarques sur la dignité, rang, preseance, autorité et iurisdiction du recteur de l'Université de Paris* (Paris, 1668), p. 82.

43. The late fifteenth century Collège de Montaigu applied for separate permission to do this. See Félibien, op. cit., V, pp. 715-716, 7 July 1495.

44. Soderini had paid the residue of the common services for the bishopric of Metz in the name of the Cardinal of Lorraine (AV, Armadio 29, 64, 167^v) and had acted again on his behalf at a consistory of 15 January 1524 (AV, Fondo Concistoriale, Acta Vicecancellari, III, 22^v).

45. ASod, III, 243^v-244^r, testimony of Staglia de Actis of 5 February 1526.

Appendix
Francesco Soderini's Will

A contemporary early sixteenth century copy of Francesco Soderini's fourth will of 22 February 1524, drawn up by the notary Domenico de Iuvenibus, is in Rome, ASod, III, 185^r-190^r. The original will is, I think, in ACap, as an early eighteenth century copy of it in ASod, III, 165^r-179^v, was made from one in ACap, Liber Extensorum no. 5. This will is untraceable for the present since the archivists of ACap claim that they do not know of such a series. Moreover the archives have been effectively closed since the late 1970s due to the collapse of the roof so that I have not been able to search for it personally. From Domenico de Iuvenibus there is only stray extant notarial material, some in AS Rome and some in AV, but it is possible to deduce that he was a much used and trusted notary for the last few years of Soderini's life.

The section relating to the bequest is on 186^v-187^r.

ITEM Reverendissimus Dominus Cardinalis testator proinde considerans quantum religioni christiane et animarum saluti viri litterarum scientia presertim in Iure Canonico et Theologia eruditi utilitati conferant desideraveritque prout cupit de presenti ut in civitate Parisiensis et eius universitate in qua cunctarum scientiarum et artium generale viget studium erigatur unum collegium pro comodo dicte civitatis et sustentatione ac alimonia pauperum scolarium in universitate eiusdem civitatis Parisiensis in Theologia et Iure Canonico studentium; et sicut asseruit idem Reverendissimus Dominus testator habere debeat in dicto Regno a diversis personis diversas pecuniarum sumas a pochis quas asseruit esse penes eximium iuris utriusque doctorem Dominum Iohannem Victorium fratrem ipsius Reverendissimi Domini testatoris. Propterea ut vere satisfiat animo ipsius testatoris si quid forte tempore vite sue non recte neque iuste a quibuscunque quicquam accepisset et remedium anime sue et peccatorum suorum veniam voluit legavit et mandavit dictas pecuniarum quantitates per christianissimum et invictissimum Dominum Francorum Regem et Rectorem dicte universitatis civitatis Parisiensis seu ab eis deputandos exigi et recuperari et de illis erigi constitui et edificari[1] sub nomine domus et familie Soderine unum collegium cum altari capella nuncupatum[2] campanali humili campana refectorio pro sustentatione dictorum pauperum scolarium in universitate Parisiensis in Theologia et Iure Canonico studentium; et in quo collegio idem testator ut si accideret quod aliquis de domo

1. MS reads: edificare.
2. The positioning of this word in the sentence appears to be particularly eccentric.

seu familia Soderina vellet studere in dicta universitate habeat in dicto collegio locum primum et habeat expensas proprias ipsius collegii et quod post illos de domo preferantur si qui sint ex prima Florentiense et post eos si qui sint ex Italia et quod pauperes scolares in eodem recipiantur et in eodem locum habeant et pro eorumdem alimonia voluit; et mandavit Dominus Reverendissimus Dominus testator ut de pecuniis restantibus emantur tot bona stabilia pro dictorum pauperum scolarium sustentatione et alimonia usque ad numerum [3] et ad effectum ut talis erectio suum sortiatur effectum. Prefatus Reverendissimus Dominus testator fecit constituit deputavit et ordinavit suos commissarios et procuratores et huiusmodi sue voluntatis executores prefatum invictissimum et christianissimum Dominum Franciscum Gallorum Regem et Rectorem dicte universitatis Parisiensis quibus et eorum cuilibet dedit omnem licentiam arbitrium potestatem mandatum et baliam dictas pecunias una cum omnibus reliquiis et arreragiis que ad Reverendissimum Dominum Cardinalem testatorem pertinere possent ratione dictarum pecuniarum et emolumentorum tam ipsius Reverendissimi Domini testatoris quam Bernardi de Verrazano nominibus per se vel alium seu alios exigendi recipiendi et recuperandi ac de exactis receptis et recuperatis quietantiam seu quietantias cum pacto de rem habitam non petendo in forma debita facienda ac in erectione constructione dotatione et fundatione dicti collegii convertendi et applicandi ac omnia alia faciendi que in comissis et circa ea necessaria fuerint et opportuna et que ipsemet Reverendissimus Dominus testator faceret in premissis personaliter adesset.

ITEM ultra premisa prefatus Reverendissimus Dominus testator dixit et asseruit se debere habere a diversis personis diversas pecuniarum quantitates et presertim a Reverendissimo Domino Archiepiscopo Bisuntinensi et a Reverendissimo Cardinali Lotharingie[4] ratione pensionis ipsi Reverendissimo Domino testatori super fructibus Prioratus Sancte Marie de Goclia ordinis Sancti Augustini Bisuntinensi et Prioratus de Goza respective debitis et reservatis et pro diversis terminis et solutionibus decursis; et propterea voluit iussit et mandavit ac legavit Reverendissimus Dominus testator dictas pecuniarum quantitates per supradictos eius executores christianissimum Dominum Francorum Regem et Rectorem universitatis Parisiensis seu per eos deputandi vel deputandos exigi et recuperari ut supra et quasquidem pecunias prefatus Reverendissimus Dominus testator voluit et mandavit exponi et exbursari similiter in tot bonis stabilibus pro dotatione et fundatione dicti collegii ac pauperum scolarium studentium ut premittitur alimonia.

3.   There is a lacuna in the MS.
4.   MS reads: Lothoringie.

Essay Review

THREE IMPORTANT PUBLICATIONS FOR UNIVERSITY HISTORY

Charles B. Schmitt

Publications on university history can take different forms. In general, I think we can identify at least three main types. First, there are the ceremonial publications, promoted wholly by the university itself and almost always designed to show the institution in the best light possible. These are frequently printed on glossy paper and contain many pictures of dignitaries and reproductions of *Cimelia*. Secondly, there are more scholarly and more objective historical studies. These vary widely both in quality and in the degree to which they are based upon a utilisation of source material. Thirdly, there are the group of publications devoted to putting into print the documentary basis for the study of university history. These can again vary widely in the quality of scholarship which has gone into them and the magnitude of the enterprise, ranging from a single unpublished document to a multi-volumed collection of relevant archival materials.

Unfortunately, the first genre is still very much with us and accounts for a distressingly large portion of publications in the field. Centenaries tend to produce such things as much today as ever. The second genre can produce magnificent results, including those books on universities which are generally discussed by historians and are reviewed in scholarly journals. They are interpretative and deal with such fashionable topics as the social background of students or the collusion between universities and the political powers of whatever stripe. They also can illuminate in the most fundamental way both the internal functioning of universities and the external impacts on educational institutions in many different contexts.

The real progress of university history as a discipline depends very heavily upon the third type of research and publication. The general availability of documents of many different universities over a substantial chronological range provides the materials for genuine syntheses and comparative history. In many ways this is the least rewarding type of research, at least in terms of immediate benefits. It involves archival research of the most single-minded type and the sort of financial support over long periods of time which is usually hard to come by these days. After the research itself has been done, the publication of the documents is itself very expensive and produces multi-volumed works with little appeal to the general public or, indeed, to the individual scholar. Such sets will find their way into at most several hundred institutional libraries, where they will hold little appeal to the undergraduates who form the bulk of readers in such libraries. Like manuscript catalogues, however, these are the sort of publications which make it possible for research and new historical interpretation to advance. With the advent of electronic methods certain types of this kind of research have been rendered much easier to carry out and less expensive to publish. Perhaps even more important is the fact that today nearly all sources of research support are more receptive to those projects involving computers than those which do not. This state of affairs is beginning to bear fruit in studies on the history of universities as the Pisan volumes to be discussed below illustrate.

Though the collection and publication of university documents, matriculation lists, graduation lists, *rotuli*, etc. go back at least to the seventeenth century, it was really about a hundred years ago that the systematic accumulation of such materials began on a broad scale.[1] The process has continued in a rather unsystematic way down to the present, though we still do not have some of the most basic information available for many of the most important universities.

Here I shall consider three recent initiatives to produce a documentary foundation for the history of individual universities in three different countries. One of these is, in fact, a reprisal of the beginnings made already at the turn of the last century, while the other two have begun *ab initio*.

*   *   *

Among the useful standard works for historians of universities has been the matriculation list for Cologne prepared by Hermann Keussen. The first three volumes covering the period from 1389 to 1559, containing 36,773 names, were published between 1892 and 1928.[2] Through Keussen had done much to prepare the list for the later period for publication, various difficulties intervened and they were left incomplete at his death in 1943. Now the remainder have been published dealing with the years 1559 until the closure of the university by the French[3]. Making use of the work already done by Keussen, Ulrike Nyassi and Mechtild Wilkes have completed the record and seen it through the press. A total of 48,274 names are contained in the record covering 238 years. On the whole the *Matrikel* follows the order and structure of handwritten lists of the archive. For the years 1709-1753 and 1789-1797 matriculation lists do not survive, but the gaps have been filled, in so far as possible, from other sources of information, e.g. from baccalaureate tables. For the missing years it can be surmised that the reconstructed list of matriculands is about 80% complete. Since the documents cover such a long period there is not an absolute uniformity in the information given. For the earlier period we are told whether the necessary oath was taken and the requisite fees paid, but this is not always indicated later. On the other hand, for the last hundred or so years matriculands are systematically divided into *nobiles, divites,* and *pauperes.*

In general we can rely upon having the names of the student and the city from where he comes. In a few exceptional cases, a certain amount of further information is given. For example, for the year 1616 (no. 414) we read:

> Andr. Kleppinck, Tremoniensis; art.; i., sed n.s., quia fr. uxoris d. Joannis ab Hardenraidt, consulus Col., 12.

This can be roughly translated as follows:

> Andreas Kleppinck of Dortmund, to study arts, swore the oath, but did not pay the fees, for he is the brother of the wife of Johann von Hardenraidt, who is a consul in Cologne, on 12 May.

The matriculation lists are prefaced by a table of the various abbreviations used in the documents, so consultation is made quite easy. The two index volumes make it possible to locate particular individuals with a minimum of effort, though there are the usual problems of variant spellings and many individuals of the same name. For example there are about 500 matriculands with the surname 'Schmitz'. A very useful feature of the index is the inclusion of geographical locations in addition to surnames. It is therefore easy to locate those students coming from Cologne (nearly 10,000), Strasbourg (10) or England [Anglus] (7), the latter group including a Thomas More, who enrolled in 1681.

During this time span, which roughly covers the period from the Council of Trent to the French Revolution, Cologne was one of the main centres of Catholicism in German speaking lands. It was also an active city in the printing of Catholic textbooks, including the Coimbra commentaries of Aristotle, which were an important feature of university education during the first half of the seventeenth century. This university itself educated many leaders of Catholic Germany, whose relation to the university can now be easily ascertained thanks to the volumes seen through the press by Nyassi and Wilkes.

*   *   *

In initiating his collection of documents on 'the Portuguese university' more than thirty years ago Arturo Moreira de Sá[4] took as his models similar collections devoted to Paris and Bologna.[5] The first volume of his own *Chartularium* appeared in 1966 and there has been a steady stream of bulky tomes ever since, volume VIII appearing in 1981. 'The Portuguese University' is the way in which one must speak of the institution since it moved frequently between Lisbon and Coimbra during the first several centuries of its existence. After being established in Lisbon in 1288, it changed places four times between then and 1377, after which it remained in Lisbon for the next 160 years until it was transferred definitively to Coimbra. It remained Portugal's only university until the foundation of Evora, as a rather minor rival a few years later. Lisbon was not re-established as a university centre until 1911. In fact, it was probably only after the definitive resettling of the institution at Coimbra that it became an intellectual centre of truly European importance. With the coming of figures such as Gouvea, Grouchy, and Buchanan at the middle of the century and the later publication of the very popular Coimbra commentaries, Coimbra took on an eminence in European intellectual life which it had scarcely had before. Nonetheless, the earlier history of the institution is not without interest, and it is noteworthy to find the initiative finally taken in Portugal to publish the documentary evidence for the early history of its university.

Professor Moreira de Sá and his team have been able to publish an immense amount in a very few years. In addition to eight volumes of the *Chartularium*, they have also produced three of an *Auctuarium*, once again following the structural model of Denifle and Chatelain. While the former is drawn from documents found in many different libraries and archives, the *Auctuarium* is drawn from two manuscript volumes in Coimbra which have the title *Livros da Universidade de Lisboa* and cover the period from 1506 to 1537, i. e. the date when the university moved to Coimbra.

Several more volumes at least of the *Chartularium* are yet to come. When it is finished it should take its place upon our shelves besides the similar collections devoted to Paris, Bologna, Montpellier, Uppsala, Salamanca, and several other institutions as fundamental tools for the study of university history. The volumes are handsomely printed with a number of illustrations and reproductions of documents. Each has a bibliography, a list of the documents printed with a brief summary of the contents of each one, and an index which makes for easy consultation. In short, the *Chartularium* and *Auctuarium* are well produced with the needs of the working scholar in mind. They should be in all libraries which have a section devoted to university history.

*   *   *

The Pisan graduation and matriculation lists were prepared by a team working under the direction of Ennio Cortese and comprised of Rodolfo del Gratta, Giuliana Volpi, Leonardo Ruta, and Margherita Giunta, in addition to several computer experts who dealt with the technical side of matters.[6] The volumes cover the period after the reopening of the *Studio* and its definitive transfer to Pisa in 1543 until 1765 for the *Acta graduum* and until 1799 for the *Liber matricularum*. The form in which the materials appear is an a computer print-out in inconsistent type faces, but the volumes are well bound and easy to use.

The *Acta graduum* are drawn from the manuscript lists preserved in the Archivio Arcivescovile of Pisa and the Archivio di Stato of the same city, with a small amount of information coming also from the Archivio di Stato of Florence. They supplement and complete several partial lists previously published by Manacorda, Lombardo Radice, and Schiaffino.[7] The relevant information can now be got with ease from a single source. The arrangement is by discipline (i.e. *in utroque iure*, philosophy and medicine, and theology) and then chronologically within each group. The information given is similar to that available in the *Acta graduum* for Padua, the publication of which has now been in progress for many years.[8] It comprises the following items: (1) the faculty in which the studies were carried out; (2) the name of the candidate; (3) the names of the promotor and chancellor for the examination; (4) the name of the candidate's father; (5) where the candidates's studies had been carried out; (6) the names of the examiners and witnesses.

Besides the lists of candidates, an alphabetical index of names is added, not only for the candidates, but also for others participating in the examinations. Thus, we can determine how frequently Andrea Cesalpino or Francesco Buonamici were involved in the procedures. A number of useful statistical tables derived from the available information are also printed. For example, there are lists of the number of graduates per year and per discipline. We can therefore see various types of fluctuations. What is clear, however, is the extent to which legal education dominated. More than 70% of the degrees awarded were in that branch of studies. Though the number of theology degrees rose dramatically in the 1570s, (as they did elsewhere in Italy), they began to fall again about 1620. But even during that period they account for only about 15% of the degrees. There are also a number of further tables devoted to the geographical origins of candidates decade by decade, family background, etc.

The *Liber matricularum* is presented in a similar fashion from materials principally in the Archivio di Stato and the Archivio Arcivescovile of Pisa. Here in most cases only the name and nationality of the students are given, as that is what the records provide.[9] The volume marks, once again, an important advance over the very fragmentary information previously in sources such as Manacorda and Weigle.[10] A comparison of the two lists show (1) that a number who entered did not receive a degree and (2) many who took degrees were not recorded at entry.

These volumes, along with those covering an earlier period for the *Studio Pisa-Firenze* undertaken by A. Verde,[11] show that after many years of neglect proper attention is now being bestowed upon the University of Pisa.

*   *   *

Each of these three enterprises provide an abundance of useful information for local and national history. The documents for Lisbon-Coimbra are a precious source for many aspects of the history of medieval Portugal. Portugal is a country not excessively rich in medieval manuscripts and one sees that much of the material published comes from distant libraries and archives, particularly from the Vatican Archive but also from Bologna, Florence, and London. The lists for Pisa and Cologne should facilitate many different research topics involving the Rhineland and Tuscany. What is more important, however, is that as more and more such material becomes available, it is easier to trace particular individuals throughout Europe. How much easier research becomes for those engaged in prosopographical studies of various sorts when such information is available in printed sources. It makes a new range of research projects viable. With the advent of the new electronic techniques one hopes that in the next generation much of the information now deposited in many European university archives will be made more generally accessible.

The Warburg Institute
Woburn Square
London WC1H 0AB

REFERENCES

1.   Among the more prominent examples are *Monumenti della Università di Padova*, ed. A. Gloria (Padua, 1884-88; repr. Bologna, 1972), 3 vols.; *Statuti delle università e dei collegi dello Studio Bolognese*, ed. C. Malagola (Bologna, 1888; repr. Bologna, 1966); *Chartularium universitatis parisiensis*, ed. H. Denifle & E. Chatelain (Paris, 1887-97; repr. Brussels, 1964), 4 vols.; and *Auctuarium chartularii universitatis parisiensis*, ed. Denifle, Chatelain and others (Paris, 1897-1964), 6 vols.

2.   H. Keussen, *Die Matrikel der Universität Köln, 1389 bis 1559* (Bonn, 1892-1928), 3 vols.

3.   H. Keussen, U. Nyassi, M. Wilkes and others, *Die Matrikel der Universität Köln, 1559-1797* (Düsseldorf, 1981), 4 vols.

4.   *Chartularium universitatis portugalensis* (1288-1537), ed. A. Moreira de Sá and others (Lisbon, 1966f.). Eight volumes covering the period up to 1490 had appeared by 1981. The companion collection is *Auctuarium chartularii universitatis portugalensis*, ed. A. Moreira de Sá and others (Lisbon, 1973-1979), in 3 vols., covering the period 1506-1537.

5.   See above, note 1.

6.   *Acta graduum academiae pisanae* (Pisa, 1979-80), 3 vols.

7.   G. Manacorda, 'Professori e studenti piemontesi, lombardi e liguri nell'Università di Pisa (1470-1600). Studio storico', *Annali delle università toscane* 22 (1899), 3-127; G. Lombardo Radice, 'I siciliani nello Studio di Pisa sino al 1600. Note d'archivio', *ibid.* 14 (1904), 4-73; E. Schiaffino, 'Elenco dei dottorati stranieri e di non toscani nell'Università di Pisa', *Bollettino storico pisano* 1-4 (1932-1935), *passim*.

8.   They begin with *Acta graduum Gymnasii Patavini ab anno 1406 ad 1450*, ed. C. Zonta & I. Brotto (Padua, 1922), but have progressed slowly only to 1550 with the volumes covering the years 1450-1500 still not published.

9.   *Libri matricularum studii pisani* (Pisa, 1983). This comprises *Libri matricularum studii pisani (1543-1609)*, ed. R. del Gratta; *Libri matricularum studii pisani* (1609-1737), ed. M. Giunta; and M. Giunta, *I collegiali di Sapienza dalla fondazione al 1618*.

10.   Manacorda, *op. cit.*; F. Weigle, 'Deutsche Studenten in Pisa', *Quellen und Forschungen aus italienischen Archiven und Bibliotheken* 39 (1959), 173-221.

11.   A. F. Verde, *Lo studio fiorentino, 1473-1503: ricerche e documenti* (Florence-Pistoia, 1973f.). Three volumes in four parts have appeared thus far.

Book Reviews

George Makdisi, *The Rise of Colleges: Institutions of Learning in Islam and the West.* Edinburgh University Press, 1981. Pp xiv + 377. £20.00.

The title of this book has been chosen with care. It is not about the origin or history of the university as such, which Makdisi accepts as an essentially Western phenomenon. The focus of the study is the college: the charitable foundation established for the benefit and communal use of students. Makdisi's thesis is that the Islamic charitable trust — or *waqf* — shows striking similarities, in its nature and legal status, to the European colleges which it precedes. Moreover, many of the aspects of the learning which took place in the *madrasas*, which were based on the law of *waqf*, match those prevalent in Europe from the twelfth century onwards. Among these he mentions the disputation-literature in which opposing arguments to a thesis are set forth without a resolution (exemplified by Peter Abelard's *Sic et Non*), which has its counterpart in the Islamic *khilaf* literature; the fondness for putting the most technical subjects into verse; and the predominance of dialectic. Makdisi lists these correspondences (which go as far as the similarities in the semantic range of the technical terms used in the Scholastic method) and suggests that, since 'the parallels are so high, the points of correspondence are so identical, and the course of development involves a time-lag of roughly a century . . . it unduly taxes the imagination to conceive parallel developments devoid of influence'. (pp. 286-7). It must be stressed that this influence cannot be proved by direct evidence. No founder of a college states that he is following an Islamic precedent, and we do not find the closest parallels in those foundations which were closest to the Islamic sphere of influence such as Spain and Southern Italy. Moreover the kind of works which were characteristic of the scholastic method in the West (Makdisi mentions the *Sic et Non* literature and the *Summae*) develop independently from the Arabic works which they most closely resemble; it was precisely the Islamic koranic and legal literature that was *not* translated into Latin in the twelfth and thirteenth centuries.

Makdisi's thesis is argued with more sophistication and understanding than those of previous apologists for the Arabic influence on the rise of universities and the origin of the scholastic method. If the reader feels disposed to reject it, he will still find a wealth of information in this book, particularly on the Islamic side (Makdisi's data on Western Europe is largely based on secondary sources). The book itself is not dissimilar to a work of *hadith* in which each point is buttressed by extensive quotation of authorities. The law of *waqf* is discussed in studious detail. Any muslim was free to endow an institution as a charitable foundation for perpetuity. Foremost among these foundations were the *madrasas* which combined the functions of places of prayer and tuition with residences for the students and their professors.

The purpose of the foundation was the teaching of the Koran and Islamic law, but other subjects (including the 'foreign sciences' based on Greek learning) were sometimes condoned. The curriculum, the status of the students and their teachers, and the methods of teaching are carefully described. The author has provided an English audience with abundant source material, much of it hidden away up to now in Arabic manuscripts, and, as such, his book should become the standard work on early Islamic colleges. The comparative material he brings forward is impressive, but not conclusive. Influence is a very hard ingredient to measure, and, as ^cAbd al-Latif wrote in the early thirteenth century 'the sciences seep away, then spring forth for a time, like vegetation or water springs; they shift from people to people, and from country to country' (p. 91).

Charles S. F. Burnett
Department of History
University of Sheffield

Manlio Bellomo, *Saggio sull'università nell'età del diritto comune.* Catania: Editrice Giannotta, 1979, pp. 290, L. 10.000.

This book is a useful up-to-date survey on the history of European universities, especially of the legal prototype, from about 1100 to 1400. It attempts to survey the various aspects of student universities, in the technical meaning of that term, from their heyday to their metamorphosis into the more modern 'università degli studi', or university, consisting of various 'faculties', beginning around 1400.

   The book consists of eleven chapters which are devoted to such subjects as a general portrait of civil law instruction in the early period, students, schools, and universities, the forms of instruction, student revolts, the nature of books in the period and implications for instruction, the nature of the professorial position and elections to the same, student corporations, the university of students, and the procedure of examinations for promotion to the doctorate, especially in civil law. One of the important merits of the book is the frequent references to and quotations from original primary material, the most conspicuous of which is the Roman Law corpus (*Iuris civilis*). Also, there are numerous quotations from the glossators. The author has used other primary sources, both clerical and secular, to document and illustrate his points. Furthermore, he has utilised both earlier and later secondary literature, including his own valuable writings. The most important part of the book is the bibliography (*indice bibliografico*, pp. 265-285), where the author lists, in one continuous alphabetical order, the items used for his study; it seems to be comprehensive and almost always exact. Bellomo's own list of relevant publications takes up almost an entire page itself (pp. 266-267) and, judging by the quality of this book, all the items listed would repay careful study.

1. As for limitations, there are a number of technical improvements one could suggest. Although a general monograph, there should be indices of *names*, of *cities* and of *subjects*. Furthermore, an index of primary texts cited would help make a good book even better. The author says (p. 265): 'Taking into consideration my readers (general university students?), I have preferred not to distinguish original sources from secondary literature'. Anzi! Neophytes, especially, could profit very early from seeing primary evidence listed first and separately, before the less valuable, derivative secondary literature.

2. In one instance, the author did not take advantage of a correction to Rashdall. On pp. 65, 78, 203, 206, 209, 221, 226 and 243, he cites Odofredus' *proemium* to *Digestum vetus*. If Powicke and Emden are right (Rashdall, I², 1936, p. 218, n. 3), this work was due, not to Odofredus, but to one of his pupils, Petrus Peregrossi of Milan (d. 1295 Chevalier II, 3577), who taught at Orléans.

3. Bellomo refers to two articles by H. Kantorowicz, viz., 'A medieval Grammarian' (p. 13, n. 24) and to the 'The Poetical Sermon' (p. 18, n. 35). In both instances he cites page numbers only. Is one to infer that both items are included in his collected papers called *Rechtshistorische Schriften*, ed. by H. Coing and G. Immel, published in 1970 (p. 276)?

4. Misprints: P. 38, last line: 'camerire' for 'cameriere'? P. 47 n. 87, 49 n. 97, 135 n. 1, 261 n. 76, 272, line 11, 275, line 12: Haskins. . .'Cultur' for '*Culture*'. P. 261 n. 76, line 1: '*cultur*' for '*students*'. P. 140 n. 21: 'CHATILLON' for 'CHATELAIN'. P. 283, line 25: '*Erfoschung*' for '*Erforschung*'; line 27: '-BEDDIES' for '-BEDDIE'.

5. Add: to p. 57 n. 121 and 144 n. 43 and 278, after MESINI, C.: MICHAUD-QUANTIN, P. *Universitas*: *expressions du mouvement communautaire dans le moyen âge latin* (Paris, 1970).

In spite of these small points, the book is a valuable addition to the scholarly literature and well deserves respectful consideration.

Herbert S. Matsen
Highland Farm
Star Route, Box 10
Bickleton, Washington 99322
U. S. A.

C.N. Constantinides, *Higher Education in Byzantium in the Thirteenth and Early Fourteenth Centuries (1204-ca. 1310)*. (Texts and Studies of the History of Cyprus, XI). Nicosia: Cyprus Research Centre, 1982.

The study of higher education and of the learned circles in Byzantium faces two main problems. First, the relevant information is scattered over an extremely varied literature. *Encomia* addressed to an emperor may refer to the state of higher education at the time and give some information on how an imperially funded school functioned. The extensive correspondence of the time may yield interesting information, but it rarely gives the modern scholar the satisfaction of knowing the whole truth regarding a particular private or public school. A comparative analysis of all the available data may give us, in the future, a much clearer picture of Byzantine education than has been possible so far. The second problem one has to face concerns the extreme conservativism — at least outwardly — of Byzantine education. The textbooks of rhetoric — to take only one example — a subject of paramount importance for the Byzantine student, were mainly the rhetorical handbooks of the Second Sophistic movement in Late Antiquity. It requires a rather minute analysis of the surviving scholia to uncover, embedded in a mass of traditional material, the timid beginnings of a proper medieval Greek 'rhetoric'.

Dr Constantinides' book, a slightly revised version of his Ph. D. thesis submitted to the University of London in 1978, makes an important contribution towards the solution of the first problem. His aim is to establish a basic narrative 'Who's Who' of the chaotic world of late Byzantine higher education from the fall of Constantinople to the Crusaders in 1204 up to the first decade of the fourteenth century. He claims that between these two dates lies an intense educational activity patronised by, or revolving around the emperors (from John III Batatzes to Andronikos II Palaeologos). This was carried on at private or imperially funded schools and in numerous learned *theatra* (= circles, we would say today) by scholarly teachers overtly emphasising the reading of and commenting upon the 'Hellenic' textual legacy, some of which had not entered the classroom since Late Antiquity.

Constantinides has read an enormous amount of the literature exchanged by teachers and pupils or members of these learned circles, not any easy task as anyone familiar with the labyrinthine, image-laden sentences of Byzantine *literati* can testify. He has traced the most prominent teacher-pupil affiliations, some for the first time, and has given us a clearer picture of their activities. Among the top teachers of the period one should mention the erratic monk Nikephoros Blemmydes (1197/8 - *ca.* 1272) with his eremitical school near Ephesos (est. *ca.* 1248); the historian of the Nicaean interlude in Byzantine administration George Akropolites (1217-1282), first professor of the re-opened imperial school of higher education in Constantinople after 1261; the future Patriarch George of Cyprus (1283-89 in office) teaching probably at the monastery of Akataleptos in Constantinople; Manuel-Maximos Holobolos at the re-opened (*ca.* 1265) Patriarchal School at the Church of St Paul in the *Orphanotropheion*; the polymath and textbook-writer George Pachymeres (1242-*ca.* 1310); and the textual scholar Maximos Planudes (*ca.* 1255-1305) who taught at an imperial monastery provided with a school.

Certain basic features of late, if not of all, Byzantine education emerge from this book. For example, it is important to remember that the graduates of private or imperially funded schools would aspire to a post in the still huge civil — or more correctly imperial — service, and perhaps later to a prominent ecclesiastical office. This is amply documented throughout the book. To rise high in this world one needed of course strong and influential patrons, but also the ability to put down on paper — at specific moments in time — the whole essence of the imperial ideology and the Byzantine *Weltanschauung.* The skill required to do that was partly learned at school, mainly through the exhaustive — and exhausting — study and practice of rhetoric as understood by the medieval Greeks. The crucial importance of rhetoric in Byzantine public and intellectual life has unfortunately not been sufficiently stressed by the author, who seems to see in it nothing but a 'fluent tongue and a convincing pen' rather than a conscious educational policy. This study would have perhaps benefitted much more had the author opted for a systematic, rather than a narrative approach to his subject. Reading through the histories of so many major and minor teachers of various subjects, one is struck by the recurring themes which could have provided the framework for the illustrative material and the critical discussions on bio-bibliographical points.

The Greek palaeographer will appreciate, I think, the rich information contained in this book which summarises and carries further recent palaeographical and codicological research, especially concerning the editorial and scribal activities of Planudes, who seems to have had problems with finding even the indispensible instruments of his trade: e.g. good parchment for his monumental edition of Plutarch *ca.* 1294/96.

An important contribution of Constantinides' book lies in his treatment of the learned circles at Nicaea and later at Constantinople. He shows that they are as important as the schools in preserving and transmitting the 'Hellenic' texts, and perhaps more important in the case of texts which were not normally read in the schools. The anecdotal side of the story is also told in detail with typical medieval Greek scholars busy collecting books of ancient and late Greek literature and science, lending them to their friends, asking for them back — sometimes in vain — recording their impressions after reading them, exchanging opinions on them — and all this for no obvious practical reason other than the honour to be called an educated man.

Further analysis of these groups can now build upon the ground cleared by Constantinides, but what is perhaps of greater urgency is a synthetic approach to the subject aiming at reconstructing for us the peculiar image of man which was fostered by Byzantine education and which was clearly at odds with the ascetic anthropology of the monastic communities.

Athanassios D. Angelou
Royal Holloway College
University of London

Walter Steffen, *Die studentische Autonomie im mittelalterlichen Bologna: Eine Untersuchung über die Stellung der Studenten und ihrer Universitas gegenüber Professoren und Stadtregierung im 13/14. Jahrhundert* [Geist und Werk der Zeiten, Arbeiten aus dem Historischen Seminar der Universität Zürich, No. 58]. Bern: Peter Lang, 1981. Pp 246. S.Fr. 44.30.

In this brief volume, Walter Steffen re-examines the published sources for and historiography of the institutional, social and economic history of the medieval schools of Bologna, with special attention to the origins and extent of student autonomy. After introductory chapters sketching the developments of civil and canon law as disciplines and the emergence of Bologna as a centre of legal studies, the author summarises what is known of the early history of the student universities of law and provides an analysis of their organisation, functions, and actual powers in the thirteenth and early fourteenth centuries. It is Steffen's contention that in this period effective organisation combined with their importance to the city's economy gave foreign students of law at Bologna real power to impose demands upon both their professors and the civic authorities. In his view, a good many of the sweeping claims to authority found in student university statutes, although still repeated in the fifteenth century long after they had become ineffective, reflect thirteenth-century realities. However, while the student universities unquestionably exercised more power in the thirteenth century — especially during its last two decades — than at any subsequent time, the evidence presented by Steffen seems to imply, even for the thirteenth century, continual tension and a measure of mutual accommodation between student universities, professors, and commune, rather than student dominance. Moreover, it is clear that in some respects the identification of the interests of citizen professors and commune was already quite close.

Despite the announced focus upon students, the longest, and in some ways the most interesting, chapter in the book concerns the professoriate, considered chiefly as a social and economic group. Steffen convincingly demonstrates that a successful career as a professor could raise the social standing not only of an individual, but of his entire family for generations to come. Furthermore, such a career brought wealth from a variety of sources — not only direct payments for teaching (*collectae* from students or, in some instances, a municipal salary) but also fees from *consilia* and the fruits of loans to students. One wishes that the collection of short biographies of professors with which the author illustrates some of these points could have included a few of the leading medical professors of the late thirteenth and early fourteenth century. While it is true, as Steffen notes, that the faculty of medicine at Bologna never achieved the level of prestige or wealth of the faculty of law, it was not as negligible as he implies. Medicine, too, was taught by some famous professors for whom their professorships were a significant avenue of social and economic advancement.

This work will be welcomed as a lively overview of early institutional developments in the schools of Bologna and a frequently perceptive account of the city's academic community in its social and economic context. Some of the same subject matter has, of course, also been recently covered in Manlio Bellomo's fine study, *Saggio sull'università nell'eta del diritto comune* (Catania, 1979). A minor feature of Steffen's book that seems distracting rather than illuminating is the incorporation of a necessarily superficial, because highly compressed, account of some of the efforts of twentieth-century students to dominate their educational environment. Berkeley in the 1960s is certainly by now as much a subject for the historian of universities as

Bologna in the thirteenth century, but the one sheds little light on the other. On the whole, however, this work provides a useful and often thought-provoking introduction to the early history of the *studium* of Bologna and its student corporations.

Nancy G. Siraisi
Department of History
Hunter College of the City University of New York
695 Park Avenue, New York, N. Y. 10021
U. S. A.

Gianfranco Fioravanti, *Università e città. Cultura umanistica e cultura scolastica a Siena nel '400.* [Quaderni di *Rinascimento*, III]. Florence: Sansoni Editore, 1981.

After many decades of neglect the history of the University of Siena in the Renaissance is again interesting a number of historians. Recent years have seen several important studies, chiefly in the series *Studi senesi* and its related *Quaderni*, and in the *Bullettino senese di storia patria*, by Bertoni, Cascio Pratilli, Catoni, Košuta, Maffei, Marrara, Nardi and most recently Mecacci and Minnucci (who has also published a valuable bibliographical survey in the 1981 volume of *Studi senesi*). A lesson to be drawn from all these studies is that the previous neglect of Renaissance Siena, and the attitude that Siena could not possibly have belonged to the 'top class' of Italian universities in this period, owe perhaps more to the daunting wealth and diversity of documentation awaiting study than to informed opinion. Above all, such studies are beginning to make serious inroads into the old dictum that the Renaissance, in terms of humanistic as well as artistic activity, largely passed Siena by.

'Alcuni aspetti della cultura umanistica sense nel '400', the first of Gianfranco Fioravanti's two articles in the 1979 and 1980 volumes of *Rinascimento*, now published together in this volume, takes this last issue as a focal point. Beginning with a discussion of Sienese civic sentiment in its political, social and economic context, Professor Fioravanti demonstrates — bringing to bear a wide range of unpublished material — the extent of Sienese interest in orations as the main vehicle for the expression of humanistic trends. This genre, however, is not only the principal but also virtually the only substantial example of Sienese humanistic output, and the rest of the article is devoted to explaining why the 'humanists' did not really go much further. A prime reason seems to have been the comparatively lowly status of humanistic studies compared to the main 'professional' disciplines which gave the Sienese *studio*, like others, its centre of gravity. Such attitudes make it possible for the loss of Filelfo (the main example, and a great blow to the city's prospects in this direction) to be laid at the door of the communal authorities. This explanation is not without its problems. Local attitudes to humanistic studies as part of university curricula are broadly similar throughout Italian *studi*, and in any case many a humanist, or humanist *manqué*, cited by Fioravanti as active in Siena did not even teach, or taught only for a short while, in the *studio*. Fioravanti returns to the *studio* at the end of the second article, on 'Pietro de' Rossi. Bibbia ed Aristotele nella Siena del '400' (in which he shows himself to be as at home with scholastic as with humanist culture), providing some more reasons for this 'non-development'. He emphasises the eclectic and uneven nature of Rossi's achievement, and goes on to ask why other teachers too have such meagre *produzione scientifica* to show for their many years of teaching. Close identification between teachers and the regime of the day, and a consequently heavy involvment in politics, curtailed such activity in many cases — Fioravanti cites and illustrates the careers of Bartolo di Tura Bandini and Bernardo Lapini in particular and others in more cursory fashion, but the examples could easily be multiplied. Thus in a sense the communal administrators of the *studio* were their own worst enemies, fighting to maintain an eminent payroll of *doctores* while at the same time constantly requiring their services elsewhere. The force of this argument is undeniable, though it could be added in parenthesis that the proportionally vast extent of territory administered by the small Sienese ruling group made it inevitable that such demands would be made on the intellectual élite, while from the point of view of the *studio* such prestigious signs of participation could be valuable and, as Zdekauer pointed out almost a century ago, at times protected the university from the force of changing winds of political fortune.

Fioravanti's thesis will be controversial, and may not entirely satisfy those who see the *studio* — and humanistic activity in Siena — in a more positive light, or those who have doubts about the importance of such external factors as administration in intellectual traditions. Nonetheless this is a bold and forceful statement which draws on an impressive spectrum of source material, touches a wide range of issues, brings to life the careers of many Sienese intellectuals of the fifteenth century, and effectively reopens a debate which it is to be hoped may at last, given the variety of present scholarly activity in this area, make further significant advances.

Peter Denley
Westfield College
(University of London)
London NW3 7ST

Celestino Piana, *Il 'Liber Secretus Iuris Caesarei' dell'Università di Bologna (1451-1500)*. Orbis Academicus. Saggi e Documenti di Storia delle Università, raccolti da Domenico Maffei, I. Giuffrè Editore, Milano, 1984. 109 + 444pp. ISBN 88-14-00098-0. Lire 50.000.

Liber Secretus Iuris Caesarei is the title of the series of official books in which were recorded the deliberations of Bologna's College of Doctors in Civil Law. An edition of the first of these volumes, which covers the years 1379 to 1512, was begun by Albano Sorbelli, two instalments appearing in 1938 and 1942. The present publication, in taking the second half of the fifteenth century, goes a substantial way towards completing the volume.

It is no exaggeration to say that this publication provides a fundamental tool for the study of late fifteenth-century civil law at Bologna. Undoubtedly of most interest to intellectual and social historians of universities will be the details of the degrees awarded by the college, which constitute most of the text. But interesting (and sometimes quite gossipy) light is thrown on the College's other activities; on elections to the college, and to its priorate, for example: on decisions about *consilia* given corporately: on strike action when salaries were not being paid: on the college's part in the ceremonial life of the city. There are several measures regulating lectures (which prove, were proof still needed, how unrealistic were the claims of the student-university, in its statutes of 1432, to control this aspect of academic life). It is interesting also to note the frequency with which dispensation was granted from one or other of the many stiff conditions which in theory had to be satisfied before a student could be awarded his degree.

But Padre Piana, as usual, has done much more than produce an edition of the text. He has painstakingly sought to identify as many of the graduands (and others) as possible, and has supplied from his deep knowledge of the sources and the literature much additional information about these individuals. The preface is, as is characteristic of his many publications, an opportunity to publish a wide variety of further documentary material. This ranges from extracts from the books of the College's notaries, which help to complete and gloss the *Liber Secretus*, to documents whose connection with the edition or even with the College of Doctors is tenuous or non-existent but which well describe the functioning of the university. Piana discusses and illustrates topics as varied as the diplomatic and other 'extra-curricular' activities of doctors, their contracts, the commune's granting to students of safe-conducts and permission to bear arms, the degree examination, the position of the student rectors, student production of university texts, Bologna's residential colleges, and the *repetitiones* which scholars gave as the means of obtaining student lectureships. The text and preface are admirably indexed, and the bibliography takes the form of an index of works cited. A well-produced volume which is a fitting and a promising beginning to this new series of texts and studies on university history, published under the auspices of the International Commission for the History of Universities.

Peter Denley
Westfield College
(University of London)
London NW3 7ST

Richard Palmer, *The 'Studio' of Venice and Its Graduates in the Sixteenth Century*. (Contributi alla storia dell'Università di Padova, 12). Trieste and Padua: Edizioni LINT, 1983. Pp. xi + 204. L. 20.000.

This is a study of the Venetian College of Physicians, an institution that until now has rested in great obscurity because it was never a complete *studio generale* and because a fire destroyed its archive in 1800. The Venetian *studio* began in the fourteenth century and later had chairs in the humanities and philosophy. It received charters to become a full *studio generale* with the power of granting degrees from Emperor Frederick III in 1469 and Pope Paul II in 1470. The first never happened, but the Venetian *studio* did grant a large number of degrees to those who did all or the bulk of their studying elsewhere. It also performed other functions: it licensed some surgical practitioners, upheld medical standards, staged an annual anatomy, and offered the opportunity for students to obtain clinical experience by working with members of the College. The College also fixed drug prices, provided physicians in times of calamity, and fought to uphold the traditional exemption from taxes of physicians and surgeons. Despite Paduan opposition, the Venetian *studio* flourished, especially as a medical degree factory.

The most useful part of Palmer's excellent study is his annotated list of the six hundred physicians who passed their examinations in Venice in the sixteenth century. Palmer describes the procedures, examinations, and cost of a Venetian degree. The last helps explain its popularity: a Venetian degree cost only half to two-thirds the expense of a Paduan degree. For this reason and because contemporaries held Venetian degrees in high esteem, a long line of physicians studied elsewhere and obtained degrees in Venice. Of the 603 identified recipients of the sixteenth century, 349 came from the Venetian Republic, 184 from elsewhere in Italy, 33 from the rest of Europe, and the places of origin of the remaining 37 remain unidentified. These graduates included some of the most important figures in sixteenth-century medicine. At least 125 either held university chairs or published in a variety of fields: Girolamo Cardano, Bassiano Lando, Girolamo Mercuriale, Giovanni Battista da Monte, Fabio Paolini, and others. The Venetian *studio* emerges as a significant and interesting institution for the history of medicine in the sixteenth century. Palmer has performed a very useful service by reconstructing its history from very scattered archival and manuscript sources.

Paul F. Grendler
Department of History
University of Toronto
Toronto, Ontario M5S 1A1
Canada

Marie-Madeleine Compère and Dominique Julia, *Les collèges français 16e-18e siècles. Répertoire 1: France du Midi.* Paris: Institut national de la recherche pédagogique/Centre national de la recherche scientifique, 1984. Pp. 758. Ff. 330.

For the past fifteen years Dominique Julia, ably assisted by his wife Marie-Madeleine Compère and a number of other colleagues attached to the I.N.R.P. and the C.N.R.S., has painstakingly combed the national departmental and municipal archives of France in an attempt to construct for the first time a social history of secondary education in the early-modern period. Julia and his associates are not the first to have begun the task. As they would readily admit they are proceeding down a trail initially pioneered by the Jesuit François de Dainville who died in 1971.[1] So far the *équipe* has produced a large number of highly interesting but very particular monographs on subjects as diverse as the pattern of recruitment to the colleges of Avallon, Gisors and Condom, and the calorific intake of *pensionnaires* at Auch, Beaumont-en-Auge, Molsheim and Toulouse.[2] In the present work the detailed research of so many years is finally brought together by this most productive of husband-and-wife teams in the first of a three-volume study devoted to the history of secondary education in its entirety. Even here though we have not yet received the synthesis which will surely come. Rather our appetites are whetted by what is primarily a work of reference, a series of potted histories of a plethora of individual institutions.

By the authors' own admission too this work (despite appearances) is not exhaustive. It merely provides a potted history of the municipal colleges, convents and seminaries that offered public courses in the Latin and Greek humanities and/or philosophy. It ignores entirely the ever-growing number of eighteenth-century private *pensionnats* that offered instruction in the modern as well as classical languages and often specialised training in mathematics, accountancy, navigation, etc.[3] But this omission, as the authors point out, was inevitable. The new eighteenth-century *maisons d'éducation* may have dramatically increased the provision of secondary education and offered an alternative syllabus. Nevertheless, by the very fact that they were in no way publically maintained they have perforce left a lamentable archival record. And the whole purpose of the research of the Julias and their associates is to establish the history of early-modern French education on a proper archival footing. It is this, the book claims in the introductory chapter (pp. 1-3), that has never been done before. During the era of the Third Republic certainly many colleges found their historians, but none was an objective searcher after truth. Each had an axe to grind, seeing

1.   Dainville's many articles have been collected and published by M. M. Compère under the title, *L'Éducation des jésuites (XVIe-XVIIIe siècles)* (Paris, 1978).

2.   W. Frijhoff and D. Julia, *École et société dans la France d'ancien régime* (Paris, 1975); W. Frijhoff and D. Julia, 'L'Alimentation des pensionnaires à la fin de l'ancien régime', *Annales, économies, sociétés, civilisations* 30 (1975), 491-504.

3.   Most fully explored so far in Ph. Marchand, 'Un modèle éducatif original à la veille de la révolution', *Revue d'histoire moderne et contemporaine* 22 (1975), 549-67.

his history as a polemical weapon in the ceaseless quarrel between right and left, Church and state, over the best form of secondary education. Hence the justification for the present and subsequent volumes, the work of late-twentieth century empiricists asking the kind of questions that interest contemporary educational historians.

Given the quality of the individual entries in volume I no one could seriously criticise the authors' decision to limit the study to public institutions of secondary education. Simply by sticking to their brief they have had more than enough institutions to investigate — some three hundred in the Midi alone. The length of an entry is determined entirely by the surviving archival information; it may run to no more than a paragraph or as much as twenty pages. But whatever the length the sources are always carefully documented and their reliability weighed. As far as possible an attempt is made to describe the chief stages in the educational history of each institution: when it was founded, whether run by seculars or regulars, the level of endowment etc. Where information is abundant the entry is headed by a résumé of the statistical data preserved such as the number of students at different times and the level of a *pension*. Above all the work is not only erudite but extremely easy to use. As a work of reference it is a model of its kind.

There can be no doubt that this three-volume work when complete will be an exceptionally useful tool to students of early-modern education. If only there was a similar work in progress on the English grammar schools and dissenting academies! One can only await with pleasure the *équipe*'s analysis of the information it has gathered. The only question-mark to be raised against the enterprise concerns its sociological bias. We learn a great deal about the administration of these institutions and the clientele they served, but little about their teaching role, after all their *raison d'etre*. We are given a skeletal framework certainly, the date that a course in philosophy was instituted for instance, but nothing more. This is to do the reader a disservice. Many of the colleges were intellectual power-houses and one would have liked more than a perfunctory comment on their contribution to the development of French science and letters. The Lyons Collège de la Trinité for example is treated to an entry of twenty pages but only a few lines are devoted to its two great seventeenth-century philosopher-mathematicians, Fabri and Milliet Dechales (p. 386). The omission too is all the more galling in that plenty of archival material survives that relates directly to the college curriculum (especially in the local *bibliothèques municipales*). Admittedly there is seldom enough to produce the curricular history of an individual college. At the very least though its existence could be referred to for the benefit of the researcher for whom this book is intended. As it stands the work as a tool of reference is seriously flawed and the unkind might even say it was a case of 'Hamlet without the prince'. Let us hope that the omission is repaired in future volumes.

L. W. B. Brockliss
Magdalen College
Oxford

Leif Grane (ed.), *University and Reformation: Lectures from the University of Copenhagen Symposium.* Leiden: E. J. Brill, 1981. Pp. 113. Guilders 32.

These are the proceedings of a conference arranged by the theological faculty at Copenhagen on the occasion of the quincentary of the university in 1979. They tell us little about Copenhagen itself (a multi-volumed history is in process of compilation), though M. S. Lausten indicates how peripheral and derivative was its experience in the age of Luther. The other contributors address wider topics. L. W. Spitz offers sound arguments for a positive view of the role of sixteenth-century universities and their symbiosis with Reformation and Counter-Reformation. D. Tamm shows that Lutheranism had a limited impact on law faculties: much traditional study survived, though the new Biblical basis brought some modifications. R. Stauffer says some fairly predictable things about the earlier history of the Genevan and French Calvinist academies. In fact, the most stimulating paper in this short and rather scrappy collection has little to do with universities at all. In it O. Pedersen re-examines the relation between modern science and the Reformation, concluding that neither the thesis of conspicuous positive correlation (the argument about the advanced character of Calvinism) nor its negative equivalent (which stresses medieval scientific origins) can be sustained. Rather, contingent factors played a decisive part, especially the rise on the (Protestant) Atlantic seaboard of economies conducive to technological change.

R. J. W. Evans
Brasenose College
Oxford

Gian Paolo Brizzi, Alessandro D'Alessandro & Alessandra Del Fante, *Università, principe, gesuiti. La politica farnesiana dell' istruzione a Parma e Piacenza (1545-1622).*[Centro studi 'Europa delle Corti'/Biblioteca del Cinquecento, 12]. Rome: Bulzoni Editore, 1980. Pp. 223. Lire 12,000.

The three short studies presented in this volume together form a rounded and stimulating introduction to the *studio* of Parma in the period during which it finally attained some continuous existence. The dates in the title, however, should not mislead. The brief reopening of the *studio* by Pier Luigi Farnese in 1545 was effective only till 1552, and for the rest of the sixteenth century the label *studio* is largely inapplicable. Foundations were being laid, though, with the growing influence of the Jesuits on the Farnese dukes, with their gradual replacement of secular teachers at all levels of education, and with the opening of the Collegio di S. Rocco in 1564 and, in 1582-3, of another Jesuit college in Piacenza where, as Alessandra del Fante shows in her 'Appunti sulla storia dello Studio di Piacenza durante l'età farnesiana', there is a modest amount of teaching at the higher level throughout this period. The true moment of the reopening of the *studio* at Parma came under Duke Ranuccio I in 1599, and more fully in 1601 (which also saw the foundation of the Collegio dei Nobili), from which time continuous and rapid expansion is traceable.

The two articles on the *studio* of Parma are written from slightly differing perspectives. Alessandro D'Alessandro's 'Materiali per la storia dello *Studium* di Parma (1545-1622)', based chiefly on material from the Archivio di Stato, the Archivio del Comune and the Biblioteca Palatina in Parma, outlines the principal developments in the history of the *studio* over the period, and will be an invaluable starting-point for future research. Ranuccio placed the refounded *studio* under more comprehensive control than had been exercised by its previous sponsors (although there was resistance from the students who attempted to gain the right to a rector or similar representative, and to more say in academic matters), but in practice ducal power was used chiefly to defend the rights of the *studio* and of the colleges of doctors. Above all D'Alessandro emphasises the crucial role, despite considerable opposition, of the Jesuits: in persuading successive dukes of the necessity for an education policy, along Jesuit lines, in establishing a predominance in teaching (and a monopoly of the subjects within their competence) and in the running of the Collegio dei Nobili, a residential college which was kept entirely separate from the rest of the *studio*. These considerations form the basis of Gian Paolo Brizzi's study, 'Educare il Principe, formare le *élites*: i Gesuiti e Ranuccio I Farnese'. Taking a narrower theme but using a wider range of sources (and it is a pity, incidentally, that no editor co-ordinated these contributions at least to the extent of facilitating cross-reference, for example when Brizzi quotes material published here by D'Alessandro), the author places early seventeenth-century developments in Parma in the context of European educational, political and social trends and stesses that ducal control — to the extent of personal supervision of admissions to the Collegio dei Nobili — was an essential part of the building of a system of patronage and of the formation of administrative cadres, a policy forged above all by the Jesuits, drawing on their ample experience at Evora, Pont-à-Mousson, Ingolstadt and elsewhere. The characteristics of their educational policy as followed in the Collegio dei Nobili are well illustrated by descriptions of Ranuccio's own sons, and the college's later reputation as the most prestigious in Italy is supported with careful analysis of the geographical provenance of its alumni.

Both these studies are accompanied by appendices which, as well as richly documenting the features stressed by the authors, provide plenty of information about the problems of university life. One is struck by the realism and sophistication with which the Jesuits planned a phased development of the *studio*, for example, while at the other extreme it is interesting to find confirmation that the proliferation of graffiti, then as now, was considered almost an occupational hazard of academic life.

Peter Denley
Westfield College
(University of London)
London NW3 7ST

The Statutes of Sir Walter Mildmay Kt. Chancellor of the Exchequer and One of Her Majesty's Privy Councillors; Authorised by Him for the Government of Emmanuel College Founded by Him. Translated with an introduction and commentary by Frank Stubbings. Cambridge: Cambridge University Press, 1983. Pp. XIV + 156. £25.00.

Mr. Stubbings, the librarian of Emmanuel, has provided in this book an accurate translation of the founder's statutes of his college. This edition is made particularly serviceable by his inclusion of a succinct introduction which describes the development of the University during the political and religious controversies of the sixteenth century, thus providing a context for Sir Walter Mildmay's college that, puritan from its inception, would soon produce so many men of influence in both England and New England.

The text is accompanied by notes which illustrate collegiate practice from archival material, and contrast the statutes with those of Christ's College, upon which they were based. Most useful are the 'College Orders of 1588', which detail how the statutes were implemented, and show more closely the academic work of the college, particularly the theological exercises. The book concludes with the Latin text of the statutes, which were originally published in a series (*Documents Relating to the University and Colleges of Cambridge* (London, 1852) 3, 483-523) that is not available in many North American libraries. Mr. Stubbings' new edition, well presented and printed, will henceforth be a standard research tool for all students of Cambridge history, as well as an accessible introduction to college practice for any scholar of Tudor-Stuart England.

Damian Riehl Leader
123 Napoleon Blvd.
South Bend, Indiana 46617
U. S. A.

Karl Mommsen, *Katalog der Basler juristischen Disputationen, 1558-1818. Aus dem Nachlass herausgegeben von Werner Kundert.* [Ius Commune. Sonderheft 9]. Frankfurt am Main: Vittorio Klostermann, 1978. Pp. 408. DM 110.

The *Katalog* is preceded by an essay by the late Karl Mommsen on the relevance of academic dissertations as a source for historical research (pp. 15-18), a detailed introduction by Werner Kundert (pp. 19-110) and several illustrations (pp. 111-128). As Mommsen tells us in his essay, the *Katalog* was a by-product of his study *Auf dem Wege zur Staatssouveranität. Staatliche Grundbegriffe in Basler juristischen Doktordisputationen des 17. and 18. Jahrhunderts* (Bern, 1970). He considers the juridical theses as a profitable source for the history of laws, as they are an accurate reflection of the average of legal and political knowledge of university graduates, and thus provide the best material for an analysis of the then prevailing conceptions of law and government. In Section I (pp. 19-42) of his introduction, Kundert gives a brief survey of Basel teaching of law between the two reorganisations of the university, 1532 and 1818, the first being inspired by the Reformation, the other by the Enlightenment. Section II (pp. 42-57) is a study of the formal aspects of the printed disputations, whereas Section III (pp. 57-71) summarises the development of disputation topics according to the juridical disciplines: *jus civile, canonicum, feudale, publicum, criminale, modernum*, and history of laws. An examination of the students' provenance in Section IV (pp. 72-82) shows that during its prosperity (until 1700) Basel was primarily a faculty of graduation for candidates from the *Imperium Romano-Germanicum* rather than from Basel itself (see also Appendix VII, pp. 104-107).

The catalogue itself (pp. 135-351) comprises 2226 entries of juridical dissertations submitted to the Basel faculty of law between 1558 and 1818. The consecutively numbered bibliography is ordered chronologically. Each entry produces the disputator's name (respective index: pp. 353-380), his provenance (index: pp. 381-391), a number referring to *Die Matrikel der Universität Basel*, ed. H. G. Wackernagel et al., vol. II-V (useful for biographical research), title of the work (subject index: pp. 392-403), type of disputation (eg. *pro gradu, pro cathedra, exercitium*), shelfmark of Basel University Library, form of *theses* (viz. *nudae* [pure assertion without referring to an authority], *vestitae* [mentioning references], *capitula* [full exposition of arguments]), size of the text.

Finally, it is to be hoped that this important bibliography will both have successors and contribute to the appreciation of academic dissertations as a valuable source for the history of ideas.

Wolfgang Rother
CH-5412 Gebenstorf
Switzerland

Mordechai Feingold, *The Mathematicians' Apprenticeship: Science, Universities and Society in England, 1560-1640.* Cambridge: Cambridge University Press, 1984. Pp.viii + 248. £22.50/$ 37.00.

The central aim of this work is to disprove the argument that during the period 1560-1640 the universities of Oxford and Cambridge provided little, if any, mathematical and scientific education for its students, and that the most important developments which contributed to the new learning took place elsewhere, particularly London. To counter such a view, put forward by, among others, Christopher Hill in his *Intellectual Origins of the English Revolution* (Oxford, 1965), Feingold has undertaken an extensive survey of both published and unpublished documents of the period. These include university statutes, student lecture notes and commonplace books, undergraduate lists, inventories, biographical material and correspondence. Feingold's conscientious investigations into this relatively uncharted area throw light on a whole network of scholars, patrons and intellectuals in the universities who were all to varying degrees educated and interested in mathematics. Although mathematics provide the focal point of the study, the material presented here would be a good starting-point for a more broadly-based study of the cultural complexion of the universities.

The first three chapters establish that despite the absence of mathematics in university and college statutes, lectures and tutorials containing new as well as traditional mathematics were given and also attended regularly at both Oxford and Cambridge. Much new information on lecturers in mathematics, college fellows and their students is given in these chapters which supplement earlier studies of the universities and their curricula such as W. T. Costello, *The Scholastic Curriculum at Early Seventeenth-Century Cambridge* (Cambridge, Mass., 1958) and C. E. Mallet, *A History of the University of Oxford*, 3 vols (repr. New York, 1968). In the fourth chapter it is argued that scholars in the English universities formed part of a single 'scientific community' not only of England but also of Europe. An interest in mathematics is regarded an an indication of an individual's membership of that community. It may be remarked, however, that the term 'intellectual community' would be more accurate, since, as Feingold acknowledges, mathematics was but one area of enquiry for the men involved in this international network of communication. Theology, philology and chronology, for example, were equally important topics for study by members of this community. The contribution of Gresham College to the advancement of science and the teaching of the theoretical foundations of the mechanical arts to common practitioners is the subject for the fifth chapter. It is argued that claims for Gresham have been exaggerated and that its chief role was as a research institute. In the final chapter the mechanics of patronage and its role in determining the activities of professional mathematicians and scientists is briefly considered. It is another area which has as yet received relatively little attention from historians.

Feingold's study contains a great deal of new information on the network of patronage and scholarship in Oxford and Cambridge during the period 1560-1640. Yet although he is concerned with mathematics, nowhere does the author provide any detailed information about the kind of material that was being studied or the use to which such knowledge might be put. In this sense it must be regarded as a socio-cultural study of groups and relationships rather than as a history of ideas.

Penelope M. Gouk
St. Hilda's College
Oxford

W. T. M. Frijhoff, *La Société néerlandaise et ses gradués, 1575-1814*
Amsterdam-Maarssen: Holland University Press, 1981. Pp. xvii +
422. Guilders 80.—

This ambitious book sets out to elucidate both the functioning of the
university as a social institution and the history of the educated elite of an
entire country by examining the size, composition and career opportunities
of graduates in the Netherlands during the 240 years between the founding of
Leiden University and the fundamental reorganisation of Dutch higher
education in the early nineteenth century. While evidently inspired by recent
historical research which concentrates, in Lawrence Stone's words, on 'the
relationship between formal education and other social processes', Frijhoff
has also drawn on the work of sociologists like Bourdieu and Passeron who
emphasise the role of education in enabling elites to perpetuate their position.

Following a discussion of university structures focused on the
institutional, confessional financial aspects of obtaining a diploma, Frijhoff
determines the number of degrees acquired by Netherlands students both
within the Republic and abroad. Careful analysis of long-term series of
quantifiable data drawn from an impressively broad range of archives,
printed sources and detailed studies, clearly presented in the text and in
numerous tables, graphs, maps and appendices, enables Frijhoff to
distinguish significant changes over time: cycles of attendance, the evolving
popularity of courses of study, the shifting balance of educational
achievement between town and country and among provinces. The final and
longest part of the book calculates proportions of graduates within the total
population and traces career patterns, particular attention being devoted to
medicine and law.

All across the period Frijhoff studies, Netherlands students pursued
degrees as much for reasons of prestige and privilege as for the sake of
knowledge. But the author's concerns lie mainly with the changing nature of
the educated stratum. Whereas during the seventeenth century, marked by
rapid growth in the number and proportion of graduates, the university
milieu proved relatively open to aspiring burgeois response to the new
Republic's demand for trained personnel, in the next century stagnating or
even declining production of degrees reflected an increasingly restricted
political order. At the same time, the ascendance of the large towns and
maritime provinces (which in any event was never as decisive as might be
imagined, depite the economic and political predominance of Holland) was
eroded in favour of interior areas and smaller centres, the effect not only of an
expanding rural economy but also of the centralisation and
bureaucratisation of provincial administration. Professionalisation equally
transformed the purpose of university education, which became a means of
access to specific careers rather than an elite's general introduction to
learning and social responsibilities.

Frijhoff's findings underline persistent variations among regions and
disciplines even while suggesting that a national, integrated and
homogeneous intellectual community had begun to emerge by the end of the
Ancien Régime. It is thus to be regretted that the author has not drawn the

comparisons which his work invites with the conclusions of scholars such as Kagan and Stone who have concentrated on aggregate national trends. In addition, the book gives a more satisfying quantitative account of the evolution of the university as a social institution. To be sure, it will not be easy to grasp the shifting curriculum and research interests of the Netherlands university, as represented, for example, by subjects chosen for theses, and Frijhoff has modestly disclaimed the ability to do so. But only by examining such topics will we be in a position fully to understand the university's function; how, that is, it affected — as well as being influenced by — the cultural and intellectual life of the larger society.

Robert S. DuPlessis
Swarthmore College
Swarthmore, PA 19081
U. S. A.

Gerhard Menk, *Die Hohe Schule Herborn in ihrer Frühzeit (1584-1660). Ein Beitrag zum Hochschulwesen des deutschen Kalvinismus im Zeitalter der Gegenreformation.* Wiesbaden: Selbstverlag der Historischen Kommission für Nassau, 1981. Pp. ix + 363. Appendix (8 plates). DM 69.

This ambitious study, which is the revised and enlarged version of a Ph. D. thesis submitted to the University of Frankfurt a. M. in 1975, provides a comprehensive account of early Herborn higher education concentrating upon institutional aspects and details rather than upon the intellectual structure. By exploring Herborn educational politics Menk intends to supply a deeper insight into the nature of Calvinism during the age of confessionalism.

First the author presents a historical survey of the High School from its foundation in 1584 until the reconstruction after the Thirty Years' War (pp. 22-96). The main part of the study (pp. 97-196) is devoted to the organisational structure of Herborn which followed the model of Strasbourg as a *Gymnasium Illustre* without the right to confer academic degrees and without the traditional division into faculties. Nonetheless philosophy (pp. 203-217), theology (pp. 231-257) as well as jurisprudence and especially political science (pp. 257-268) were taught throughout the whole period.

The characteristic feature of philosophical teaching was Ramism as the basic scientific approach. With the foundation of the Calvinist academy in Herborn Ramist philosophy received a new centre in Germany which, however, turned out to be a bulwark less against Aristotelianism than against Cartesianism during the 1650s. In this Ramist context humanist learning culminated in Johann Heinrich Alsted's (1588-1638) encyclopedism, finally tending to transgress confessionalism. Herborn theology, being primarily directed against Catholic and Lutheran dogmatics, had been established by the early federal theologian Caspar Olevian (1536-1587) and the controversialist Johannes Piscator (1546-1625), also a loyal Ramist. The outstanding figure of political science was the famous representative of popular sovereignty Johannes Althusius (1557?-1638), who provided a Calvinist theory of a republican commonwealth.

The last chapter deals with the influence of Herborn scholarship on other Calvinist academies (pp. 282-326), especially in Germany upon the Arnoldinum in Steinfurt, the Bremen Gymnasium, and the Hanau High School. Several Herborn professors taught in the Netherlands, particularly at Franeker, but also at Groningen, and many Swiss students came to Herborn School, whose teachers had close contacts with colleagues in Basel, Zürich and Bern. In 1630 a number of former Herborn professors moved to the newly founded academy in Transylvania, and philosophy teaching in Sweden had the stamp of both Althusius and Alsted. Herborn influences can be also traced to St Andrews and Edinburgh, to English Puritanism and, last but not least, to Harvard and later to Yale. Altogether this broad and well-documented study is a valuable contribution to the historical research on early modern universities.

Wolfgang Rother
CH-5412 Gebenstorf
Switzerland

Erhard Cellius, *Imagines professorum tubingensium 1596*. 2 Vols.: H. Decker-Hauff and W. Setzler (eds), Vol. I: *Faksimile*, pp. 139; Vol. II: *Kommentar und Text in Übersetzung*, pp. 170. Sigmaringen: Jan Thorbeck Verlag, 1981. DM 94.

After taking his BA and MA at Tübingen, Erhard Cellius (1546-1606) was appointed to a junior post there as Latin teacher. At the same time he began writing speeches and *Gelegenheitsgedichte* for ceremonies within the life of the University, such as anniversaries, graduation days, marriages and funerals. Many of these speeches were printed, some by his own press. In 1582 he became professor of poetry and history.

Already in 1577 Cellius had composed a long poem to mark the centenary of the University's foundation. The same occasion saw the commissioning of portraits of some of the professors. Subsequently, Cellius persuaded others to sit for portraits, and woodcut copies of these began to appear with his various speeches. From here it was but a short step to compose a larger work in celebration of the centenary: for each of thirty-five professors, the *Imagines* juxtaposes a verse biography of thirty lines with a portrait of its subject.

Volume I is a facsimile of the original. First Cellius works through the four faculties in turn as they stand in 1596, prefacing each with additional verses and testimonia to its ancient origins: Theology (four professors), Laws (eight), Medicine (three) and Arts (seven). For each professor, Cellius includes such information as places of study, appointments held and authors or subjects taught. Among the better known names here are those of Jakob

Heerbrand, Andreas Planer, Martin Crusius and Michael Mästlin. Then Cellius continues with those professors who were teaching in 1577, but have since died. Included here are Jakob Andreae, Jakob Schegk and Philip Apian. Volume II contains a translation by Volker Trugenberger and Uwe Jens Wandel, and supplementary material. Wilfried Setzler provides a concise essay on the University of Tübingen at the end of the sixteenth century; Werner Fleischhauer gives the history of the portraits and the woodcuts; Trugenberger discusses models for Cellius's biographies, and analyses their language, style and metre. Lastly, Gudrun Emberger supplements each biography with a chronological outline and a genealogy. Footnotes are given throughout, and an index of persons and place-names completes the volume.

The *Imagines* is valuable in several ways. Its assembly of a complete professoriate provides a well focussed view of the University as a whole, while also facilitating study of its individual members. Familiar figures are placed in a collegiate context, and unfamiliar ones emerge from obscurity — foremost among these being Cellius himself. It is full of hints as to the intellectual climate of Tübingen at the time, and as it would have been experienced by its students, especially those that came under Cellius's influence. One of his students was Johannes Kepler, who contributed to Cellius's funeral oration for Samuel Heiland (1533-1592), professor of ethics and Master of the evangelical seminary in which the future astronomer lived. Johann Valentin Andreae was also taught by several of the professors found here.

The *Imagines professorum tubingensium* is a sixteenth-century contribution to university history. The editors are to be congratulated for having made available this rich source for the University of Tübingen, and for setting it in its historical and cultural context.

P. M. Sanders
The Warburg Institute
Woburn Square
London WC1H 0AB

Norman Fiering, *Moral Philosophy at Seventeenth-Century Harvard. A Discipline in Transition.* Chapel Hill: University of North Carolina Press, 1981. Pp. xi + 323. £19.20.

Though much effort has been expended upon the study of the institutions and culture of Colonial America, a good deal remains to be done as this volume so clearly shows. Professor Fiering's study of moral philosophy at Harvard breaks new ground and indicates a number of directions for future research. The situation at seventeenth-century Harvard was very similar to that of a number of contemporary European universities, paralleling most closely the Protestant institutions of northern Europe. The same battles were fought and the same texts read at Harvard as in England, Lutheran Germany and

Calvinist Holland. The first chapter sketches the lively controversy over whether there remained the necessity for a secular (i.e. Greek-derived) moral philosophy after the promulgation of Christian Scripture. The battle was decided for the New World following the European pattern, and the textbooks used at Harvard were generally the same Aristotelian ones read by European students. Fiering analyses four of them written by Theophilus Golius, Eustachius a S. Paulo, Franco Burgersdijck, and Adriaan Heereboord. All were widely diffused in seventeenth-century New England, as they were also in Protestant Europe. Though Stoic, Platonic and other moral systems were avidly discussed, the basis for moral philosophy instruction was Aristotelian of the modified and eclectic sort found in the four authors already mentioned. The transition point came — at Harvard, as in European universities — at the turn of the eighteenth century. As Fiering notes (p. 4) 'the moral philosophy texts in use at Harvard in 1650 were vastly different from those in use in 1710'.

A particularly interesting chapter is devoted to Charles Morton (1627-1698), 'America's first professional philosopher', who before emigrating had been a teacher of Samuel Wesley. The authors he used on both sides of the Atlantic (p. 214) were largely of the same scholastic Aristotelian fabric (Suarez, Zabarella, Keckermann, Heereboord, Crakanthorpe, Scheibler, Smiglecki), though the education was leavened by the more modern tendencies of Gassendi and Stahl. When the break with Aristotelian scholasticism came, it was Henry More's *Enchiridium ethicum* which proclaimed the new age, being a set text at Harvard from 1690 to 1730. During those years ended — as in most parts of Europe as well — the Aristotelian domination of the universities.

It is fascinating to see just how closely the Harvard pattern followed the European one. Of course, at the time the Colonies were very much under British domination, but nonetheless there seems to have been very little 'cultural lag' of colony with mother country. Professor Fiering has written an extremely useful and balanced account of the situation. He is far better informed on relevant Continental matters than many who work on similar aspects of British history. Even if his grasp of the earlier history of university philosophy occasionally falters, it is most welcome to see a work of American intellectual history so accurately related to the European context of the same period. The study is an important contribution to seventeenth-century university history.

C. B. Schmitt
The Warburg Institute
Woburn Square
London WC1H 0AB

Jurgen Herbst, *From Crisis to Crisis: American College Government 1636-1819*. Cambridge, Mass.-London: Harvard University Press, 1982. Pp. xvi + 301. £17.50.

This book had its origins in the campus unrest that accompanied the Vietnam war. The unrest itself raised issues of university autonomy and of the relationship between civil and academic jurisdiction that were to act as the starting-point for Professor Herbst's investigation into the legal and governmental history of the early American college and university. His book begins in 1636, when the General Court of the Massachusetts Bay Company agreed to appropriate £400 to contribute to the expense of a school or college, thereby founding what would in time become Harvard University. It ends in 1819, with the Dartmouth College case, in which the Supreme Court recognised that Dartmouth was a private rather than a public foundation and consequently not subject to interference by the state legislature. In the 183 years between these two events, American perceptions of the nature and appropriate method of governance for higher education changed a great deal. The first colleges were the product of a compromise between the European tradition, which regarded a college as a civil corporation to be jointly supervised by secular and ecclesiastical authorities, and the English view which saw the privately endowed colleges of Oxford and Cambridge as elemosynary corporations. Herbst argues that the commonly-held but erroneous assumption that American colonial colleges were religious and charitable foundations rather than the public corporations they were chartered to be 'has prevented an appreciation of just how radical an innovation the American private college was when it first emerged at the end of the eighteenth century' (p. x). The private college would indeed be 'one of the country's most characteristic and unique institutions' (p. 242).

Early American colleges like Harvard and William and Mary in Virginia tended to be governed by secular and ecclesiastical representatives in tandem. The Great Awakening in the middle years of the eighteenth century, by fostering a greater degree of religious heterogeneity, weakened the hold of ecclesiastical authority and led to increasing demands for secular control over college government. But the attempt to prevent one sect from dominating a particular institution broadened out after the Revolution into a movement to found new private colleges, most of which were staffed, governed and funded by a particular church or denomination. In 1770, there were 9 colleges altogether, only one of which (Queen's College, now Rutgers University) was the preserve of the members of one church. By the early 1820s, there were more than 40 colleges in all. In terms of ownership and government, they offered a bewildering variety. The Dartmouth college decisions, by protecting the chartered rights of private corporations, regularised the position to some extent and laid the legal basis for the two-pronged system of American higher education, with both public and private institutions, which persists to this day.

Herbst's book is an excellent contribution to our knowledge of early American higher education. It offers a powerful and sustained analysis, based on informed and rigorous scholarship. The only mild cavil that might be entered by this reviewer is that by concentrating so exclusively on college governance, to the exclusion of curricular and social matters, some important issues which bear on the argument of the book have been ignored or discussed only superficially. Herbst does not explain, for example, how Americans of the colonial and early national eras differentiated in their own minds between colleges, academies and grammar schools. Colleges alone were empowered by their charters to give degrees, but the curriculum they followed (as Herbst himself seems to concede on p. 159) was sometimes very little removed from that of other educational institutions. Moreover, without some attention to the curricular and social side of college life, it is difficult to understand early examples of student militancy such as the revolt which brought down President Clap of Yale in 1766 and led to the state legislature reasserting its claim to general supervision of the college.

Melvyn Stokes
University College London

Robert G. Frank, Jr. *Harvey and the Oxford Physiologists. A Study of Scientific Ideas.* Berkeley, Los Angeles and London: University of California Press, 1980. Pp. xviii + 368. $34.40/£19.25.
Thomas Willis's Oxford Lectures, edited and translated with an introduction and notes by Kenneth Dewhurst. Oxford: Sandford Publications, 1980. Pp. x + 182. £9.00.

It was not until the seventeenth century, the second half especially, that England regained a major role in the development of European science similar to the one she had enjoyed during the hey-day of the Merton School some 300 years earlier. Significant contributions to the mathematical and physical sciences were made by Gilbert, Briggs, Oughtred, Wallis, Ward, Wren, Hooke, Barrow, Newton and Halley. Botany, geology and zoology benefitted from the research of Ray, Willoughby, Lhuyd and Woodward, while the corpus of the biological, medical and chemical sciences were greatly expanded by Harvey, Lower, Willis, Mayow, Hooke and Boyle. The analogy with the Merton School can be carried one step further. Like their medieval predecessors, most of these seventeenth-century men of science conducted their investigations at the universities, or at least in conjunction with Oxbridge men. Also noteworthy is the similarity between the two periods in terms of the versatility of their scientific contributors and the well-developed networks of association they formed among themselves.

Unfortunately, apart from studies of the major scientific personalities — for the most part limited to the hard-core physical and mathematical sciences — little attention has been given to the English scientific community as a whole. And the universities, which traditionally have been regarded as conservative, if not reactionary, institutions, reluctant to embrace any meaningful programme of innovation or reform, have suffered most in this respect. For this reason Robert Frank's *Harvey and the Oxford Physiologists* is an important contribution to our understanding of a crucial period in the annals of English science, and should lead to a better assessment of the interplay between ideas, individuals and educational institutions. Frank's line of argument is simple and forceful. The startling achievements produced by English physiologists in the period after 1640 can be traced through a distinct and direct lineage to William Harvey. It was the lingering impact of the latter's personal influence — as well as his writings — that provided his 'apostles' with the topics to be investigated, and the methodologies and experimental techniques to be employed. Most important, these scientists, even if they no longer subscribed to the traditional, mainly Aristotelian, natural philosophy adhered to by Harvey, could bring about the completion of the intellectual revolution initiated, but not resolved, in *De motu cordis* and *De generatione*. Thus, according to Frank the extensive research conducted by Boyle, Willis, Lower, Mayow, Hooke, etc., on such topics as the nature of blood, injection and transfusion, respiration, fermentation and muscular motion, is derived from issues raised and left open by Harvey, even if much of this 'new physiology was based on atomic and chemical view of matter' foreign to Harvey himself. And Frank devotes the greater part of the book to a detailed and fascinating portrayal of this academic scientific community in action: the men involved, the topics they pursued, their relationships, teachings and writings, and their impact on the surrounding environment.

It would not be difficult to fault Frank, as in fact some of his reviewers have, for being too outright and forceful in his presentation. Indeed, he may have exaggerated the degree to which Harvey's personal influence was crucial for the conversion and future work of his followers as well as created too sharp a distinction between the period before and after 1640; between the Oxford group and their counterparts at Cambridge, in London and on the Continent; and between competing world views. Yet, such criticism — justified as it may be — seems to miss the major objectives of the book. Frank's purpose was not to write a general history of physiology, but to focus on the inception, development, and reception of a specific world view; en route he provides us with a fine and sensitive study of an intellectual community firmly embedded in the social context of seventeenth-century England. The result is a solid foundation for future historians to build upon in their studies of the scientific enterprise and its network of associations, both within and without the academic community.

Kenneth Dewhurst's edition of Thomas Willis's Oxford lectures provides a good illustration of many of the issues raised by Frank. Willis's lectures were delivered in the early 1660s as part of his duties as Sedleian Professor of Natural Philosophy at Oxford, and were devoted to the function of the brain and various neurological disorders. These, and other lectures, formed the basis of Willis's *De anima brutorum*, which was published in 1672. The significance of these lectures lies in the way they elucidate Willis's work and scientific frame of mind in the decade prior to the publication of his *De anima* as well as in the light they cast on Willis's students and colleagues, and the Oxford in which he worked. Important is the fact that Willis was lecturing on the very topics he himself was investigating at the time, and that his colleagues at Oxford helped him to reformulate and improve upon his ideas. Such lectures further teach us to proceed with caution when discussing the university statutes. Although the statutes continued to prescribe Aristotle as the authority to be adhered to, great latitude was allowed to lecturers, as demonstrated by the chance survival of Willis's lectures. Once again we are offered proof of the adage, 'new wine in old bottles'. The fact that the lectures notes were taken by John Locke and Richard Lower and that other attendants included such Oxford men as John Ward suggests the close association between students and teachers, between men of science and local 'virtuosi'.

Clearly, the general scientific picture drawn by Frank and the careful study of one component in that picture by Dewhurst's rendering of Willis's lectures will force us to look afresh at the role of English universities in fostering scientific activity.

Mordechai Feingold
Department of History
Boston University
Boston, Massachusetts 002215
U. S. A.

Hanspeter Marti, *Philosophische Dissertationen deutscher Universitäten 1660-1750. Eine Auswahlbibliographie unter Mitarbeit von Karin Marti*. Munich - New York - London - Paris: Saur, 1982. Pp. 705. 168.- DM.

Cum grano salis, it can be maintained that, up to the present, early modern teaching of philosophy has hardly attracted the attention of those engaged in the study of the history of ideas, and the scholar willing to devote himself seriously to this subject must realise that usually the required sources are insufficiently opened up. Marti's bibliography proves to be a very useful attempt to take remedial measures.

Marti's list comprises 9818 entries of philosophical dissertations submitted to German universities in the post-Cartesian era, 1660-1750. The author sifted the inventories of about fifty libraries, mainly in the Federal Republic of Germany and the German Democratic Republic. Details about those libraries are rendered at full length in a *Bibliographical Account* (pp. 32-51).

Each entry reproduces all information which can be gained from the title-pages: names and provenance of *Praeses* and *Respondens*, full title of the dissertation, date of submission, place of publication, printer's name. Then Marti notes the size of the text (generally very brief), as well as the libraries where he found a copy.

The consectively numbered bibliography is ordered alphabetically according to the names of *Praesides*. Marti chose this criterion because of its suitability for library cataloguing though being conscious of the problem of authorship. The *Respondentes* are listed in a separate index (pp. 582-648).

Useful information is provided by the *Index of Universities* (pp. 548-581), which reflects the importance of each faculty of art in post Thirty Years' War Germany. The lion's share of dissertations were submitted in Wittenberg, Jena, Leipzig, Königsberg, Helmstedt and Altdorf, but there are also many texts originating from Halle, Strasbourg, Giessen, Marburg, Tübingen and Rostock. Finally, the *Subject Index* (pp. 649-701) comprising more than three thousand entries turns out to be a veritable mine for historians of philosophy. It is to be hoped that Marti's pioneering work will stimulate research in two regards. First, considering the international character of the *Respublica litteraria*, the limitation to 'German' universities seems to be as arbitrary as the temporal caesura 1660, being in the midst of an era of philosophical and scientific upheaval. For this reason, it would be desirable to have the bibliography extended geographically and temporally to the learned world of the whole of Europe and to all printed dissertations extant since the mid-16th-century. This extension could be informative for the academic reception of Aristotle. But secondly and finally, this limitation should not prevent philosophical research from a material analysis of the sources now made available.

Wolfgang Rother
CH-5412 Gebenstorf
Switzerland

Stefano De Rosa, *Una biblioteca universitaria del secondo '600: La libreria di Sapienza dello studio Pisano (1666-1700)*. Preface by Charles B. Schmitt (Collana di monografie delle biblioteche d'Italia, VIII). Florence: Leo S. Olschki Editore, 1983. Pp. 177.

The history of university libraries is an important branch of the intellectual history of universities. Much is revealed about the intellectual milieu of an institution of higher education by the contents, acquisitions policy, and level of funding of its library. Hence a valuable addition to our knowledge of the early modern history of the University of Pisa is provided by Stefano De Rosa's edition and erudite analysis of some hitherto unstudied records of the library of the Collegio di Sapienza in the years 1666-1700. From an account book kept by successive rectors of the Sapienza, De Rosa has reconstructed a partial catalogue of the contents of the library. Since the officials who kept the records were concerned primarily with meticulous book-keeping rather than with describing books, they listed names of authors and titles of books bought in extremely abbreviated form; in most instances, however, these references have been sufficient for De Rosa to identify author, work, and edition. In only one case, however, was he definitely able to identify a volume listed in the seventeenth-century account book with one now in the Pisa University Library.

In thirty-five years the Sapienza acquired somewhat over 180 books. De Rosa classifies them in three main categories, namely law, 'science' (including philosophy, medicine, and mathematics) and 'theology' (including apologetics and ecclesiastical history). Of the three law was the largest, its predominance increasing toward the end of the century. The great majority of the books bought were the work of sixteenth or seventeenth-century authors; however, Aristotle, Plato, Galen, Hippocrates and Apollonius were also represented. Nicholas of Cusa seems to have been the only medieval author present. Among seventeenth-century scientific authors whose works were purchased were Magini, Sennert, Borelli, Francesco Redi, and Malpighi.

The edition and catalogue are prefaced by an illuminating analytical essay which draws on numerous other archival sources, including the correspondence of Federigo Nomi, Rector of the Sapienza, with his friend and patron Antonio Magliabechi. Numerous constraints affected the acquisition of books for the Sapienza. Among these were the stocks available via the chosen suppliers, book prices, and the state of the book trade in general; intellectual disputes within the university (especially the attacks on the *galileiani* in 1669-70); and, in the last two decades of the century, severe inflation which eroded the purchasing power of the college. Above all, there was the increasingly direct control of university affairs by officials of the Grand Ducal government in Florence, a control which both bureaucratised the process of buying books and limited local autonomy in choosing them. As De Rosa points out, the Florentine authorities sought to ensure that the university would turn out public servants and professsional men of unimpeachable religious orthodoxy and solid practical training, rather than humanistically educated scholars or scientists. These goals certainly appear to be reflected in some of the book purchases.

Now that we have available De Rosa's study of the library of the Sapienza and Tiziana Pesenti's monograph on the early history of the library of the University of Padua, it is to be hoped that more researchers will be encouraged to turn their attention to parallel studies of other early modern university libraries. The present work constitutes a useful contribution to both the administrative and the intellectual history of the University of Pisa.

Nancy G. Siraisi
Department of History
Hunter College of the City University of New York
695 Park Avenue, New York, N. Y. 10021
U. S. A.

Emil Kuhn-Schnyder, *Lorenz Oken (1779-1851); erster Rektor der Universität Zürich; Festvortrag zur Feier seines 200. Geburtstages, von Emil Kuhn-Schnyder. Mit Eröffnungsansprache des Rektors Peter G. Waser und Zusammenfassung von Heinz Balmer [Schriften zur Züricher Universitäts- und Gelehrtengeschichte, 3]*. Zürich: Rohr, 1980, pp. 71.

This brief tract is what its subtitle indicates, and it has all the vices and virtues of the genre. It began as a ceremonial lecture delivered at Zürich University to honour the memory of Lorenz Oken, and it has been slightly expanded, decorated with extensive footnotes and a brief bibliography, and published. It contains a brief account of Oken's life, a surprisingly sympathetic treatment of his scientific ideas under the influence of *Naturphilosophie*, and a short summary of his political difficulties at Jena and Bavaria. Oddly, the lecture has least to say about what would have been of greatest interest to historians of universities, namely Oken's administrative work as rector of Zürich following his appointment in 1833. In general the treatment of Oken rises above the temptation to hagiography, but not above historical amateurishness. Readers seeking a short introduction to Oken's life and thought would do better to consult the *Allgemeine deutsche Biographie* and the *Dictionary of Scientific Biography*.

R. Steven Turner
Department of History
University of New Brunswick
Frederickton, N. B.
Canada E3B 5A3

Kenneth Dewhurst and Nigel Reeves, *Friedrich Schiller. Medicine, Psychology and Literature with the First English Edition of His Complete Medical and Psychological Writings*. Oxford: Sandford Publications, 1978. Pp. xii + 413. £12.00.

The authors of this interesting volume perform two important services. By carefully tracing Schiller's medical education and the ideas to which he was exposed, they show that far from an unrecognised precursor of Freud or Pavlov, Schiller creatively responded to theories of psychosomatic medicine typical of the German Enlightenment. By undertaking the by no means straightforward task of translating Schiller's writings as a medical student, they perform a useful service in making these accessible to English readers.

Readers of this *Journal* will be interested in Schiller's education as a cadet at the Military Academy established by Karl Eugen of Württemburg between 1770-73. Student life was regulated by harsh military discipline, providing a contrast, typical for the age, to an enlightened curriculum. Daily life at the Academy is vividly described, as are Schiller's responses from 1773-80, as expressed in the personal analyses students were compelled to write. Biographical information is included on Schiller's professors, and there is an especially interesting chapter on Jakob Friedrich Abel, who was Schiller's most inspiring teacher. Comparison of this to other academies is not made, however, nor are the implications assessed for this type of professional training for the stratification and practices of medical practitioners. The Academy's *Krankenjournal* is a valuable source which could be exploited for socio-historical investigation of student illnesses, and so deepen the book's rather impressionistic comments on student melancholy as a symptom of the *Sturm und Drang* reaction to Englightened rationalism. Schiller's analysis of a fellow student's depression is among the translations. His theses on the animal and spiritual nature of man are fascinating not only for the insight they provide on Schiller, but also into the examiners who rejected the first draft. The authors argue that Schiller's literary works were infected by his medical theories, but they also concede that a major stimulus was escapism from the rigours of the Academy and the monotony of duties as regimental doctor from 1780-82. The only evidence translated of Schiller's medical practice is one autopsy report and one prescription. But the evidence suggests that far from having the insight and sympathy expected of modern psychiatry, Schiller as a practitioner was arrogant, contentious and drunken.

Paul Weindling
Wellcome Unit for the History of Medicine
University of Oxford
47 Banbury Road
Oxford OX2 6PE

Konrad H. Jarausch, *Students, Society, and Politics in Imperial Germany. The Rise of Academic Illiberalism.* Princeton, N. J.: Princeton University Press, 1982. Pp. xvi + 448. Cloth: £28.20. Paper: £11.70.

Jarausch's study is an effort to explain the 'ideological reversal' of the German university, its professoriate and student body, from the liberal corporate institution of the early 19th century to 'the vanguard of national socialism' a century later (p. 12). For Jarausch, the shift in values occurred as part of the corporate reaction to an irreversible movement toward greater social, political, and cultural pluralism during the Second Empire. For students and professors this meant opposing: the expansion of the university to a 'mass' university, the development of technical and scientific education threatening the humanist synthesis of the early 19th century, the admission of greater numbers of 'minorities' — Catholics, women, German Jews, and foreigners — who competed for positions in relatively static markets. The outlines of this history have been available to the English reader from earlier works (e.g. F. Lilge, F. Ringer, C. McClelland, M. Steinberg), and Jarausch's work provides few interpretive surprises.

Still Jarausch contributes to the literature on the German university in two distinct areas. The first is his search for greater historical precision through quantification. Using the Prussian universities of Bonn, Berlin, and, to a lesser extent, Marburg, Jarausch reconstructs over the later 19th century the statistical patterns of student and professorial demography (sex, ages of matriculation, religious affiliation, urban and rural origins, choices of study and profession), and he examines fluctuations in enrollment and the overcrowding within fields. In this dimension the book is impressive, though, curiously, the author does not create a broad comparative institutional framework within which to place the statistics from these universities. Both Berlin and Bonn, for instance, were new universities founded between 1810 and 1818. Bonn, in addition was an outpost in Prussia's liberal, Catholic western provinces. Would comparisons to other universities founded in the 19th century — Catholic Münster and Munich — or to older important universities — Halle, Tübingen, Göttingen, Jena — reveal the same patterns? The nature of Jarausch's second contribution is less problematic: his work is one of the first in English to examine student organisations and official student political life. In two lengthy chapters Jarausch describes the duelling and non-duelling fraternities, corporations and student associations of the Second Empire. Again using quantitative techniques he traces the fluctuating pattern of allegiance to the fraternities and associations. He shows persuasively that a certain sector of student society, that of the joiners and climbers who sought careers in the army, bureaucracy, and Protestant church through their student affiliations, succumbed to a growing conservatism and nationalism. Whether, however, these students comprised 'the' university is to be doubted, even by the author's own account in chapters five and six. Lost in the statistical analysis are those students who comprised the new 'mass' university; lost are the students at the technical universities and those in the hard sciences and medicine. Not all students and fields fell equally under the sway of extreme nationalism, as the intellectual migration of the 1930s demonstrates.

The chief difficulty of Jarausch's book is that by itself the statistical evidence does not produce an historical explanation and that as an explanation of higher education in imperial Germany the book delivers far less than the title promises. Certain key phenomena are not treated adequately. For example, that the pre-industrial educated elite (*Bildungsbürgertum*) formed a cohesive stratum (pp. 82-3) and reacted defensively as a group in the midst of dramatic social change is assumed but not really shown. Jarausch demonstrates convincingly that the educated perpetuated themselves by sending their male offspring and, increasingly, their female offspring to the university but this does not prove the lack of significant adaptation through marriage with other social strata — the nobility, the entrepreneurial elite, or the free intelligentsia. Surprisingly Jarausch uses only matriculation lists but no genealogical evidence to support his arguments about mobility. Also the central term 'illiberalism', which Jarausch takes from F. Stern, is not carefully developed. To have any explanatory power the phenomenon of 'illiberalism' must be carefully located within the changing historical pattern of liberalism during the period. The author does this only in the most cursory manner. I can only suggest that the phrase is quite inadequate for describing the growing pluralism and crisis in imperial Germany. It is insufficient for the author to state that his own critical reservations of his central concept rest in an unpublished paper and not in his book (p. 229). In addition, since liberalism remained more dynamic in the regions outside Prussia during these years, the author should have looked comparatively at non-Prussian universities and paid greater systematic attention to the survival of liberal views within the Prussian harmony, despite Pevsner's justified strictures on some affronts offered to the enviroment in the 1960s; certainly the academic enclave contrasts well with the urban dereliction outside it. And in the century the growth in numbers — in students, staff, departments and financial turnover — has been spectacular. Kelly chronicles this institutional progress very adroitly. He uses a variety of published sources and the university's own archives, weaving a considerable mass of awkward detail into a fluent narrative. Skilful in terse judgment, he is as candid about shortcomings as he is enthusiastic about successes. For example, he sketches the distinguished contributions to English studies made in the university by Raleigh, the Allotts, and Muir (among others), but also the friction between the department's two professors that was thirty years ago a byword among the undergraduates who suffered its effects. He mentions the achievements in civic design (a field which Liverpool might almost be said to have invented) and also the regrettable early history of the law faculty, which for decades control by the city's solicitors kept in intellectual poverty. Kelly's lengthy account has style and balance. Only occasionally does its inclusiveness make it seem rather like a catalogue of names, dates and new buildings, as French succeeds classics and biochemistry overtakes philosophy.

The approach matches the fragmented, multi-faceted semblance of a civic university, and the way most members of it feel their careers are shaped. Liverpool's unit of teaching and professional relationships is the department. It has usually worked very well, and often more helpfully than Oxbridge's looser and more untidy pattern that leaves a lot of holes for discontent to moulder in; the department gives undergraduates and teachers a secure intellectual home, and fosters the research that Kelly pays tribute to. But the structure has flaws. For most of the period Kelly surveys the average department was very small, containing perhaps only one or two teachers. Enjoying autonomy yet too restricted for effective intellectual cross-fertilisation, some departments were until recently somewhat isolated from developments in their field. Notable at Liverpool in the 1950s, for example, was the old-fashioned philological approach of some language departments, on which Kelly makes brief and telling comment. Thirty years ago some anti-expansionists argued that bigger would mean worse. In the event, in the civic universities bigger has meant better.

Behind the university's many departments are its central officers and institutions. It is disappointing that there is comparatively little about them in the book, and that we are given only an intermittent account of financial opportunities and constraints, or the thrust of university policy. Though there are hints that at times Liverpool has been more cautious than other universities, for example over expansion in the early 1960s, it is hard to tell who was responsible for this strategy and to what extent it was long-term in character. University policy-making has certainly been a complex process, the result of conflict and consensus between permanent officials, Senate, and Council, representing various sorts of lay and academic opinion. One constant area of dispute has been competing claims for funding, the sharpest struggle sometimes being not between departments, but between their collective demands and those of the university's common agencies like university. There is, in general, a surprising amount of evidence within the book that liberal values did not disappear and, in fact, that the social and ideological process was far more complex than the author indicates. The chapter on the political values of the professoriate is especially unpersuasive.

The author argues by building a mosaic of quotations from famous contemporary scholars to demonstrate their overt political beliefs, but he does not actually situate those beliefs in the struggles within their fields. The result is a one-dimensional treatment of the professoriate in which speeches at ceremonial occasions or in politically sensitive lecture courses are made representative for all the faculties. There are numerous examples of individuals and controversies — in Protestant theology (Overbeck), Neo-Kantian philosophy (Lange, H. Cohen, the pre-war Lukacs), history (Lamprecht controversy), national economy (free trade debate), the emerging social sciences (Tönnies, Sombart) — which show far greater pluralism and internal pressure to change in a liberal direction than Jarausch indicates.

Lastly, I must note that the copious footnotes reveal a startling lack of care and precision in a work concerned with statistical exactitude. The loose use of collective footnotes, missing or only approximate page numbers even for direct quotations, and numerous errors in citation make the scholarly apparatus largely unusable.

J. B. Knudsen
Department of History
Wellesley College
Wellesley, Massachusetts 02181
U. S. A.

Thomas Kelly, *For Advancement of Learning. The University of Liverpool 1881-1981.* Liverpool: Liverpool University Press, 1981. Pp. xvi + 560. £18.00 (cloth), £12.50 (paper).

Few chapters in Liverpool's record in the last century encourage a comforting interpretation of British history. Once the country's second port, its ships dominated the Atlantic routes and created the prosperity still reflected in its Victorian architecture. The ships have left, the warehouses are being converted to museums and flats, and Liverpool's unemployment rate is among the highest. The university is one of the city's rare long-term successes. Like so many provincial colleges its beginnings were in the rich and diverse culture that sustained in mid-Victorian times a medical school and several colleges for higher education. As a result of intense civic effort these institutions combined to form the university college in 1881. Thomas Kelly's book was written to commemorate its first centenary.

Since its origins in small and mostly makeshift premises, including a disused lunatic asylum, the university has come to possess an extensive campus where restored Georgian and purpose-built Modern mingle with fair libraries and places of assembly. Such a battle, described in unusual detail by Kelly, marked the period as Vice Chancellor of the tough and combative Hector Hetherington in the 1920s and 1930s — a time of financial stringency, rather like the present, when arguments over money are naturally at their keenest. In his campaign for the common agencies Hetherington was supported by laymen (notably Fred Marquis, later Lord Woolton) and by some academics with narrower vision. The episode, like others, does not suggest that universities are best left in the total control of academics.

Not of course that they every have been: in Liverpool as elsewhere there was considerable local involvement in the university's business in the early years, replaced in this century by central institutions of the State, first the UGC and more recently the DES. From the 1920s onwards UGC funding was far more significant than local for any university, and so the UGC was increasingly a voice to be heeded. Since the 1950s the DES has steadily encroached on the UGC's area of decision, indeed in very recent years supplanting it altogether over matters of principle. The trajectory of State participation, from persuasion to command, is another dimension of Liverpool's history which is treated too cursorily by Kelly. In giving less than due attention to the forces that have played on British higher education as a whole the book in effect isolates Liverpool from other universities, which it makes sense to study for some of the time together. Kelly raises in one's mind the perennial question, of how far one institution among many is an intelligible field of study, and he cannot be said to have answered it in a totally convincing way.

The book's greatest strength is its description of individual departments and their teachers, who have included some strange and unusual people. One such was E. Allison Peers, remembered by this reviewer as a laconic and old-fashioned Hispanicist, thirty-five years ago. Nothing about him suggested the mole of academe he proved all the time to have been. His *Guardian* obituary revealed that he was Bruce Truscot, in whose books about 'Redbrick' malicious comment about his Liverpool colleagues may by the knowledgeable be detected. Liverpool, the original Redbrick University, now has in Kelly's lively and wide-ranging history a happy celebration of its first century.

Peter Searby
Fitzwilliam College
Cambridge

Publications Received

This list includes those publications received by the Editor before January 1985. Books to be reviewed in future volumes of *History of Universities* are not included.

Emma Baeri, 'Una riforma caraccioliana: le scuole normali di Sicilia (1788-1810)', *Università di Catania, Annali della facoltà di scienze politiche* (1980), 87-157.

Batavia Academica. Bulletin van de nederlandse werkgroep universiteitsgeschiedenis. Vol. I (1983). Pp. 40.

Roberto P. Ciardi, 'La pubblica utilità delle arti: una giustificazione per l'esistenza delle accademie nell'estetica tra Sette- e Ottocento', in *Scritti in onore di Ottavio Morisani* (Catania, 1982) 427-53.

Alan B. Cobban, 'Theology and Law in Medieval Colleges of Oxford and Cambridge', *Bulletin of the John Rylands University Library of Manchester* 65 (1982), 57-77.

Peter Denley, 'The Social Function of Italian Renaissance Universities: Prospects for Research', *Town and Gown: The University in Search of its Origins. CRE Information* 62 (1983), 47-58.

Brendan Dooley, 'Giornalismo, università e organizzazione della scienza: tentativi di formare una accademia scientifica veneta all'inizio del Settecento', *Archivio veneto*, ser. V, vol. 120 (1983), 5-39.

Kostas Gavroglu, 'Certain Features of Higher Education in Greece and the Failure of the Attempts to Reform It', *Journal of the Hellenic Diaspora* 8 (1981), 95-108.

Luce Giard, 'Histoire de l'université et histoire de savoir: Padoue (XIVe-XVIe siècle) (I)', *Revue de synthèse* 104 (1983), 139-69.

Nokter Hammerstein, 'Jubiläumsschrift und Alltagsarbeit. Tendenzen Bildungsgeschichtlicher Literatur', *Historische Zeitschrift* 236 (1983), 601-33.

Nokter Hammerstein, 'Universitäten des Heiligen Römischen Reiches deutscher Nation als Ort der Philosophie des Barock', *Studia Leibnitiana* 13 (1981), 242-66.

History of Education Quarterly 23 (1983)

History of Education Quarterly 24 (1984)

Peter Jones, 'The Scottish Professorate and the Polite Academy, 1720-46', in *Wealth and Virtue. The Shaping of Political Economy in the Scottish Enlightenment*, ed. I. Hont and M. Ignatieff (Cambridge, 1983), 89-117.

P. Osmund Lewry, 'Rhetoric at Paris and Oxford in the Mid-Thirteenth Century', *Rhetorica* 1 (1983), 45-63.

Medische microscopie in de negentiende eeuw. Thematic number of *Tijdschrift voor de geschiedenis der geneeskunde, naturwetenschappen, wiskunde en techniek*, vol. 6, n. 2 (1983), pp. 57-120. Hfl. 12--.

G. Minnucci, *Le lauree dello Studio Senese alla fine del secolo XV* [Quaderni di 'Studi Senesi', 51]. Milan: Giuffrè Editore, 1981.

Rosario Moscheo, 'Melchior Inchofer (1585-1648) ed un suo inedito corso messinese di logica dell'anno 1617', *Quaderni dell'Istituto Galvano della Volpe* 3 (1982), 181-94.

Daniela Mugnai Carrara, 'Una polemica umanistico-scolastica circa l'interpretazione delle tre dottrine ordinate di Galeno', *Annali dell'Istituto e Museo di Storia della Scienza di Firenze* 8 (1983), 31-57.

Rivista española de teologia vol. 43, fasc. 2 (1983).

Agostino Sottili, 'Le contestate elezioni rettorali di Paul van Baenst e Johannes von Dalberg all'università di Pavia', *Humanistica Lovaniensia* 31 (1982), 29-75.

Grazia Tomasi Stussi, 'Per la storia dell'Accademia Imperiale di Pisa (1810-1814)', *Critica storica* 20 (1983), 60-120.

Lucia Tongiorgi Tomasi, 'Projects for Botanical and Other Gardens: a 16th Century Manual', *Journal of Garden History* 3 (1983), 1-34.

Lucia Tongiorgi Tomasi, 'Un "florilegio" pisano del XVII secolo', *Bollettino storico pisano* 52 (1983), 199-209.

Paul Trio, 'De statuten van de laat-middeleeuwse clericale O. L. V. -broederschap van de studenten van Parijs te Ieper', *Handlingen van de Koninklijke Commissie voor Geschiedenis* 148 (1982), 91-142.

Giuliana Volpi, 'Lineamenti per uno studio sull'Università di Pisa nel XVII secolo', in *Scritti in onore di Dante Gaeta* (Milan, 1984), 639-783.

THE HISTORY OF
THE UNIVERSITY OF
OXFORD

General editor: T.H. Aston

A completely new, full-scale history of the university
in eight chronologically arranged volumes

VOLUME I
The Early Oxford Schools

Edited by J.I. Catto

Covers the establishment of the University in the twelfth and
thirteenth centuries and the development of its studies, up to the great
philosophical debate between William of Ockham and his Mertonian
opponents in the fourteenth century.

£55   Clarendon Press   0 19 951011 3

For detailed information please apply to the Publicity Department

Oxford University Press